Neurolinguistic Psychothe

Neurolinguistic Psychotherapy offers a unique and exciting postmodern perspective on an advancing model of therapy. It places neurolinguistic psychotherapy in context and considers the history of NLP and its relationship to psychotherapy. Presented as an effective model for facilitating neurological change through the therapeutic relationship, this book challenges therapists to incorporate a psychodynamic approach within their work.

In addition the book also presents:

- A model of the developing personality and the relationship to attachment theory and emerging theories of neuroscience.
- A discussion of the linguistic components of NLP and the effectiveness of utilising the language patterns offered by NLP.
- A challenge to neurolinguistic psychotherapists – asking them to consider the benefits of including relational approaches to therapy above that offered by a programmatic model of change.

This book will be of great interest to all psychotherapeutic practitioners and trainers, students and academics.

Lisa Wake is a Neurolinguistic Psychotherapist, and an internationally recognised Master Trainer of NLP. She is Director of Awaken Consulting and Training Services Ltd, which offers corporate consultancy, training, coaching and psychotherapy services. She is also Director of Awaken School of Outcome Oriented Psychotherapies Ltd, which provides UKCP accredited psychotherapy trainings. Lisa has also served as Vice Chair and Chair of UKCP.

Advancing Theory in Therapy
Series Editor: Keith Tudor

Most books covering individual therapeutic approaches are aimed at the trainee/student market. This series, however, is concerned with *advanced* and *advancing* theory, offering the reader comparative and comparable coverage of a number of therapeutic approaches.

Aimed at professionals and postgraduates, *Advancing Theory in Therapy* will cover an impressive range of theories. With full reference to case studies throughout, each title will

- present cutting-edge research findings
- locate each theory and its application within cultural context
- develop a critical view of theory and practice.

Titles in the series

Neurolinguistic Psychotherapy

A Postmodern Perspective

Lisa Wake

Routledge
Taylor & Francis Group

LONDON AND NEW YORK

First published 2008 by Routledge
27 Church Road, Hove, East Sussex BN3 2FA

Simultaneously published in the USA and Canada
by Routledge
270 Madison Avenue, New York NY 10016

Routledge is an imprint of the Taylor & Francis Group, an Informa business

© 2008 Lisa Wake

Typeset in Times by Garfield Morgan, Swansea, West Glamorgan
Printed and bound in Great Britain by TJ International Ltd, Padstow, Cornwall
Paperback cover design by Sandra Heath

This publication has been produced with paper manufactured to strict
environmental standards and with pulp derived from sustainable forests.

British Library Cataloguing in Publication Data
A catalogue record for this book is available from the British Library

Library of Congress Cataloging-in-Publication Data
Wake, Lisa, 1962–
 Neurolinguistic psychotherapy : a postmodern perspective / Lisa Wake.
   p. ; cm.
 Includes bibliographical references.
 ISBN 978-0-415-42540-7 (hbk) – ISBN 978-0-415-42541-4 (pbk.)
1. Neurolinguistic programming. 2. Psychotherapy. I. Title.
 [DNLM: 1. Psychotherapy–methods. 2. Neurolinguistic programming.
 WM 420 W146n 2008]
 RC489.N47W35 2008
 616.89'14–dc22
                                                          2007029198

ISBN: 978–0–415–42540–7 (hbk)
ISBN: 978–0–415–42541–4 (pbk)

Contents

Acknowledgements

This book has emerged out of many years of thinking, learning, teaching and dialoguing with friends, colleagues and students about neurolinguistic psychotherapy. My greatest frustration has been translating my understanding of neurolinguistic psychotherapy at an unconscious level into the written form. I am grateful to my dearest friend and colleague Jeremy Lazarus who sat me down one day and challenged me to write this book; he didn't let me off the hook and I created a goal. Within a week of this happening, Keith Tudor approached me at the UKCP AGM to write this book for the series. Thank you Jeremy, Keith and my unconscious for manifesting my goal.

My greatest appreciation is to my clients who have given me their permission to use their experiences in this work, and to my students who have encouraged me incessantly to write down my thoughts from the classroom environment.

Thank you to Annette Gamston whose persistent critique, demanding timescales and honest feedback on the written word has helped me enormously to make sense of my work. I am grateful to Pam Gawler-Wright for encouraging me to complete this work, and for challenging my thinking during the creative process. To Nici Evans, who has provided invaluable feedback and has also aided the transition of neurolinguistic psychotherapy into the academic world. To Keith Tudor, as series editor for your critique, feedback and commitment to my writing. To Judith DeLozier who assisted me by confirming factual historical details.

To my husband Mark, and daughters Rebecca and Hannah for your support, patience and for creating the space in our life for me to achieve this.

Finally, within the neurolinguistic psychotherapy community, three souls have acted as unconscious sponsors in their own way. Bill O'Hanlon for showing me what is possible, and for opening my eyes to my Self; Robert Dilts for the spirit, love and ecology that you bring to the world of neurolinguistic psychotherapy; and Steve Gilligan for your humour, warmth and compassion.

Series preface

This series focuses on advanced and advancing theory in psychotherapy. Its aims are: to present theory and practice within a specific theoretical orientation or approach at an advanced, postgraduate level; to advance theory by presenting and evaluating new ideas and their relation to the approach; to locate the orientation and its applications within cultural contexts, both historically in terms of the origins of the approach, and contemporarily in terms of current debates about philosophy, theory, society and therapy; and, finally, to present and develop a critical view of theory and practice, especially in the context of debates about power, organization and the increasing professionalization of therapy.

I am delighted to introduce this volume and its author, Lisa Wake, who is well known and well respected in psychotherapy circles in the UK as formerly representing the Neurolinguistic Psychotherapy and Counselling Association as its Chair, in which capacity she also served on the UKCP NHS Committee and, later, the United Kingdom Council for Psychotherapy as its Vice Chair and then Chair. In this book she also reveals herself to be a leading exponent of and writer on neurolinguistic psychotherapy.

While there are numerous books on neurolinguistic programming (NLP), this is the first book to consider NLP as a psychotherapeutic modality. It moves beyond the basic application of material studied at traditional NLP practitioner and master practitioner levels and, consistent with the purpose of the series, advances the theory and field of neurolinguistic psychotherapy (NLPt). It traces the history of NLPt and its emergence – theoretically, practically and organizationally – as a therapeutic modality. NLPt spans a number of different therapeutic philosophies and is directly influenced by the work of Milton Erickson, Virginia Satir and Fritz Perls, therapists and theorists to whom the present author returns throughout the book in order to explore the roots of NLPt and its relationship with other psychotherapy approaches. This informs a wider purpose of the book: to consider the relationship between NLPt and psychotherapy in general. Wake explores the principles of constructivism as a philosophical base to NLPt and its therapeutic approach, tracing these as far back as Socrates. Later, in three separate chapters, she deconstructs the components of NLP, namely neurology, linguistics and programming. Other highlights include a model of the mind for NLPt which incorporates an alignment between the conscious and unconscious; the integration of current thinking on neuroscience to the practice of NLPt and, specifically, the importance of rapport; an ecological discussion of the role of the therapist within an ethical framework; and a concluding chapter on the author's views on the future of NLPt within a postmodern paradigm.

While this book is highly theoretical, it is also highly practical. The author presents her practice, including some extended case studies, as well as a wide range of theory in a straightforward, accessible and lively manner. Psychotherapists across all theoretical orientations will find this an invaluable contribution to their thinking and practice.

Keith Tudor

Introduction

Erickson told a story about when he was growing up.

Erickson had polio when he was 17, but before that he was a fairly active kid who lived in a farming area in Wisconsin for much of his growing-up years.

He told a story about how he was with friends one time a few miles away from his home. People didn't travel very far from their homes at that point and he and his friends were unfamiliar with this area.

They were travelling down a country road and a horse which had obviously thrown its rider ran past them. Its reins were all askew and it was very skittish. He and his friends chased the horse into a farmyard, and when they got into the farmyard, they caught the horse and calmed it down. Then Erickson announced, 'I'm going to take this horse back home, back to its owner.' His friends said, 'We don't even know whose horse this is. How're you gonna do that?' Erickson said, 'That's all right.' He jumped up on the horse, told the horse to giddyup and the horse went out of the farmyard and took a right turn onto the road. Erickson spurred him on down the road. As they were riding down the road, every once in a while the horse tried to go off the road and eat some wheat or some hay. Erickson just steered him back on the road and spurred him on. A few miles down the road, the horse turned and went into another farmyard. The farmer heard the commotion and came out and exclaimed, 'That there's my horse. How did you know how to bring my horse home? I've never met you. You didn't know that was my horse.' Erickson said 'That's right, I didn't know where to bring the horse, but the horse knew the way. All I did was to keep him on the road and keep him moving.'

When he told that story, Erickson ended with the moral, 'I think that's how you do psychotherapy.'

(O'Hanlon & Bertolino, 1992, pp. 15–16)

The discipline known as NLP began, before it had a name, with an interdisciplinary community of people (Richard Bandler, John Grinder,

Leslie Cameron, Mary Beth Megus, David Gordon, Robert Dilts, and myself, to name but a few). We were motivated by a shared curiosity about how we know, about how we learn, how we communicate, and how we change. And how we can influence the process of change in a well-formed, ecological way. The patterns of NLP were not imparted to us, but unfolded in our learning.

(DeLozier, 1995)

The emergence of neurolinguistic psychotherapy as a therapeutic modality

Neurolinguistic psychotherapy emerged out of the development of neuro-linguistic programming (NLP), a psychology of performance excellence that was developed by Bandler and Grinder.* In the mid-1980s therapists within the UK became interested in NLP and started to integrate some of the underlying principles of the technology into their psychotherapeutic prac-tice. As this interest developed over time, the Association of NLP (ANLP) formed a counselling and psychotherapy section and joined UKCP (UK Council for Psychotherapy) in 1992. By 1996 this section of ANLP started to separate from mainstream NLP and a formal division, ANLP-PCS (Associ-ation for NLP – Psychotherapy and Counselling Section), was created that could represent neurolinguistic psychotherapy in the wider therapy field. Therapists such as Brion, Burtt, Chalfont, Clarkson, Gawler-Wright, Janes and Lawley recognised that there was a need for neurolinguistic psycho-therapy to be developed separately to NLP and an independent legal entity was set up, formally separating ANLP-PCS from ANLP in 2000. By 2002, ANLP-PCS changed its name and became The Neurolinguistic Psychother-apy and Counselling Association (NLPtCA), representing approximately 70 therapists registered with UKCP. During this time, my role was initially that of training standards officer, and I worked closely with Gawler-Wright to consider how standards could be developed to ensure that they were more flexible and had a greater emphasis on generic psychotherapy rather than proceduralised models generated from the methodology of NLP. Later in 2002, I served as Chair of NLPtCA and represented the modality within UKCP, particularly on the NHS Committee prior to being elected as Vice Chair and then Chair of UKCP. This platform has enabled neurolinguistic psychotherapy to be represented at a number of levels and has been used to inform the development of the field.

Since 2000, there has been a considerable expansion in the number of psychotherapists from a range of modalities using neurolinguistic psycho-therapy as an additional skill set. Neurolinguistic psychotherapy is currently

* Please note that the abbreviation 'NLP' throughout this book refers to neurolinguistic programming as opposed to neurolinguistic psychotherapy.

represented by an accrediting member organisation within the Experiential Constructivist Section of UKCP and there are also two Member Organisations that represent neurolinguistic psychotherapy as a wider therapeutic approach within the Hypnopsychotherapy Section of UKCP. These two institutes are BeeLeaf Institute for Contemporary Psychotherapy and my own Awaken School of Outcome Oriented Psychotherapy, which I run with my husband and other colleagues. Awaken and BeeLeaf, founded by Pamela Gawler-Wright in 1993, continue to collaborate in the development of training and registration of psychotherapists in the modality, as well as furthering the community's commitment to enhancing its theoretical and research basis.

Purpose of the book

The purpose of this book is to consider the relationship between neurolinguistic psychotherapy and psychotherapy in general. The field of neurolinguistic psychotherapy, as alluded to earlier, is represented within two sections of UKCP. There are a number of reasons why the modality is held within these two sections, as follows:

- Neurolinguistic psychotherapy has emerged from the work of three therapists: Erickson, a psychiatrist and hypnotherapist; Satir, a family therapist; and Perls, a gestalt therapist. As a modality it could be represented through family and systemic therapy, humanistic and integrative therapy (the preferred home of gestalt therapists), or hypnotherapy.
- Neurolinguistic psychotherapy is a brief outcome-oriented therapy, therefore a few individuals in the field have argued that there is little need for personal therapy as part of the training requirement, while most regard the weekly commitment to therapy to be contrary to strategic therapeutic treatment plans, hence it will not meet the needs required of humanistic and integrative psychotherapists.
- Only a very small amount of Perls's work is credited within the modality, although much of it is grounded in his practices of skilled facilitation of experiential sensing of reality, therefore it cannot be seen to represent accurately the entirety of gestalt therapy.
- The work of Satir that predominantly influenced Bandler and Grinder was her use of specific questioning processes, later referred to as the meta-model, and her work on parts or roles that individuals adopted within families. Although she worked systemically with her clients, this has not been incorporated significantly within NLP and therefore is under-represented in some presentations of neurolinguistic psychotherapy. The systemic aspects that neurolinguistic psychotherapy has

adopted more widely are those of Bateson and Dilts and working with the ecology of the self system. This has been added to by Gilligan and his theories on self-relations.

- In considering the influence that Erickson has had on the development of neurolinguistic psychotherapy, and in particular some of his students and contemporaries, such as Haley, Rossi, Rosen, O'Hanlon and Gilligan, there has been a natural leaning towards more unconscious communication and integration. This has influenced considerably the work of Gawler-Wright, who represents contemporary neurolinguistic psychotherapy within the Hypnopsychotherapy Section of UKCP, as do my own trainings.
- One of the basic philosophical tenets of neurolinguistic psychotherapy that underpinned the work of Erickson, Satir and Perls was that *everyone lives in their own model of the world*. This forms the basis of constructivism, and NLPtCA continues to find its home within the experiential and constructivist section of UKCP.
- The modality as it is represented in its purest sense is struggling to find its place within the wider theoretical models represented in psychotherapy. There is very little literature available that references neurolinguistic psychotherapy, and I would hope that this book will encourage a wider debate within the field. McDermott and Jago co-authored a book in 2001 on *Brief NLP Therapy*, and there is also literature by Gawler-Wright, and Lawley and Tomkins that has added to the field. Gawler-Wright is a well-respected Ericksonian therapist and her thinking moves neurolinguistic psychotherapy into the contemporary world through the work of Erickson, Rossi and Gilligan. Lawley and Tompkins have developed further the work of Grove and there is now an increasing level of interest in the use of Clean Language processes as a therapeutic model. Kostere and Malatesta, Bolstad and NLPtCA have stayed closer to a later modelling of NLP by such contributors as Andreas, James and Woodsmall as a psychology that offers a set of applications and procedures within psychotherapy rather than a psychotherapeutic process.

Within the book, I present developing and new ideas in the work of neurolinguistic psychotherapy, and bring together the founding principles of the therapists as originally modelled by Bandler and Grinder. The book considers the roots of constructivism and systems thinking as a basis for a therapeutic model. It includes the concept that neurolinguistic psychotherapy is a methodology rather than just a method applied within a given context, and what this means for the therapist in practice. It also aims to raise questions in the reader's mind about the place of unconscious processes and depth relational therapy within the context of neurolinguistic psychotherapy.

Psychotherapy or applied psychology?

A dichotomy exists within the neurolinguistic psychotherapy field that creates a challenge for neurolinguistic psychotherapists. There is a tendency by some therapists to develop neurolinguistic psychotherapy as a behaviourist model of an applied psychology, whereas others, and I include myself here, prefer to see neurolinguistic psychotherapy embedded in the roots of constructivism, hypnopsychotherapy and relational psychotherapy. I aim to present a debate on these apparent opposites and build on the work of Lawley and Tompkins (2006), who conceptualise the two approaches as being synergistic. They refer to the main principle of neurolinguistic psychotherapy as enabling the client to *change their existing model of the world* (p. 35). This means that any model that the therapist builds changes as they work with clients. By using 'the client's patterns of behaviour . . . to construct a model of the client's internal processes . . . the therapist attempts to figure out *how the structure* of the client's subjective experience so consistently gets them the results they get' (p. 35). The therapist works with the subjective experience of the client to 'direct the client's attention' (p. 35) and to 'use their own body and voice for maximum therapeutic effect' (p. 35).

Just as NLP is a model of a model, and is based on subjective experience, so is my own interpretation of neurolinguistic psychotherapy. I wish to respect the range of maps that currently exist within neurolinguistic psychotherapy and hope to create a space whereby more maps might be considered, while at the same time recognising that the only territory that matters in therapy is that of the client and much of that lies undiscovered.

NLP per se is portrayed as a methodology, which, when applied, can be effective in facilitating a client to change their behaviours and thereby their results. What is missing from this and mainstream literature on NLP is the wider therapeutic perspective of Erickson, Satir and Perls. This was over and above the aspects that Bandler and Grinder modelled, with various elements from each of the therapists originally modelled now influencing the work of therapists today. Chapter 1 provides the historical and conceptual overview of NLP from its roots through to a model of psychotherapy. The remainder of the book will consider a wider perspective of psychotherapy and bring in new theories to enhance the original model of NLP and neurolinguistic psychotherapy.

Although Bandler and Grinder modelled the linguistic components of Erickson's work, and this rightly has its place in the success of NLP today, it would be naïve to consider that this is 'all' that made Erickson's work a success. In this book, I aim to develop this early work, by bringing to mind the work of Erickson that has been so elegantly captured by Rossi, Haley and O'Hanlon. To consider only the linguistic structure of Erickson's work is to leave out the essence of what made him such an effective therapist who dared to go to places that many therapists are reluctant to consider. I would hope that in this book I will encourage therapists to look beyond the method, tools and techniques that are now the trademark of NLP and bring to life much of what was successful in Erickson's work.

For a number of years, books on NLP were relegated to the 'black magic' section of the bookshop, and NLP has not helped itself by portraying the methodology as a panacea. Within the NLP community, therapists started to recognise the benefits of NLP in a therapy setting, and were able to extract and utilise certain aspects of the model to facilitate change in their clients. Many more therapists from a huge variety of modalities, deliberately or intuitively utilising the principles and skills that NLP described, found the clarity of these descriptions highly useful in aiding cognitive awareness of what made the psychotherapy they practised successful. Over the past ten years there has been a groundswell of therapists who continue to influence neurolinguistic psychotherapy as a therapy that is robust, ecological and effective at facilitating spiritual, mental, emotional and physical well-being in clients. The concept of modelling has remained at the core of the therapists' work, integrating the work of others who modelled Erickson at a similar time to Bandler and Grinder, such as Rossi, Haley, Rosen, O'Hanlon and Gilligan.

A second generation of Ericksonian psychotherapists, schooled in both psychotherapy and NLP, are building on the principles of systemic NLP. They emphasise the purpose of psychotherapy as building the relationship, or co-created 'field', between cognitive (linguistic) and somatic (neurological/emotional) intelligence. Encapsulated in Stephen Gilligan's term 'self-relations', and highlighted in the work of Gawler-Wright (1999), this development reclaims Erickson's sense that the purpose of psychotherapy is to rebuild the supportive rapport between conscious and unconscious mind. These interdependent minds can lose communication and come into conflict because they have different characteristics, language and function, and because they are differently received and expressed in the person's social and cultural environment. While bearing some resemblance to Freud's id–ego–superego conflict (regarded as an ultimately pessimistic standpoint), systemic NLP and self-relations embrace Erickson's incorrigible optimism in the human being as a creative, autonomous and self-balancing system that is seeking well-being, even in the presentation of symptoms. Through a process of 'sponsorship' between the cognitive and somatic minds, self-relations seeks to promote a creative dialogue of appreciation and wonder, expressing itself through the humane languages of sensation, metaphor and behavioural autopoeisis.

Returning then to the work of Erickson: in his foreword to Bandler and Grinder's (1975a) modelling of his language patterns, he expressed caution about assuming that it was the linguistic patterns that were the key to the success of his work.

Although this book by Richard Bandler and John Grinder . . . is far from being a complete description of my methodologies, as they so clearly state it is a much better explanation of how I work than I, myself, can give. I know what I do, but to explain how I do it is much too difficult for me . . . While I would like still further analyses of the complexities of communication for hypnotic purposes, which would require much more than this book by Bandler and Grinder can encompass, I would also like an analysis of how and why carefully structured communications can elicit such extensive and effective patient responses, often not actually requested.

(p. ix)

Haley commented similarly in the preface to Bandler and Grinder (1986), 'I think Erickson would be pleased that his years of hard work, innovating new ways to influence people, have resulted in such a following. He might be less pleased about the cult being built around him, since he was such a practical man' (p. 9).

Approaches in neurolinguistic psychotherapy

Neurolinguistic psychotherapy finds itself spanning a number of different therapeutic philosophies and is directly influenced by the work of Erickson, Satir and Perls. As the modality has developed, the influences of systems theory, cybernetics, use of metaphor, the unconscious, and solution-focused work all add to the repertoire of skills and approaches of the neuro-linguistic psychotherapist. In essence, neurolinguistic psychotherapy finds itself split into two main schools of thought. The more cognitive and programmatic approach has close links to cognitive and behavioural therapies and builds on the programmatic and modelling work of Bandler, by utilising strategies to affect and influence therapeutic outcome. In this approach the therapist stays outside of the relationship with the client and operates from a model of facilitating change in 'how' the client does what he/she does.

The more unconscious hypnopsychotherapeutic approach involves the therapist as a core element of the therapeutic process and recognises that all behaviour and therefore all change lies within the unconscious, and it is only through direct communication with the unconscious that change can occur. In *Uncommon Therapy* Haley (1993) emphasises Erickson's strategic aspect and the idea that 'the clinician initiates what happens during therapy and designs a particular approach for each problem' (p. 17). Haley points out that Erickson not only communicates with patients in metaphors, but also used metaphor to facilitate unconscious change. He notes that Erickson avoids interpretations and that he would feel that 'typical insight interpretations of unconscious communication are absurdly reductionistic, like summarising a Shakespearean play in a sentence' (p. 29). Yet it would seem that this is what programmatic therapists who adhere strictly to the model portrayed by Bandler and Grinder are at risk of doing.

In understanding this perspective of working within the metaphor, Lawley and Tompkins (2005) have integrated the work of Grove with the metaphorical work of Erickson and developed a therapeutic method of modelling the client's inner landscape through their work on symbolic modelling.

Bateson adds much to the epistemological aspects of neurolinguistic psychotherapy through his work on cybernetics. His influence on both neurolinguistic psychotherapy and family therapy enables a common grounding for the two modalities. His perspective is that each of us is connected through a series of interrelationships within a system and it is only by influencing the greater system that we will create a sense of balance in the system.

O'Hanlon's development of Erickson's work has brought both inclusive and possibility therapy, and solution-focused therapy to the realm of neurolinguistic psychotherapy. O'Hanlon's use of splitting, validation and permission has enabled therapists to work in the client's realm of past, present and future in ways that engender ecological and sustainable change.

Beyond these more widely acknowledged approaches to the application of the principles of NLP, I add the work of Schore, Edelman and Pert and the recent thinking on neuroscience as being core components of neurolinguistic psychotherapy. Pert (1997, p. 305) remarks:

> The approach that I've been trained in, traditional talk therapy, doesn't seem to impact the mind–body level. We often hear our patients say, 'I know I shouldn't feel this way, but I *do!*' Knowing something doesn't always impact how we feel, and we may have to get past purely verbal communication to access our emotions. Some of the approaches I have found effective at getting to deeper, more fundamental levels are storytelling, hypnotherapy, neurolinguistic programming, and any of the expressive therapies that employ visualization, music and art.

The success of neurolinguistic psychotherapy to speak to and through the somatic intelligence of both client and therapist was perhaps pre-empted by where its originals placed their attention in the psychotherapeutic setting. Perls's emphasis was on the reality of sensory experience in the here and now, Satir's trademark was sensitivity to body, voice and touch in the exchange of emotional meaning and Erickson was almost fixated in his attention to the expression of internal events through observable physiological events which he greeted as sincere and eloquent communications from the unconscious mind. In neurolinguistic psychotherapy the main modeller of these somatic processes was one of the women in the original team of developers, Judith DeLozier; previous training in both dance and anthropology ensured that these vital elements were not lost to the more cognitive bias of Bandler and Grinder (Gawler-Wright, 2007, p. 36).

Structure of the book

The chapters of the book move beyond the basic application of material learnt at traditional practitioner and master practitioner levels. It brings in perspectives from other modalities that were not modelled by Bandler and Grinder and yet were inherent components of the work of Erickson, Satir and Perls.

In Chapter 1, the subjectivity of experience is discussed within the construct of the communication model and how this is influenced according to a person's relationship to the subjective 'now' of our reality. I provide a brief overview of the historical therapeutic roots of Erickson, Satir and Perls and how these are represented within neurolinguistic psychotherapy. The chapter concludes with a comprehensive review of the presuppositions of NLP as they are presented by Dilts, and within the construct of the world of psychotherapy.

Chapter 2 places neurolinguistic psychotherapy within constructivist principles and the perspectives of Socrates, Piaget, Korzybski and Schrödinger. The discussion goes wider than purist constructivism and considers the development of NLP as an epistemological philosophy, which is brought to life through the presentation of case studies from Erickson's and my own therapy. Neurolinguistic psychotherapy is considered in relationship to other modalities of therapy, particularly those that have also emerged through constructivist principles. As the book considers throughout each chapter the dichotomy of programmatic versus unconscious relational therapy, I compare neurolinguistic psychotherapy with the psychodynamic therapies of Freud, Adler, Jung and Klein, through to the humanistic therapies of transactional analysis and person-centred therapy, to consider its relationship to other methods of unconscious and relational therapy. Additionally, neurolinguistic psychotherapy is considered alongside the cognitive therapies of cognitive behavioural therapy and rational emotive behavioural therapy.

Theories on development of the personality are considered in Chapter 3. NLP was originally developed as a modelling project looking at the linguistic structure of three therapists. At the time it was never the intent of Bandler and Grinder to include any theories around the development of the personality. Theories have been harnessed by therapists in the field and are utilised as a framework to understand the development of the individual. I recognise the limitations and opportunities presented by a model that has little theory concerning development of the personality, and I introduce the theories of personality as they are presented by Erickson, Satir and Perls, while recognising that a constructivist's view would encourage working with no such theory. Massey's influence of the three developmental stages of 'imprinting', 'modelling' and 'socialisation' is included, as is the work of Lorenz on imprinting, which was integrated within NLP models by Dilts, who relates it back to psychoanalytic theory and offers powerful utilisations of these for the neurolinguistic psychotherapist. Deeper underlying personality structures are also considered, particularly the work of Massey and Graves on the development of values, which are considered to provide the fundamental motivational factors to our behaviour. Graves has influenced therapists to consider the evolutionary process of values inherent within individuals. Some therapists are also encouraged to offer a spiritual dimension to their work with clients and have brought in the notion of the development of the physical, emotional, mental and spiritual aspects of self alongside conscious, unconscious and higher conscious processes, through the work of Dilts. Beyond this are the more complex underlying personality structures known as metaprogrammes, attributed to an early developer of NLP, Leslie Cameron. The relationship of metaprogrammes to Jung's personality typology is considered, along with the relationship to the Myers Briggs's personality typing. Understanding these aspects of personality development may influence the work of the therapist, in enabling the client to develop a greater understanding of themselves and their own traits, but also in working with clients to develop more useful behavioural responses. The latest theory on neuroscience is introduced at this stage in the light of what is known about the developing brain and the regulating self system. The chapter concludes with a case history demonstrating how the personality can be reformed by working interrelationally while adhering to the principles of constructivist psychotherapy.

Chapter 4 places the neurological components of neurolinguistic psychotherapy within Korzybski's work *Science and Sanity* (1933), and goes on to include the work of Carroll, Damasio, Edelman, Gerhardt, Heylighen, Panksepp, Pert, Schore and Von Foerster. The chapter recognises the inherent link between programmatic therapy and neurological processes, and the reader is encouraged to move beyond the concepts offered within traditional NLP and anchoring of states and responses as developed initially by Twitmeyer, and then by Pavlov. The chapter reviews the theory of neurology that sits behind some of the techniques that make up the model of NLP. The reader is asked to consider neurology and the developing brain, including the effect that stress and increased levels of cortisol can have on the brain of the developing infant. This is likely to challenge the reader who may prefer a purist view that all clients have all the resources inside themselves to succeed. The chapter debates this notion and asks the reader to consider some of the recent work around neuroscience and attachment theory in the light of this presupposition.

The concept that all molecules within the human body are capable of responding at an emotional level takes anchoring to a new level. The reader is encouraged to consider the possibilities that this affords within the therapeutic setting, including working with the somatisation of emotional distress. I include within this work a case history of the neurological re-patterning and developmental work with a client over an extensive period of time in therapy, setting aside the notion that neurolinguistic psychotherapy is always brief therapy. A contrast is given to this case history towards the end of the chapter when a case is discussed that only uses future-oriented work and the possibilities in enabling neurological re-patterning from a solution-oriented approach.

Chapter 5 begins with a reminder of the theoretical components that make up the linguistic processes of NLP and the need to utilise the powerful structures of language in NLP within an ecological frame. The linguistic structures are reviewed from each of the original therapists' perspectives, with connections made to the work of Watzlawick and the psychology of linguistic structure. Each of the linguistic aspects is considered in the light of the therapist who works from a constructivist's viewpoint, and a case study is used to highlight the effects of working with the linguistic structure of the client's reality. The case study is continued into the exploration of the paradoxes that exist in the client's world and how these are represented through linguistic double binds, which are then facilitated through the theory afforded by quantum linguistics. An alternative perspective to the resolution of such paradoxes is considered in the recent work of Tompkins and Lawley on clean language. The chapter concludes with an extensive case summary of a client's linguistic representation of their therapeutic process.

The use of programming within NLP is placed within the context of programmatic models of change in Chapter 6 and a dialogue is conducted to consider the limitations of a programmatic model. A wider perspective is given, bringing in the systemic narrative of Bateson as an anthropologist. The systemic approach is taken beyond this and considered within the model of solution-oriented therapy which emerged out of the original modelling of Erickson by O'Hanlon. This is represented in a brief case history that demonstrates the power of facilitating change at a systemic level by transferring existing resources across contexts. Behaviourist theory and the work of Pavlov, Skinner and Lazarus are considered, with Bolstad providing a comparison of working with anchored behavioural responses across a range of modalities. The systemic patterns of Bateson re-emerge in Dilts's work, which is considered in depth and linked back to the theory of development of the personality, particularly the evolutionary aspects that would be considered to be an inherent part of the personality among NLP therapists.

Patterns are considered within the context of the generalisation process that is core to NLP, and a case history is presented that demonstrates the opportunity afforded within neurolinguistic psychotherapy to resolve ingrained patterns of behaviours. The chapter is completed with a review of the power of working with goals, including the connections with solution-focused therapy.

Much of the work of the neurolinguistic psychotherapist is to enable clients to reframe their belief structures and resolve negative emotions. In Chapter 7, this is placed in the context of a theoretical framework and the development of emotional constructs as they are presented by Erickson and Satir. The reader is reminded of the therapeutic techniques that are core to NLP, particularly the work of Dilts, Bodenhamer, Hall and James, all of which use time code work to reframe a client's experience of their past relationship to emotions and experiences. Each of these techniques is programmatic in nature and the reader is asked to consider how they might be used in a less programmatic way to enable the client to gain more insight and understanding with regard to their own inner landscape. The opportunity that is afforded through time line interventions and the scientific rationale for these methodologies is discussed.

Programmes of personality from Chapter 3 are revisited, with this moving on to the development of patterns of identity. The notion of the development of the self is considered, as is the development of parts or splitting. A range of theories are presented, including the resolution of parts through some of the techniques available within NLP. This theory is then reconnected to current thinking on neuroscience and the potential of repair of neural synapses through the therapeutic relationship. The chapter concludes with an ecological review of prime concern and core belief processes, and how these can be assisted within the therapeutic relationship.

An ecological discussion is held as the introduction to Chapter 8, reminding readers of the presuppositions of neurolinguistic psychotherapy work, the basis of constructivist thinking and the role of the therapist within an ethical framework. Rapport was a core aspect of the work particularly of Erickson and this is revisited in the light of what we now know about neuroscience and the effect that rapport has on reducing cortisol levels in the brain.

The reader is given insight into two case studies that represent the various components of neurolinguistic psychotherapy and the role that the therapist has had in each of these relationships. One case demonstrates work with complex psychological problems and the inclusion of a relational approach, whereas the second case demonstrates a more programmatic way of working that facilitates the client towards her outcome. They show how the therapeutic work modelled from Erickson, Satir and Perls is brought to life in the therapy setting. A model of therapy process is presented for therapists who wish to have a structured methodology to refer to.

Chapter 9 reviews neurolinguistic psychotherapy as a postmodern approach. The debate between constructivism and behaviourist approaches is concluded. The reader is reminded again of the subjectivity of the therapist with case studies that demonstrate how the internal world of the therapist can add to or take away from the therapy relationship. A summary of the research within NLP is discussed and I make recommendations on how the modality can be advanced through the use of empirical research methodologies.

The chapter concludes with a summary of neurolinguistic psychotherapy principally as a therapeutic process that works to facilitate change through the unconscious as demonstrated by Erickson, Satir and Perls. It is presented as an advancing model of therapy and challenges the reader to advance their own work by considering how it can be merged with and complement other approaches.

Chapter 1

Founding principles of NLP

> Two important characteristics of maps should be noticed. A map is not the territory it represents, but, if correct, it has a similar structure to the territory, which accounts for its usefulness. If the map could be ideally correct, it would include, in a reduced scale, the map of the map; the map of the map of the map; and so on, endlessly, a fact first noticed by Royce.
>
> (Korzybski, 1948, p. 38)

Within this chapter, the founding principles of NLP are considered as a psychological model that enables the understanding of subjective experience. The theory of NLP is presented as an overview, including the historical influence that Erickson, Satir and Perls had on the work of Bandler and Grinder. The philosophical principles of the work of each of these three therapists is initially considered and expanded further within subsequent chapters. Each of the therapists worked with the subjectivity of their client's experience and Erickson in particular utilised this subjectivity of the client's presented reality to therapeutic advantage. Over the past 15 years, NLP has developed into a therapeutic model and I have linked the presuppositions of NLP to neurolinguistic psychotherapy, providing case examples of how these are incorporated into everyday practice.

Historical roots of NLP

It is important to consider the historical background of the development of NLP, as NLP in itself is not a psychotherapy, but has developed through Bandler and Grinder's modelling of the work of three therapists: Milton Erickson, a psychiatrist and hypnotherapist; Virginia Satir, a family therapist; and Fritz Perls, a gestalt therapist. It is mainly Erickson's work that has influenced the neurolinguistic psychotherapist today.

Bodenhamer and Hall (1999) define modelling as 'the process of observing and replicating the successful actions and behaviours of others; the process of discerning the sequence of internal representations and behaviours that enable someone to accomplish a task' (p. 395). Through modelling, Bandler and Grinder were utilising Pareto's (1935) principle that 80% of any results of a given behaviour will be produced by only 20% of input. They were able to successfully identify the 20% of Erickson's, Satir's and Perls's linguistic behaviours that made a difference to their therapy work, separate these from the idiosyncratic, install them in themselves and achieve the same results.

Over the next few years, Bandler and Grinder continued to develop the model to include further work on programming through language, including the work of Korzybski and Watzlawick. They also incorporated systematic behavioural studies building on the theories of the physiologist and psychologist Pavlov, and the programming and strategy work of Miller and Galanter. Since Bandler and Grinder's early work, NLP has expanded to include cybernetics and systems theory, philosophy, unconscious processes, cognitive psychology, neuroscience and spirituality.

Milton Erickson

Erickson had suffered from poliomyelitis as a young man and had learnt much of what later came to influence his work during his recovery from this illness. His inability to move freely meant that he observed very closely the non-verbal and verbal interactions of those around him and began to recognise that there were frequently contradictions between the verbal and non-verbal patterns. He used this heightened acuity to inform his therapeutic work later on, often bringing to consciousness unconscious patterns of behaviour.

Erickson began his career as a medical doctor, and a Masters graduate in psychology. He started to practise hypnosis in the 1920s and worked as a psychiatrist in the 1930s in Massachusetts. He developed a particular interest in the use of hypnosis in a therapy setting and spent much of his time researching and teaching therapeutic hypnosis, as well as working from a private practice in Phoenix, Arizona. Although he was initially considered a controversial figure, his work in the latter years of his life achieved considerable recognition. He has directly influenced the work of the well-respected therapists Rossi, Haley, O'Hanlon and Gilligan, among others, and his approaches continue to influence a range of psychotherapies today.

Virginia Satir

Satir was a therapist who was strongly influenced by the notion of the interdependence of people within a system. The main focus of her work was to use different perspectives to aid people to gain greater self-esteem, and she encouraged people to achieve balance between their own natural drives for personal development and the need to respect other people. Her work with families brought the notion of parts therapy to life and she would often encourage individuals to negotiate with more destructive aspects of their personality that were imprints from their own early influences. She also found herself acting the 'Leveller' to the different family roles that were acted out in the therapy room, those of 'Placater', often attributed to the mother/wife, the 'Blamer', often attributed to the father or head of the family, and the child roles of 'Distracter' for the younger child and 'Computer' for the older child.

Fritz Perls

Fritz Perls brought some of the principal components of gestalt therapy to NLP. His model of gestalt therapy moved away from its early aggressive and provocative tendencies and towards a place that respected the integrity of the individual through integration of mind and emotions. He utilised neurological processing of our sensory experiences and was one of the first therapists to actively include the senses of sight, sound, touch and feelings in his communication with clients.

Theory of NLP

> You cannot pin NLP down to a single definition. There are many explanations of NLP, each like a light shining from a different angle, picking out the whole shape and shadow of the subject.
>
> (O'Connor, 2001, p. 1)

Probably the most difficult thing to describe in NLP is what it is. There are a vast array of descriptions and each person who utilises the methodology will often have their own interpretation of what it is, based on their subjective experience. O'Connor (2001), in *NLP Workbook*, presents the following series of definitions as giving 'a good idea of the field' (p. 2).

- NLP is the study of the structure of subjective experience.
- NLP is an accelerated learning strategy for the detection and utilisation of patterns in the world (John Grinder).
- NLP is the epistemology of returning to what we have lost – a state of grace (John Grinder).
- NLP is an attitude and a methodology that leaves behind a trail of techniques (Richard Bandler).
- NLP is the influence of language on our mind and subsequent behaviour.
- NLP is the systemic study of human communication (Alex Von Uhde).
- NLP is the method for modelling excellence so it can be duplicated.

Each of these definitions goes only some way towards describing what NLP is and attempts to provide a summary of the subjectivity of human experience and how one can work with this subjectivity to facilitate more choice.

NLP is made up of three core components:

- neurology
- linguistics
- programming.

In the context of NLP, neurology is the study of the mind and how a person thinks and codes information at a neurological level; linguistics is how language is used to directly affect the internal landscape, state and behaviours; programming is how the internal and external behaviours are programmed or sequenced to achieve specific results.

Theory of neurolinguistic psychotherapy

McDermott and Jago (2001) define neurolinguistic psychotherapy as 'a therapy of what is possible; it opens for the client and therapist a voyage which is genuinely into the unknown' (p. 11). Neurolinguistic psychotherapy operates from the assumption that 'a client should always leave the therapist's room with more choices than they came in with' (p. 11). The purpose of neurolinguistic psychotherapy is to create more choice while at the same time working towards the client's outcome. McDermott and Jago recognise that this potential for growth towards outcome occurs if the fundamental survival needs are met and that because neurolinguistic psychotherapy works towards outcomes and considers the subjective nature of a client's experience, it does not 'identify or label a hitherto unremarked upon part of the client's pathology' (p. 11).

Kostere and Malatesta (1990) also view neurolinguistic psychotherapy as a model that facilitates choice for the client by assisting clients to change the 'limits in their model of the world' (p. 20). They view the purpose of therapy as 'working with clients in order to facilitate the expansion of their world model, that is, to open new possibilities, to broaden the scope and depth of their world views, and to expand their models' (p. 20).

The European Association for Neurolinguistic Psychotherapy (EANLPt) defines neurolinguistic psychotherapy as follows:

Neurolinguistic Psychotherapy is a systemic imaginative method of psychotherapy with an integrative-cognitive approach. The principal idea of Neurolinguistic Psychotherapy (NLPt) is the goal-orientated work with a person paying particular regard to his/her representation systems, metaphors and relation matrices. In the course of the therapeutical work in NLPt the verbal and analogue shaping and the integration of the expressions of one's life and digital information processes is given an equal share of attention. The aim of the method consists in accompanying and giving support to human beings so that they can obtain ecologically compatible goals. Further the method helps to position the subjectively good intentions underlying the symptoms of illness and/or dysfunction so that old fixations about inner and outer unproductive behaviour and beliefs can be dissociated and new subjectively and intersubjectively sound behaviours and beliefs can be established and integrated.

(Jelem & Schutz, 2007)

The Neurolinguistic Psychotherapy and Counselling Association (NLPtCA) stays closer to NLP and defines neurolinguistic psychotherapy as:

A specialised form of Neuro Linguistic Programming (NLP). The idea is that we work from and react to the world as we construct it from our experiences rather than directly from the 'real world.' We build our own unique models or maps of the world. Although all such maps are genuine to each of us, no one map is fully able to represent the 'real world.' Further, NLP is a way of exploring how people think, identifying success and then applying these successful actions or even beliefs in ways that work. This has proved practical and effective in a wide range of applications and situations. Using this form of what is called 'modelling' change can be quite quick. NLPt is broad based and draws on concepts from many areas of psychology and psychotherapy. Influences stem from the Gestalt 'school', the family therapy of Virginia Satir, Ericksonian brief therapy, and humanistic psychology. There are also clear links with the fields of systems theory, behavioural psychology and linguistics.

(NLPtCA, 2006)

Neurolinguistic psychotherapy is a model of therapy that makes a series of assumptions about a client, even before the client arrives for therapy.

- The client is the expert on their problem and therefore the expert on the solution. (If they knew how to create the problem, they will equally know how to 'un-create' the problem.)
- The client's problem is how they structure their subjective experience, and it is therefore possible to change their subjective view, through 'how' rather than 'why' questions.
- The client has unlimited resources and flexibility of behaviour; it is a matter of facilitating the client to access and utilise these resources.

- The client will have their own internal map of the presenting 'problem' and will have developed a series of behaviours in response to this map.
- These behaviours have been generalised over time.
- Each of the behaviours that the client presents with will have a purpose and function.
- The purpose and function of each of the behaviours will have been positive for the client at some point in time.
- Behaviour is precisely that; it is not the identity of the person and the person is always more than their behaviour.
- Behaviours are contextually dependent, therefore there will be a time when they don't 'do' the behaviour, i.e., the solution already exists.
- The client will communicate their internal landscape or 'map' in ways that are both conscious and unconscious.
- The purpose of therapy is to increase choice for a client and facilitate them to a more resourceful state than they currently have access to.
- A small change in the structure of the client's reality can result in a major change in their subjective experience.
- The therapist can't not project their perception of the client onto the client.
- The main focus of therapy is towards outcomes.

Each of these assumptions recognises the subjectivity of a client's experience and assists the therapist to respect and acknowledge the subjective reality that their clients present in therapy.

The map is not the territory – the subjectivity of experience

Korzybski's 'the map is not the territory' underpins neurolinguistic psychotherapy as a therapeutic model that works with the subjectivity of a client's experience. The structural components of the NLP communication model (Figure 1.1) presuppose that there are a set of filters that directly influence the internal representation of the external world. Although the communication model is thought to be unique to NLP, similar concepts are described in the work of Gerhardt (2004, p. 24), who has researched the developing brain of an infant:

> Unconsciously acquired, non-verbal patterns and expectations have been described by various writers in different ways. Daniel Stern (1985) calls them representations of interactions that have been generalised (RIGs). John Bowlby calls them 'internal working models'. Wilma Bucci calls them 'emotional schemas' (1997). Robert Clyman calls them 'procedural memory' (1991).

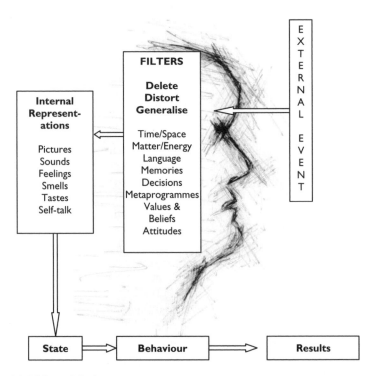

Figure 1.1 NLP model of communication

However these filters are developed, they will each affect the behavioural responses of an individual based on the individual's subjective experience.

Within the NLP communication model, it is recognised that a person determines their construct of the external world via a series of filtering processes: deleting portions of experience determined by the ability to handle abstract data and a preference for absorbing information in manageable chunks; generalising on past learned experiences and behavioural responses; and distorting the event by interpreting it in a way that fits the internal world.

The basis for the filtering of information is found in Korzybski's (1948) review on general semantics where he proposes that deletion is an affective disturbance causing people to fail to recognise the intention, goal or meaning of information that they receive from another individual, 'Disturbances of the semantic reactions in connection with faulty education and ignorance must be considered in 1933 as sub-microscopic colloidal lesions' (p. 20). The neuroscientific component of this is supported in Rothschild's (2000) work on trauma. Neural synapses connect both cognitive and somatic memory to the brain, but Rothschild states that 'nothing is fixed about the sequence of synapses . . . . New learning is achieved through the creation of new synapse strings, or adaptation of existing ones. Forgetting . . . is the result of disuse of synapse strings – as the saying goes, "use it or lose it"' (p. 19). She continues by connecting this to the NLP concept of distortion: 'It is also, for better or worse, through the alteration of synapses that memory can be distorted' (p. 20).

Additionally, there are a number of subjective factors within an individual's personal construct that directly influence how information is filtered – time/space/matter/energy, language, memories, decisions, metaprogrammes, values, beliefs, attitudes. These will be considered in depth throughout the relevant chapters in the book. The filter of time/space/matter/energy supports the ability to reason and make logical one's experiences, i.e., consciousness. Einstein's theory of special relativity, whereby life is viewed in terms of a four-dimensional world, proposes that it is through experiences that two people will observe the same thing differently – an optical illusion of consciousness.

Kovelman (1998, p. 13) elegantly presents this in an interpretation of consciousness:

> In order to get anywhere in our four-dimensional world one needs to know where he is at a particular moment, and where he wishes to be in the next. Hence, location and place are determined by the relative placement of at least two points in space. Without a here, we cannot go there. Without a there, we will never arrive here. Further, the neurological system of an observer interacts with externally perceived objects in order to create an inner experience of places and objects existing in four-dimensional space-time. It is our neurological apparatus which allows us to perceive imperceptibly discrete, small movements occurring in time and space, as continuous and smooth. It is our brain, in here, which interprets sensory information out there, and determines how we understand and see our physical world.

In the context of psychotherapy, one then has to question the concept of 'now'. How does the therapist come to know the 'now' that exists for a client? How can the therapist determine that the 'now' that they *think* exists for the client is not, in fact, their own interpretation of their 'now' in relation to how they have interpreted the client's 'now'?

Haley (1993) summarises how Erickson utilised the concept of working with space and time to facilitate change in his clients. He recognises that Erickson's 'strategic therapy' was often about using hypnotic trance: 'transforming a severe symptom into a milder one, or one of shorter duration, he can think of shifting an interpersonal problem into an advantage' (p. 18). An example of how Erickson used this in a family context is given by Haley (1993). Erickson begins by explaining how he would have seen a family together initially to 'lay down a foundation' (p. 32) of the family dynamic and would use the chairs that each member of the family sat in as spatial indicators of the family roles: 'that spatial compartmentalisation usually prevents the others from barging into the conversation, and it forces the others unmercifully to take a more objective view' (p. 33). He would ensure that he was also able to send 'members in and out of the office' (p. 33). He was then able to use the spatial relationships within the family as a way of enabling a client to see things from the perspective of another family member. 'I carefully move father from his chair and put him into mother's chair . . . I might put mother in the child's chair, at least temporarily. Sometimes I comment on this by saying, 'As you sit where your son was sitting, you can think more clearly about him' (p. 33). He summarises the aim of this family work as follows: 'the family grouping is being rearranged, which is what you are after when changing a family' (p. 33).

Perceptions of reality

> We are what we think.
> All that we are arises with our thoughts.
> With our thoughts we make the world.
>   (The Buddha, quoted by Byrom, 1976)

One of the definitions of NLP is the study of subjective experience; it holds within it the notion that we all have differing perceptions of reality. We use these perceptions of reality to project our lived experience onto the outside world, leading us to the concept of 'Perception is Projection'. Neuro-linguistic psychotherapists often reference Jung as the influence behind this notion, yet historically Freud, as an influencer of Jung, already assumed that judgement is the rejection of stimuli. He postulated that perception is more than just reception, rather it already consists of a judgement that functions as a barrier against stimuli. In her biography of Klein, Kristeva (2001, pp. 172–173) builds on this in her summary of Klein's work on negation and symbolism:

> That is what is reflected in the mechanism of Freud's *Verneinung*: the patient can name sexual stimulation or confess to it only if he denies it. (On: 'You ask who this person in the dream can be. It's *not* his mother.' We emend this to; 'so it *is* his mother.') (emphasis in original)

Bateson, who has strongly influenced the systemic and cybernetic aspects of NLP, picked up on this and utilised the Greek philosophical concepts of Creatura and Pleroma in Jung's 'The Seven Sermons to the Dead'. This idea accepts that meaning and organisation are projected onto the world, with Creatura defining the perceived world, subject to difference, distinction and information, and Pleroma referring to the world that is undifferentiated by subjectivity.

The concept that a person creates reality based on the need to project their subjective experience onto the outside world is common across many different schools of psychotherapy. It naturally links to Einstein's theory on special relativity and Heisenberg's (1932) principle that the conception of objective reality is based in uncertainty. Heisenberg determined that any reality will be dependent on the position from which it is observed. The electron can act as a wave or a particle depending on the point of view, and whenever reality is observed, the observer will always influence it.

Both psychoanalytic and analytic psychotherapy practice hold similar concepts to the neurolinguistic notions of perception and reality represented in the work of Freud and Jung, and at the opposite end of the therapeutic spectrum within person-centred therapy there exists the notion of Rogers' 'Perception is reality'. Tudor and Worrall (2006) comment that 'language is not so much a device for reporting one's experience, but a defining framework for it. If we agree that perception is reality . . . then the language we use to describe that perception is also reality' (p. 40).

Irrespective of how the notion of 'Perception is Projection' has come about, the neurolinguistic therapist has a responsibility to hold in mind the subjectivity of their own and their client's experience. They are as likely to project their reality onto a client as the client is to project their reality onto their own subjective experience of the world.

Within this concept of 'Perception is Projection', I include Aristotle's (384–322 BCE) principles of cause and effect – *All causes of things are beginnings; that we have scientific knowledge when we know the cause; that to know a thing's existence is to know the reason why it is*. Within a neurolinguistic framework, this principle presupposes that a client needs to be *at cause* to enable change to happen. One could say that a client is already at cause because they have made the first step in seeking assistance through therapy, yet others would hesitate on this point, and postulate that if the client were truly at cause, they would have resolved the issue that has brought them to therapy, therefore they must be *at the effect* of their subjective experience.

Presuppositions in the context of neurolinguistic psychotherapy

Erickson, Perls and Satir operated from within a series of belief structures that later became adopted as the presuppositions of NLP, i.e., useful assumptions that aid the communication process. Dilts (in Dilts & Delozier, 2000, pp. 1001–1002) divides the presuppositions into two components, that of 'The Map is Not the Territory' and 'Biological Interactions are Systemic

(Cybernetic) as Opposed to Linear'. Bodenhamer and Hall (1999, pp. 64–65) divide the presuppositions into four components, linking with different aspects of the model for communication. Both of these definitions set the presuppositions within a non-therapeutic frame, and I have considered them here in the light of psychotherapeutic process.

1. The 'map' is not the 'territory' – people respond to their own perceptions of reality

As already acknowledged, clients will present with a subjective map of their reality in the 'here and now'. The map is a representation of the client's deep structure after it has gone through the filtering processes of deletion, distortion and generalisation. The map, if carefully considered, will hold clues to what is going on at a deep structure level.

Erickson was particularly adept at noticing clues within the map that gave an indication of what might be occurring in the deeper unconscious structures of a client. An example cited by Rosen (1982) in *My Voice Will Go With You* refers to a client that has consulted 26 doctors, none of whom could find anything wrong with her; she was eventually referred to a psychiatrist. When Erickson investigated what had happened with each of the doctors, she responded, 'Well, I always sneezed when they started to examine my right breast' (p. 190). On hearing this, Erickson immediately called a gynaecologist and arranged for a full examination of the client's breasts, suggesting that she had a lump in her right breast. When she was examined, a malignancy of her right breast was found and treated.

The role of the therapist is to relate to the presented map in a way that engenders useful change for the client. This may be by the client gaining more 'knowing' about their own internal landscapes, or it may be for the client to choose to change their map in response to what they know about the maps of others based on their projected reality. Or, as demonstrated here with Erickson, it may be about noticing what is present in the map that provides clues to deeper processes.

2. The meaning of a communication to another person is the response it elicits in that person, regardless of the intent of the communicator

Each therapist holds 100% responsibility for their communication with clients, in the same way that clients hold 100% responsibility for their communication with the therapist. Much of Satir's work in family therapy was to enable individuals to accept responsibility for their communication. She was a proponent of the view that all people are interdependent with each other, and she worked with individuals to increase their self-esteem and to enable them to gain understanding of the point of view of other people. She did this by enabling her clients to alter their perspective through acting out the different roles within the family. This then resulted in a change in the individual's perception of themselves through the eyes of the interdependent 'other'. The meta-model, as it was elicited by Bandler and Grinder through modelling Satir, facilitated clients to reconnect with the deep structure of their experience. In doing this, Satir enabled them to create more choice in their communications to the outside world, and at the same time reframed their internal subjective experience by reconnecting them to the source of their disabling constructs.

3. No response, experience, behaviour is meaningful outside of the context in which it was established, or the response it elicits next

A therapist will observe many meanings that the client holds within their subjective experience. If the therapist were to 'try them on' in their model of the world, with a different set of life experiences, a different set of filters and no gestalt formed from an experience, they could seem almost meaningless. And even as the client presents them in their current reality, the meaning that the client applies to the event that they are referring to will be contextually tied to their reactions to the event as it first occurred. Gerhardt (2004, p. 143) comments:

> From an adult perspective, 'abuse' tends to mean the more gross and visible examples of maltreatment such as hitting and injuring children, or violating them sexually. It is much harder, I think, for some adults to appreciate that being told you are a 'stupid waste of space' or being left unattended or alone are also traumatic for dependent children. The essential aspect of trauma is that it generates doubts about surviving – either as a body, but equally as a psychological self. As one survivor put it: 'I had to believe I was hurt and hated myself because I was so bad, and so all these years I hurt and hated myself.'

I experienced a client who attended a series of sessions with me, always referring obliquely to the 'thing that she couldn't tell me as it was so awful'. I paced her model of the world through these sessions, developing a relationship of trust whereby she could disclose this most 'awful thing'. Her 'awful thing' was dyslexia and her experiences of being isolated, picked on and marginalised at school had created such a gestalt of abuse and shame that it took her some time before she could entrust me with that information.

---

4. Mind-and-body form a cybernetic system

Much of Erickson's work utilised the mind–body system based on his own auto-hypnotic experiences of mind–body communication. He included this self-experience in his clinical work with patients and would communicate with one component of a person's physiological or emotional make-up to directly influence another aspect. The rationale behind this has been advanced through the work of Chopra. Chopra (1989) brought the principles of Ayurvedic medicine into western thinking and introduced three concepts of the mind–body system:

1   that intelligence is present everywhere in our bodies
2   that our own inner intelligence is superior to any that we try to substitute from outside
3   that intelligence is more important than the matter of the body, as without the intelligence the body would be redundant.

Chopra's (1989, pp. 41–42) definition of the intelligence of the mind–body is:

> Every cell in the body is programmed by its DNA, for example, to divide at a certain rate, producing two new cells after the mother cell splits in half. Like everything else regulated by our inner intelligence, this process is not purely mechanical. A cell divides in response to its own internal need, combined signals generated from cells around it, the brain, the faraway organs that are 'talking' to it via chemical messengers.

Pert (1997) has added to Chopra's work with her studies on the emotion-carrying neuropeptides. Her research has demonstrated that the core limbic brain structures that are the basis of our emotions – the amygdala, hippocampus, and limbic cortex – contain up to 95% of neuropeptide receptors. She provides a tongue-in-cheek interpretation of this finding in relation to psychoanalysis:

> If we accept the idea that peptides and other informational substances are the biochemicals of emotion, their distribution in the body's nerves has all kinds of significance, which Sigmund Freud, were he alive today, would gleefully point out as the molecular confirmation of his theories. The body is the unconscious mind!
>
> (p. 141)

These concepts will be explored further in Chapter 4, where I discuss the neurological aspects of neurolinguistic psychotherapy in detail.

5. The processes that take place within a person and between people and their environment are systemic. Our bodies, our societies and our universe form an ecology of systems and subsystems all of which interact with and mutually influence each other and a pattern of associations (anchors) may be set up through a single trial experience in contrast to linear repetitions

This presupposition is embedded in the concept of operant conditioning (Skinner, 1961). The principle accepts that all behaviour is generated via a cause/effect system of either positive or negative reinforcement and is the basis of behaviour modification programmes. Skinner shows that a random behaviour that results in a reward will be repeated to see if the same reward can be elicited. This is the basis of generalised behavioural responses in NLP. Once the behaviour is set, the strategy that generated the behaviour in the first instance often disappears from consciousness. It is thought that positive stimuli such as pleasure, emotional contact or physical contact will increase the likelihood of the behaviour being replicated, and pain or emotional and physical withdrawal will reduce the chance of the behaviour being replicated.

By understanding how a client has sequenced their representation systems, resulting in specific behaviours, it is then possible to change the sequence to facilitate a different result. O'Hanlon (2000) has developed Erickson's work by formulating a model of Possibility Therapy that is covered in depth in his book *Do One Thing Different*. He proposes that if clients either change one aspect of the 'doing' of the situation, or one aspect of the 'viewing' of the situation, then the problem will change.

O'Hanlon and Weiner-Davis (2003, pp. 130–131) list eight ways of changing the 'doing' or 'viewing' of the problem or complaint as it is perceived by the client:

- change the frequency or rate of the performance of the complaint
- change the timing of performance of the complaint
- change the duration of the performance of the complaint
- change the location of the performance of the complaint
- add (at least) one element to the complaint pattern
- change the sequence of elements/events in the complaint pattern
- break the complaint pattern into smaller pieces or elements
- link the complaint performance to the performance of some burdensome activity.

A mother of a 12-year-old boy consulted me for therapy for her son. He had been diagnosed with Tourette's syndrome some time ago and she was finding his behaviour increasingly difficult. When the young man arrived for therapy, he was uncommunicative, sullen in appearance and avoided eye contact or meaningful dialogue. He reluctantly told me a little about his experiences in the family; he felt that he was given everything that he wanted and apart from being irritated by his little sister, could not see that there was a problem. He was having difficulties at school, was being picked on because of his spontaneous tics and vocal eruptions and was being increasingly excluded for bad behaviour. After a time, we found some areas that he did want to share with me, and he became quite animated as he told me about a 24-hour rowing competition that he was entering for charity. He was proud that he was preparing for it by getting up an hour earlier each day and practising on his rowing machine before going to school. I suggested to him that he should get up an hour earlier than this, and use the time to 'do' his tics and vocal eruptions each time he pulled the row bar. This was to be the only time that he could do this, and not at any other time, and he could do it as much as he liked. In fact the faster he rowed, the fitter he would become and the more times he could 'do' his tics and vocal eruptions. Two weeks after this session his mother called to say that he did not want to return for a further session as he did not consider that I had helped him. He was doing his tics more than ever now as he understood that I had given him 'permission' to do them as often as he wanted. The tics were now getting on his nerves and he wanted to stop. One evening he took a hammer and, every time he did a tic, he hit his leg with the hammer. His symptoms stopped completely from that evening and he has remained symptom-free.

I saw him fairly recently, five years after this therapy. He has grown to be a delightful young man, and fondly recalls how mad he was with me for not sorting him out and how he managed to 'fix' himself. In essence, I changed one aspect of his 'doing' of the problem, and with some hypnotic suggestion, facilitated him to a place where he could no longer 'do' the original complaint.

6. We respect each person's model of the world – no individual map is any more 'real' or 'true' than any other. All maps have some validity

Erickson was a master at finding new and creative ways of demonstrating respect for his client's world view and utilising it to therapeutic advantage.

In the example given below by Haley (1993, p. 28), he enables his client to move to a position of useful activity within the therapeutic community.

> Erickson's willingness to accept working within metaphors applies not only to verbal interchange but even to persons who live a metaphoric life. Such a style of life is typical of schizophrenics, and Erickson assumes that with a schizophrenic the important message is the metaphor. For example, when Erickson was on the staff of Worcester State Hospital, there was a young patient who called himself Jesus. He paraded about as the Messiah, wore a sheet draped round him, and attempted to impose Christianity on people. Erickson approached him on the hospital grounds and said, 'I understand you have had an experience as a carpenter?' The patient could only reply that he had. Erickson involved the young man in a special project of building a bookcase and shifted him to productive labour.

In the discussion on constructivism and the subjective nature of reality in Chapter 2, it is essential that therapists demonstrate respect for clients' model of the world, even if the model of the world is creating difficulty for the therapist or those around the client. How easily a therapist can do this will be determined by their own willingness to operate from within constructivist principles, accepting that even as the observer a therapist is likely to influence the system. What do therapists hold within their own unwritten rules and expectations that might affect how another person's reality is perceived?

7. Not all interactions in a system are on the same level. What is positive on one level may be negative on another level. It is useful to separate behaviour from 'self', to separate the positive intention, function, belief, etc., that generates the behaviour from the behaviour itself

Bateson refers to 'I' as the ultimate nominalisation or abstraction beyond any objective form of meaning. As soon as a description is attributed to a person's identity it becomes a major influence on their subjective experience. Korzybski (1948, p. xxix) wrestled with the concept of identity and held the view that identity was non-existent except in the minds of philosophers and the mentally ill:

> These 'philosophers', etc., seem unaware, to give a single example, that by teaching and preaching 'identity', which is empirically non-existent in this actual world, they are *neurologically* training future generations

in the pathological identifications found in the 'mentally' ill or mal-adjusted . . . whatever we may *say* an object *'is, it is not,'* because the statement is verbal, and the facts are not. (emphasis in original)

Neurolinguistic psychotherapy would propose accepting the territory of the individual and assume that people are much more than their behaviour. Within a programmatic model of therapy, if therapy builds on the work of Dilts and effects change to facilitate the formation and reconnection of an identity that is beyond the presenting problem, then the client may well be setting up future problems with the newly forged identity, particularly if the client has secondary gain at identity level from the existing problem.

> I recall a student of mine on a practitioner course in the late 1990s. She became quite distressed towards the end of the programme; she was concerned that 'I am doing it again – I always end up saying "Look at me, poor K – attention-seeking, I always end up attention seeking".' K was wrestling with a behaviour that she was holding at identity level. She worked through the rest of her course to deal with this. She formulated a more ecological identity for herself and in her mind, and integrated the attention-seeking behaviour. A couple of years after this event, she returned to see me for therapy. Again, she was wrestling with her need for attention and had tried a series of processes with herself to deal with it, all to no avail. She worked through a number of issues and I did not see her again for another couple of years.

She has returned recently into therapy and this time has learnt to accept that her behaviour is just that, her identity is what it is, and that to try and change either would keep her in the same loop of 'insanity' that she has spent 30 years trying to get out of. The client is no longer working at identity level and attributing importance to this; she has learnt to live with who she is, accept her own behaviours and find new choices just by 'being', beyond any need to label her identity.

8. At some level all behaviour is (or was at one time) 'positively intended' and people make the best choices available to them, given the possibilities and capabilities that they perceive available to them from their model of the world

As originally coined by Rogers (1951, p. 491) in his theory of the personality, 'Behaviour is basically the goal-directed attempt of the organism to satisfy its needs as experienced, in the field as perceived'. Tudor and Worrall (2006, p. 88) have expanded on this within the field of person-centred therapy, referring to 'bizarre, destructive or self-defeating' behaviour as being 'an expression of [the client's] tendency to actualise'.

Haley (1993) had also identified this in Erickson's work, providing an alternative perspective to that offered through psychodynamic therapies, noting that 'Erickson relabels what people do in a positive way to encourage change' (p. 34). Haley acknowledged that Erickson used an aspect of the difficulties that a client presented with in therapy as a way of improving functioning of the individual. 'Rather than assuming there is something hostile in the unconscious that must be brought out, he assumes there are positive forces there that need to be freed for the person's future development' (p. 34). This sponsoring or acknowledging of the positive attributes of unuseful aspects of a person's behaviour is seen in second-generation Ericksonian therapists who have brought Gilligan's (1997) theory on self-relations into the arena of neurolinguistic psychotherapy.

To return to K, mentioned above: she has now learnt to accept her need for attention and has turned this into how she can give attention to herself. She has considered how she might give attention to and validate her own feelings of being isolated and alone when her husband is away. She has considered how she might like to receive attention when he returns home and which specific behaviours she could adopt that are most likely to attract positive behaviours from him. The client has now moved to 'cause' in her life choices and is no longer 'at the effect' of her environment or her internal negative responses.

9. The processes that take place within a person, and between people and their environment, are systemic. Our bodies, our societies and our universe form an ecology of systems and subsystems all of which interact with and mutually influence each other

Bateson (2000) held the view that the mind operates within an ecological system, and that where ideas are introduced to it, it is like introducing seeds to an environment. The seeds can only root, grow and flourish if the system is supportive. Therefore any change work that is undertaken with a client needs to be considered in the light of the wider system. To offer any change to a client without considering the ecological perspectives of the client's existing state and patterns of behaviour may result in the client creating a bigger problem than the one they originally had. Alternatively the client may bring to consciousness underlying repressed processes that the existing behaviour had kept submerged, i.e., the notion of secondary gain whereby the client may develop more complex problems if they resolve the presenting behaviour.

10. It is not possible to completely isolate any part of a system from the rest of the system. People cannot not influence each other and people respond to their own perceptions of reality

Most therapists understand the surface-level aspects of this presupposition and acknowledge that the client will communicate in ways that enable understanding. I would prefer to consider this presupposition from two perspectives, the first being its intended meaning, that clients will find ways to communicate their internal landscape; the second to look at a more complex process of communication and how Watzlawick interpreted this presupposition before it was adopted by NLP.

Clients often use creative and unconscious ways to relay their internal landscape in therapy. O'Hanlon (2002, p. 41) demonstrates this presupposition in practice where he refers to a young girl that has consulted him for therapy but is 'agitated and . . . terrified to talk about it'. A dialogue continues for some time between O'Hanlon and the girl, until finally he says 'Okay, I know this may not make sense, but what I want to say can be understood somewhere deeply inside. You can tell me and not tell me at the same time.' This created a double bind for the client in that she was enabled to keep her secret, while at the same time telling her story to the therapist unconsciously, which she promptly did through her hands. When she had finished and her hands had stopped moving, 'she opened her eyes and smiled, obviously relieved. "There," she said, "you were right. I told you and didn't tell you at the same time. My hands told you the whole story of my abuse. Now I can tell you in words."'

There are many ways that therapists can enable clients to communicate, and by respecting their map of the world, and holding true to this presupposition, with sufficient rapport and linguistic skill, it is possible to work with the deeper subjective experience of clients. Watzlawick's (1978) view of this presupposition utilises Plato's influence on Perls to consider the possibility that the communication that therapists have with clients could border on manipulation and abuse of power. He summarises his rather passionate view on this to say: 'One cannot not influence. It is, therefore, absurd to ask how influence and manipulation can be avoided, and we are left with the inescapable responsibility of deciding for ourselves how this basic law of human communication may be obeyed in the most humane, ethical and effective manner' (pp. 10–11).

This then takes me to the subjective experience of reality as a therapist. How can a therapist recognise when their own subjective map is creating complexities within a client that the therapist is remaining blind to? This raises questions concerning the role of supervision and how it might be used to understand the subjective experiences that a therapist might bring to their work. It also raises questions regarding the need or not of personal therapy for a therapist working in a more brief way with clients. Both

supervision and personal therapy provide an opportunity for a neurolinguistic psychotherapist to explore their own subjective reality and become
aware of their potential blind spots.

11. Systems are 'self-organising' and naturally seek states of balance and stability. There are no failures, only feedback

NLP is frequently portrayed as a rapid form of change work, and I know of
some therapists who have been berated by their colleagues for taking longer
than a few hours to complete therapy with a particular client. In some of
the cases that are relayed in Erickson's work with clients, he has worked
with clients over a number of years.

Erickson also viewed failure of a client to respond to therapy as being
feedback on the client's current situation. In Rosen (1982), Erickson relates
the story of an alcoholic who wanted to stop drinking. Rather than focusing
on the drinking, Erickson works strategically with the client and identifies
resources within the client's life that he could bring into the therapeutic
relationship. The client is married and he and his wife have purchased a
holiday home that they have made suitable for long visits during the
summer. The client refers to the level of freedom that he experiences at his
holiday home. 'There's no telephone. We're ten miles from civilisation. It's
beautifully furnished. Every kind of food and booze that can be brought is
up there. And every summer my wife and I spend about two or three weeks
there in the nude, really enjoying life' (p. 128). Erickson utilised this as a
potential resource and suggested to the client a strategy for ensuring that he
could not access alcohol while spending time at the holiday home. The
client's response to this was, 'Doctor, I think I'm mistaken about wanting to
quit drinking' (p. 128). Erickson always used feedback with his clients
during therapy to assess their willingness to change and the effect that his
therapeutic approach was having at different points in time.

Identifying any secondary gain that a client may have with regard to
letting go or stopping their existing pattern of behaviour is one key element
of assessing the client's willingness to change. In Chapter 8 I consider
additional processes that enable the assessment of a client's willingness to
change.

12. The law of requisite variety – the part of the system with the most flexibility of behaviour will be the controlling or catalytic element in the system

Grounded in cybernetics and systems theory, this presupposition accepts
the principle that the more flexible in communication the therapist is, the
more likely they are to direct influence over the client's system. In therapy,

it is important to consider the notion that the client has already exerted an inordinate amount of unconscious control over retaining their present state and circumstances; otherwise they would not be seeking external assistance to deal with the problem. There are a number of processes within the methodology of NLP that, if taught to a client, will enable greater choice within their own system, including any that facilitate dissociation from the current state and association into a future desired state.

13. People already have (or potentially have) all of the resources they need to act effectively

This presupposition formed the basis of Erickson's work, with him working from the principle that not only do people have all the resources that they need, but also people are not broken and therefore do not need fixing. By resources I refer to internal resources rather than those in the external world. Reframing plays a part here, in that something that a client may perceive as a problem, if reframed appropriately, can actually be utilised as a resource that aids recovery and growth of the individual: as in the case of K, who learnt to use her previous problem of attention-seeking as an effective calibrator of her internal state, so that when she needed to give attention to herself, her internal mechanism would communicate this need to her.

Rothschild (2000, pp. 88–92) suggests that we have five major classes of resources: functional, physical, psychological, interpersonal and spiritual. When related to Dilts's neurological levels, functional resources would be those held at environmental levels, and would include factors such as contracts for therapy. The client is encouraged to work within a contract that includes contact outside of therapy or other factors that might act as a protection mechanism when working through trauma, e.g., sleeping with a phone next to them at night after being burgled. Physical resources are those held at a behavioural level and within the physical body such as utilisation of resource anchors or taking up new physical activities that aid resolution of the problem. Psychological resources relate to those held at capability, value and belief levels. These include the innate psychological strengths that an individual has, but also those resources that have up to now been used as defence mechanisms. Rothschild (2000) proposes that finding the opposite of a defence mechanism creates choice and balance as well as a potential resource. An example that she gives is that of dissociation, whereby she considers that dissociation can be a useful strategy for dental work, yet if left 'unchecked dissociation of that calibre can cause problems in other areas of daily functioning. What is needed . . . is to help the client learn to control his dissociation, maintaining the ability to do it when it is useful . . . and being able to stay present when that is safer or more useful' (p. 90).

Interpersonal resources are those derived at identity level and involve individuals with whom a person identifies, in the here and now or from the past. Spiritual resources are those that involve belief beyond identity, such as belief in a higher power. Rothschild raises a concern about the therapist's countertransferential response where the therapist's belief system is contrary to that of the client. By working in a constructivist way, and recognising one's own prejudices as a therapist, this risk can be minimised and clients can be enabled to utilise whatever spiritual resources are appropriate for them at a given time.

14. The 'wisest' and most 'compassionate' maps are those that make available the widest and richest range of choices, as opposed to being the most 'real' or 'accurate'

The idea that all communication and work with clients should increase choice and, more importantly, that a client will always leave in a better state and with more choices than when they arrived, is not new to neurolinguistic psychotherapy. Bateson (1972, p. 487) proposes that, 'As therapists, clearly we have a duty. First, to achieve clarity in ourselves; and then to look for every sign of clarity in others and to implement them and reinforce them in whatever is sane in them.'

Rather than focusing on 'why' things are the way they are with clients, the question of 'how' things are and 'how' they could be different is a process that inevitably expands the map and frame of reference for a client. Bringing solution-focused work into the therapeutic relationship with a client creates an environment where choice is inevitably opened up for the client. The basic tenets of solution-focused therapy as outlined by O'Hanlon and Weiner-Davis (2003, pp. 32–50), which were initially developed from Erickson's solution-focused hypnosis, are:

- clients have resources and strengths to resolve complaints
- change is constant
- the therapist's job is to identify and amplify change
- it is usually not necessary to know a great deal about the complaint in order to resolve it
- it is not necessary to know the cause or function of a complaint to resolve it
- a small change is all that is necessary; a change in one part of the system can effect change in another part of the system
- clients define the goal
- rapid change or resolution of problems is possible
- there is no one 'right' way to view things; different views may be just as valid and may fit the facts just as well

- focus is on what is possible and changeable, rather than what is impossible and intractable.

15. Individual skills are a function of the development and sequencing of representational systems

Dilts (in Dilts & Delozier, 2000) suggests that it is the sequencing and utilisation of representational systems, i.e., the ability to process information in visual, auditory and kinaesthetic systems, that enables a person to get the results that they get, and it is the ability to access and utilise these that is the basis for generating positive life experiences. He also utilises this presupposition to suggest that as individuals have the ability to utilise all representational systems, it is possible to model the sequencing and order of the representational systems within an inherent model, and install this in someone else. From a therapeutic perspective, this would encourage the development of outcomes, identify the sequencing of representational systems within the outcome and assist the client to install this in themselves.

Bandler (1985, p. 7) rather provocatively said:

> Most people don't actively and deliberately use their own brains. Your brain is a like a machine without an 'off' switch. If you don't give it something to do, it just runs on and on until it gets bored. If you put someone in a sensory deprivation tank where there's no external experience, he'll start generating internal experience. If your brain is sitting around without anything to do, it's going to start doing something, and it doesn't seem to care what it is. *You* may care, but *it* doesn't.

How often does a person actually think about what their brain is doing? It has been demonstrated through neurological research that with guidance and support it is possible to re-programme brains to achieve different results. Neurolinguistic therapy offers a series of processes to clients whereby they can start to have more control over how they choose to use their brains and thereby affect the results that they are getting. Korzybski (1948, p. 62) had already alluded to this in his work *Science and Sanity*, commenting that we are '*linguistically* prevented from supplying the potentially "rational" being with the means for rationality'. He likens the human nervous system to that of animal functioning and suggests that most people live in a state of 'arrested development or regression, and, in general, disturbances of some sort' (p. 62).

In essence, what Korzybski is referring to is that the more people try to rationalise and control unconscious urges through ordered processes, the more likely they are to end up with some form of suppressed or repressed neurosis or behavioural disturbance. Hence Erickson's desire to work only with the unconscious and to make existing patterns of behaviour acceptable in some reframed way.

Neurolinguistic psychotherapy as a therapeutic model

The basic principle of NLP is the ability to model specific behaviours and replicate this into other contexts. Neurolinguistic psychotherapists have taken the fundamental principles of NLP and adapted them to work effectively in a therapeutic context. The subjectivity of an individual's experience acts as the basis for any change work that is offered within psychotherapy and in the next chapter I consider the subjective process within constructivism, hypnotherapy and a wider psychotherapeutic frame.

Chapter 2

Neurolinguistic psychotherapy in context

> The first [rule] was never to accept anything as true if I did not have
> evident knowledge of its truth; that is, carefully to avoid precipitate
> conclusions and preconceptions, and to include nothing more in my
> judgements than what presented itself to my mind so clearly and
> distinctly that I had no occasion to doubt it.
>
> (Descartes, trans. 1991, I, 120)

This chapter explores the principles of constructivism as a philosophical
base and a therapeutic approach. Neurolinguistic psychotherapy could find
a natural home in a range of therapies, but it has historically been associated with constructivism. More recently, particularly with the increasing
interest in the work of Erickson as it is portrayed by Rossi, Haley,
O'Hanlon and Gilligan, more and more neurolinguistic psychotherapists
are experiencing greater resonance with their work within the hypnopsychotherapy world. By bringing in the original work of Erickson, Satir and
Perls and the various influences on their own particular approaches in
therapy, I continue an exploration of the relationship of neurolinguistic
psychotherapy to other psychotherapy approaches. From this position, I
then present a model of the mind for neurolinguistic psychotherapy that
incorporates an alignment between the conscious and unconscious.

Constructivism as a philosophical base

Constructivist therapies have emerged out of the principles of phenomenology, which require that the therapist put aside what they know of the
world to then discover it through a clean set of filters. The therapist's role is
to make no assumptions about what they might find and certainly hold no
judgement about matters as they are discovered in therapy. Rather than
analysing a client and making meaning of the client's world as it is presented,
a therapist operating from a phenomenological base will work with the

description of the client's world as it is verbally and non-verbally portrayed in the session.

The approach for the majority of neurolinguistic psychotherapists aligns closely with the work of Kelly and personal construct therapy. Kelly was a contemporary of Piaget and it was their combined thinking that led to the development of constructivist therapies. Personal construct therapy assumes that we have a direct impact on our world and literally create it as we perceive it; in the words of Kelly (1991, p. 50), 'a person's processes are psychologically channelized by the ways in which he anticipates events'.

Here Kelly has reconnected with a philosophical perspective that has been debated since Socrates (470–399 BCE) encouraged his students to utilise his method to form a conclusion, only to point out that *since he had reported no facts, the students must have known the conclusion all along.* The purpose then of working from a constructivist principle is to assist a client to find their own solution, and assumes that the solution already exists in the client's psyche.

Constructivist therapies were strongly influenced by Piaget and Schrödinger during the second half of the twentieth century. Schrödinger's (1958) view that *Every man's world picture is and always remains a construct of his mind and cannot be proved to have any other existence* was developed by Piaget in his perspective on genetic epistemology during a series of lectures that he delivered at Columbia University in 1968. Piaget held the view that everything changes from day to day, that nothing stays fixed and that 'the current state of knowledge is a moment in history, changing just as rapidly as the state of knowledge in the past has ever changed, and, in many instances, more rapidly' (Piaget, 1968, p. 1). Both of these views are present within neurolinguistic psychotherapy and are seen through the concept that our 'now' as it exists is based on how we are currently viewing the world. A person will always filter their experience of the world according to their own internal set of personal constructs that have been developed through time. These constructs will change from moment to moment, providing an opportunity for change to occur within a short space of time. When a person is tired, emotional or particularly stressed their experience of their current reality will be different from the reality that they perceive when they are elated, relaxed or joyful. Clients may also present their construct of 'now' as a set of beliefs or emotions that were formed at a young age and have become part of their construct of 'now' with their past being lived in the present reality. Alternatively, some clients may present their 'now' as a future desired state and focus all their attention on how things 'might' be. The purpose of neurolinguistic psychotherapy is to utilise this knowledge of the current construct for the positive benefit of the client, assisting the client to achieve greater neurological, psychological and emotional choice.

Recognition of the complexity of internal constructs was the basis of Korzybski's research into general semantics, *Science and Sanity*, which later went on to inform the work of the pioneers of NLP who were keen to understand the epistemological perspective of Korzybski. Korzybski coined the term 'neurolinguistics' as a way of coding information and made reference to the world outside of us as being 'what is going on', and the world before it is experienced. It is the way that we then make sense of the world that is the basis of constructivist thinking.

The aim of constructivist therapies is to facilitate a client to gain greater insight into their own subjective experience and from this to redefine old constructs or develop new constructs and ways of being to enable greater personal choice. Building on the concepts that Piaget has presented, it would seem sensible to consider all therapeutic interventions as being determined by the client's immediate construct of now. Neurolinguistic psychotherapy concerns itself with facilitating a client to develop greater congruence within their subjective experience. As demonstrated in the communication model (Figure 1.1), there is no such thing as reality, only a construct of our perceptions based on our internal filtering mechanisms.

Milton Erickson

Bandler and Grinder (1975) identified Erickson as a master at working with the subjective experience of a client, who utilised all his observational skills to identify the many varying subjective perceptions that a client might make at any given moment. Erickson refers to these as 'double takes' that are based on 'totally different experiential associations' (p. vii). On occasions he recognised that a client might have several differing perceptions of their experience and he began to utilise language patterns that could create a range of perceptions that were frequently contradictory to enable communication at a number of different levels, notably confusing the conscious mind to then communicate directly to the unconscious mind. His high levels of sensory acuity in recognising the different forms of verbal and non-verbal communication enabled him to work with the multiple facets within a personality to therapeutic success.

An example of this is given in Rosen's (1982) description of how Erickson worked with alternative levels of meaning with a young girl who had freckles. She was becoming increasingly distressed and wanted to change her appearance as she was being mercilessly teased at school. This was having a direct effect on her behaviour and she was very angry with everybody around her. At her first session with Erickson she appeared as a very angry young lady, obviously 'ready for a fight' (p. 154). Rather than trying to pacify or sympathise with her, Erickson responded by giving her something to fight about, accusing her of being a thief. This demonstrates Erickson entering her constructed reality: she wanted to fight, so he gave her something to fight about. An argument ensued between Erickson and the girl until finally Erickson told her that he was aware of precisely what she had stolen. Erickson then utilised her negative perception of her freckles, giving them a different meaning. He told her that she had stolen 'cinnamon cookies, cinnamon buns, cinnamon rolls – and you spilled some cinnamon on your face – you're a Cinnamon Face' (p. 154).

Erickson successfully worked with and validated his client's current and past knowledge state. She hated everyone and he made sure that she took her hate and anger and placed it on him – he didn't try to change her existing construct by bringing to mind her anger towards those around her and its relationship to her freckles and the teasing she had experienced at school. Rather, he opted to reframe her constructed meaning of the freckles into something that she held in her construct as a positive reference, i.e., cinnamon. He later commented on his work with her 'You also ought to learn that it's not what you do, it's not what you say, but what the patient does, what the patient understands' (p. 154).

An epistemological viewpoint

Constructivism as a philosophical principle is closely connected to epistemology, which is found within the theories presented by Piaget (1968). Purist epistemology would determine that we will consciously only consider a piece of knowledge as it exists in the moment. When the knowledge that we have is not held within the conscious mind but is unconscious, it will have limited impact on our current reality. This raises questions, then, for the notion that all our behaviours are unconsciously driven. An alternative perspective is that we create our current reality out of our past experiences held within the unconscious. As the different philosophical tenets of NLP are considered there is a spectrum of perspectives, ranging from those who would say there is only the construct of the client's now and any historical influences are immaterial in determining how you work with the client's subjective reality, through to those who would adhere more closely to Piaget's genetic epistemology, which recognises that it is our entire history, social upbringing and associated psychological thought patterns that influence our current reality.

The therapeutic models of Erickson, Satir and Perls align themselves closely to the epistemological perspective of Piaget. The client, as they present in the now, has a social, psychological and emotional history that has influenced their current subjective reality. The role of the therapist includes the modelling or 'mapping' out of the internal subjective reality of the client, including all the historical 'landmarks' that have facilitated their experience of now as it has presented in the therapeutic space. When I explain this process to students it reminds me of my high school biology field trip. The purpose of the 'mapping' of a particular landscape to study marine life was to view the microcosmic world of the rock pool without disturbing any of the intricacies of its ecosystem. We learnt to notice where each of the various organisms was, and what was required to sustain equilibrium within the pool. It was only when we had mapped this in its entirety that we could immerse ourselves in studying the finer aspects of an anemone, or sea urchin. In working with clients, as soon as the therapist starts to make meaning of a client's presented reality, or offers an intervention for a perceived block or problem, the constructed reality of a client will change. These interventions then become part of the client's representation of their reality.

The main focus of Erickson's work was to map the internal world of his clients. He would understand their world sufficiently so that he would know that if he presented a certain symbol or idea, the client's unconscious, through a process of free association, would make meaning of the association and access their own internal resources to resolve the problem. Returning to the example of the young girl with freckles, he assisted her to access a positive reference for an alternative meaning for her freckles, and created an association between cinnamon cookies and freckles, rather than teasing, anger and freckles.

Roots within constructivist therapies

Personal construct therapy

As I identified at the beginning of this chapter, there is a considerable correlation between neurolinguistic psychotherapy and Kelly's personal construct therapy. Kelly was influenced by Piaget's views on constructivism and developed a model of therapy that recognised that there are a variety of ways in which any event can be viewed. He also worked from a principle that people acted 'as if' something were possible or true, whereby they would hold a certain perception in their mind of the world, and then would act out this hypothesis through a series of personal constructs, whether for the positive or the negative. This resonates well with neurolinguistic psychotherapy, which operates from a belief that the unconscious mind cannot determine the difference between pretend and reality, therefore if a client could act 'as if' something were possible, then their neurology would find a way to make it become possible. Both Erickson and Satir assumed that the client already had the solution to their presenting problem and would often encourage clients to tell their 'story' as if they had already resolved it. Satir did this in her use of chairs work, where she would get her clients to act as if they were being the alternative family member with whom the conflict had occurred and encouraged them to speak as if they were that person, and then respond from their own perspective, thereby altering their constructed reality.

Personal construct therapy is also similar to neurolinguistic psychotherapy in that it operates from a position of enabling people to change their individual constructs by recognising and working through their patterns of 'stuckness'. The question 'how else might you achieve this?' in goal-setting within neurolinguistic psychotherapy provides an ideal environment for the client to move beyond the presenting problem and consider alternative solutions. Also, the use of alternative perspectives such as 'how will someone else know you have achieved this?' encourages a client to dissociate from their current reality and consider their situation from an alternative, yet to be recognised, reality.

Where neurolinguistic psychotherapy and personal construct therapy can be seen to differ is the notion that within personal construct therapy, the therapist will work through a series of therapeutic theoretical constructs that enable understanding and inclusion of the client's constructs, which includes the trying out of unverbalised hunches – which could be perceived as 'mind-reads' for neurolinguistic psychotherapists. A fundamental aspect of neurolinguistic psychotherapy is that the therapist may only offer to the client something that has already been presented from their existing reality. By testing out hunches or intuitive interpretations, there is a risk that this then becomes part of the client's reality, when it was not there previously, setting up the possibility of false memories.

There is also a range of therapeutic interventions within personal construct therapy that mirror and support the work of the neurolinguistic therapist. A process known as 'laddering' considers the relationship between personal constructs and the reason why they were constructed in the first place. This is similar to the notion of 'chunking' in neurolinguistic psychotherapy, whereby if the therapist chunks up on a specific behaviour the client will eventually end up at a place where there is only positive intention for the behaviour and the client utilises this as a reframe to change their existing behaviour. This positive intention will have been the reason why the behaviour was initially created.

'Pyramiding' involves pursuing information in the opposite direction and moving constructs that are held at identity, value or belief level down to capability or behavioural level by asking the questions 'how?' or 'what?' rather than 'why?'. Within neurolinguistic psychotherapy this process occurs with the use of the meta-model, and is seen within Satir's work whereby she would ask her clients how they knew they were not loved, rather than accepting their mind-read that they were not loved. She recognised that if she asked them why they felt this way they would reply in a way that kept them *at effect* and this would stop them reconnecting with the original source of their belief.

The 'ABC' model of questioning takes clients through the varying poles of their constructs, which, from a neurolinguistic psychotherapy perspective, mirrors the work that is done in identifying the ecology of given behaviours including the identification of any secondary gain. In identifying secondary gain within neurolinguistic psychotherapy, the client is asked:

- What will happen if you achieve this/do this?
- What will happen if you don't achieve this/do this?
- What won't happen if you achieve this/do this?
- What won't happen if you don't achieve this/do this?

Similarly to the 'ABC' model, the client is connected with any of their existing constructs that may prevent them achieving resolution of the presenting problem, and accessing a solution state.

Existential therapy

Existential therapy is a similar therapy to personal construct therapy. The basic premise of existential therapy is that the self does not exist, and that people move through life having to create 'our-self' on a daily basis. The basic assumptions of existential therapy are that there are four dimensions to being:

- physical, which includes the environment and physical presence of an individual
- social, which concerns how people relate in social interactions
- psychological, which includes cognitive relationship to the world
- spiritual, which incorporates one's relationship with the unknown.

In considering these four dimensions from a neurolinguistic viewpoint, there is a direct relationship to the notion of the four bodies: the physical, emotional, mental and spiritual. Within neurolinguistic psychotherapy the aim of the therapy is to assist integration and alignment with each of the four bodies, and to ensure that a similar emphasis is given to each. Conflict or even disintegration of the self can occur if too much emphasis is given to a particular aspect; for example, a client may be too connected to an emotional construct and therefore spend too much energy focusing on resolving this particular issue, or they may dwell on it too much to the exclusion of the remaining bodies.

Other aspects within existential therapy that are parallel to those within neurolinguistic psychotherapy include working to gain different interpretations of emotions, beliefs, talents and recollection of memories through processes that involve reframing.

Influence of hypnotherapy

Although there are many different approaches and utilisations of hypnosis and hypnotherapy, it is mainly Erickson's work that influences neurolinguistic psychotherapy.

As the notion of the unconscious was debated in the late nineteenth century, and a split developed between those that pursued behaviourism through the work of Pavlov and Salter and those that continued with analysis and the development of Freud's work through Jung and Adler, a third stream emerged that developed hypnosis further into the twentieth century. Erickson found an affinity with the work of therapists such as Charcot and continued to research hypnosis during his time at Worcester State Hospital.

The key elements of Ericksonian therapy that have been adopted by neurolinguistic psychotherapy stem from the personal beliefs that supported Erickson's work. Erickson believed in the notion of ecology, and much of his therapy involved working with the system. This may be the family system, whereby he would encourage behavioural change in the family and not just the individual with the presenting problem. Sometimes he would talk directly to the 'problem' person, while inducing trance in another member of the family who would be sitting at the opposite end of the room. On other occasions he would involve patients in the 'cure' of another; for example, he would arrange for a patient that had social difficulties to take a walk near the home of another patient who was seeking a new relationship. He also viewed his own role as being integral to the therapy and would often include personal reflection or disclosure in his metaphors.

What neurolinguistic psychotherapy has also taken out of Erickson's work is his ability to observe the most minute elements of detail in his clients and utilise these to therapeutic advantage, and out of this came the presupposition that you can't not communicate. He accepted the principle of resistance and, as I have alluded to in Chapter 1, he utilised this in three different ways. He also recognised that people were naturally goal-oriented and that by using a process of association his clients were enabled to access their own internal resources to aid problem resolution.

Historical roots of gestalt therapy

Bandler's very early work that influenced the development of NLP was based on his modelling of Perls. Bandler studied much of Perls's linguistic patterns through papers that he had written as well as some video recordings of his case material. Within the history of the development of gestalt therapy, there are other parallels with neurolinguistic psychotherapy that are not as apparent in the historical perspective of NLP as it is presented today from the original modelling work of Bandler and Grinder.

Gestalt therapy emerged from an increasing level of interest in phenomenology and existentialism, and Perls, with his wife, Laura, built on the work of Wertheimer, Kohler, Koffka and Lewin and brought gestalt therapy forward by publishing his first work on *Ego, Hunger and Aggression* in 1969. A number of misconceptions built up around gestalt therapy at the time, particularly the perception that it was confrontational in approach. Although originally designed for group work, it now has its place as a respected therapy for both individuals and groups.

Perls recognised that individuals are constantly developing and will devise behaviours that are continually self-organising and self-actualising. He also believed that people do not need fixing, which forms the basis of the presupposition that 'People work perfectly, we are all executing our strategies perfectly, but the strategies may be poorly designed and ineffective.'

The processes that are common to neurolinguistic psychotherapy and gestalt therapy are found particularly in the notion of working with polarities, or opposing and conflicting aspects of the personality. This process brings to mind what is missing for the person, and recognises, much in the way that Jungian analysis does, that one's psyche is made up of polar opposites, the purpose being to create equilibrium between these opposite parts. Parts therapy and resolution of core belief structures are discussed further in Chapter 7. Interruptions and avoidances are also important to the neurolinguistic therapist; often it is what is not said that gives a clue to the deeper structure of the client's subjective reality. Clients will miss out portions of their sentence as they relay their story in therapy, or they may divert and present a different chain of thought to avoid answering a specific question. Resistance too, has its place in gestalt therapy, as discussed in Chapter 1, and within neurolinguistic psychotherapy the role of the therapist is to utilise rapport and hypnotic language patterns to bypass conscious resistance and access deeper unconscious resources to aid problem resolution.

Finally, I want to consider Bandler's description of the attitude required in NLP, that of 'wanton curiosity and experimentation'. This notion was derived from gestalt therapy that advocated experimentation and techniques. Parlett and Hemming (1996, p. 203) refer to this as working with a client by 'undoing or deconstructing . . . a fixed gestalt [and] experimenting with a novel solution'. It is from this model that the notion of perceptual positions or chairs work was derived. This has similarities to the role work of Satir who encouraged her clients to adopt the different roles within their family to gain a different perspective on their situation.

The position of cybernetics within systemic and family therapy

Cybernetics or systems theory would say that no matter how complex a system, if you start to understand the laws of the system, it is possible to change any aspect of the presenting problem by changing any part of the existing system. Systems theory in itself looks at the structure of the system and how it might be changed, whereas cybernetics considers more the functions within different aspects of the system.

Satir was an advocate of systems therapy and her work often involved changing either the structure of the system or the functions of individuals within the system. Systemically she might change how people viewed their experience; for example, her work on self-esteem, where she related to the 'pot' of self-esteem. She encouraged families to refer to how much their behaviour towards each other added to or took away from the 'pot'. At a functional level, Satir would consider the roles within the families that she worked with and how, by changing these, the family system would then change. Evidence of her systemic work is found in the linguistic structure of the meta-model where she challenged the family rules of deletions, distortions and generalisations. She would use language patterns to assist a client to reconnect with the original source of their distorted beliefs and then reframe this so that the client could change their constructed reality.

Bateson's (2000) view of cybernetics brought a depth to systems theory that had hitherto been missing within neurolinguistic psychotherapy. His view that difference is the analogue of cause, i.e., the difference that makes the difference, ensures that NLP holds within it sufficient understanding of systems theory to enable patterning and re-patterning to be considered a major component of neurolinguistic psychotherapy. This principle considers that if change is introduced anywhere within the system, this will cause change within the entire system.

Modelling from other therapies

NLP would claim that it is modelled from the linguistic behavioural strategies of Erickson, Satir and Perls, and it is worth considering the relationship between neurolinguistic psychotherapy and many of the other therapies that exist today. Commencing with the three therapists originally modelled, Erickson was a psychiatrist before he developed his work in hypnotherapy and had also completed a Masters degree in psychology while at the same time studying for his medical degree. Satir started her therapy career with alcoholics and the homeless, and it was from this work that she developed an interest in family therapy. Perls, a neuropsychiatrist, studied the work of Freud and Reich; however, along with his wife, he preferred the philosophies of existentialism and phenomenology which later became strong influences in his development of gestalt therapy.

Each of these therapists will have been influenced during their early training and clinical years by a range of therapies, and within the next section I provide a brief summary of the main modalities of psychotherapy and some of the parallels between the approaches.

The influence of psychodynamic therapies on neurolinguistic psychotherapy

Psychoanalysis

Historically, both Erickson and Perls spent time learning from psycho-analysis. Perls had analysis with a number of Freudian analysts including Reich; and Erickson, during his medical psychiatry training, would have encountered the work of Freud, Adler and Jung. Satir was strongly influenced by the family therapists of the day, who would also have studied analytic approaches to therapy. Many neurolinguistic psychotherapists prefer to see their therapeutic work at the opposite end of the spectrum to analytic approaches and more closely aligned to briefer models of therapy, yet the work of Freud, Jung, Adler and Klein shows some considerable parallels in philosophical approaches as well as methodologies.

Freud was intrigued by the notion of hypnosis and, in the mid-1880s, studied hypnosis with Charcot. He experimented with this for a while with Breuer and they published their *Studies on Hysteria* in 1895. Following this work he developed his own theories of the unconscious and its role in repressing memories that were too painful for the conscious rational self to deal with. The main principle of Freud's (1904) theory at this point was that the mind consisted of three states: the unconscious, the preconscious and the conscious. He later coined the terms, Id, Ego and Superego as representatives of these states. From a neurolinguistic perspective there is a general acceptance of the unconscious and the influence that this has in driving our behaviours. Some neurolinguistic psychotherapists have adopted the notion that the mind also consists of three aspects, or 'bodies': the unconscious, the conscious and the higher conscious.

The unconscious mind would parallel Freud's unconscious in that this state of mind is outside of conscious awareness, and Freud would say it was 'inaccessible' to consciousness. Through the use of hypnotic processes inherent in neurolinguistic psychotherapy, it is possible to gain direct communication with the unconscious. The conscious mind parallels Freud's conscious or Ego state. From a neurolinguistic perspective the conscious mind is the mind that makes rational our life experiences, and is the determinant of free will. From a Freudian perspective, the Ego is the part of the personality that maintains a relationship between the internal and external reality. Freud's Superego is determined as the part of the mind that holds the opposites of good and bad. Within neurolinguistic psychotherapy this would parallel the concept of the higher conscious mind, for some, and the collective consciousness for others, although there is no notion of reproach or reward – rather unconditional acceptance. Freudian analysis also recognises that clients will present with a series of defence mechanisms, some of which are recognised within neurolinguistic psychotherapy. Some of these are anathemas; others have parallels with processes that are embedded within neurolinguistic psychotherapy. The mechanisms that Freud (1926) postulated to have the closest parallels to neurolinguistic psychotherapy are as follows.

- *Repression.* Repression is dealing with unwelcome or distressing unconscious thoughts by repressing them. The notion of repression is recognised as one of the prime directives of the unconscious mind (see Chapter 7) within neurolinguistic psychotherapy, suggesting that we will repress memories and emotions as a protection mechanism.
- *Projection.* Projection is well recognised as being a process whereby we will attribute negative or disturbing aspects of ourselves onto others, and contrary to Freud's notion, we will also project the more positive or pleasing aspects of ourselves onto others.
- *Introjection.* Introjection within analysis theorises that we will emulate aspects of others including our parents and early value systems. When viewed from a neurolinguistic perspective this is seen as a client holding as their own some of the negative aspects of those around them, often represented when working with splitting or 'parts' of the personality.
- *Isolation.* Isolation as determined by Freud is the ability to dissociate from feelings, most often at times of distress when the cognitive strategies to deal with it more appropriately, for example in distressing situations as a child, are not present, which may be seen as a dissociative state or, in more severe circumstances, the creation of 'parts'.
- *Negation.* Freud's notion of negation to avoid acknowledging the less positive aspects within a personality sits well with the presupposition that we can't not communicate and is analogous with the notion that something must be present in our neurology in order for us to negate it and deny its existence.
- *Rationalisation.* Rationalisation operates from the principle that we find false reason for our negative behaviours, and although neurolinguistic psychotherapy would prefer to deny that negative behaviour exists, it does hold the presupposition that every behaviour has a positive intention, even the most abhorrent. The role of therapy therefore is to enable clients to recognise the positive intent behind unuseful behaviours and find different ways to gain the same benefit through a different behavioural response.
- *Conversion.* Conversion recognises that individuals will often somatise psychological distress into physical disorders such that they do not have to deal with the distress, which may be seen in the neurolinguistic notion of secondary gain, or have parallels with the mind–body connection.

Kleinian therapy

Klein (1952) was an advocate of Freud and continued daily analysis for much of her life. Although some of her work is considered controversial, particularly her analysis of her children, she does bring some notions to analysis that have parallels with those in neurolinguistic psychotherapy. She recognises that much of our behaviour is driven by goals; however, she assumes that our aggressive tendencies will provide the main focus for our actions. There is a model within neurolinguistic psychotherapy that works with a client's values, the primary aim being to enable a resolution of the 'away from' aspects of their values, i.e., the values that underpin our motivation and behaviour and where we are motivated by avoiding negative stimuli.

Klein's (1932) work also focused on the role of the mother and the infantile anxieties that a person may have as a result of the mother's neuroses. In neurolinguistic psychotherapy these are picked up in a minimal way in the history of a client's early 'imprint' period, with the mother playing only a minor role in formulating the way that the personality has developed. Klein also brings in an additional component to the development of the personality at the imprint stage, through her work on projective identification, where the child creates a relationship with the mother for his inner world to be experienced by the mother. This projection enables the child to project into his mother something that he does not like about himself. Within a therapeutic context this is realised as the expression of experiences that the patient cannot hold within their linguistic structure; the patient therefore projects them into the therapist.

Jungian analysis

Jungian analysis, on the other hand, works with the theory of opposites. In terms of the theory of parts therapy and the notion of understanding the higher intent of a given behaviour, which is usually dichotomous to the identified behaviour, there are strong parallels between Jungian analysis and neurolinguistic psychotherapy. Also familiar to the neurolinguistic psychotherapist is the work of Jung (1971) on archetypes that has so strongly influenced Myers (1962) and the Myers-Briggs Type Indicator (MBTI) personality profile. This model is based on two specific principles, first our orientation to the world through our tendency to extrovert or introvert our energy, and second how we function in the world, i.e., how we perceive information through either our senses or our intuition, how that information affects our state, whether this is associated in feeling, or dissociated in thinking and logic, and then how we adapt our response according to our perceptions and internal state.

Jung's theory would support the notion that our behaviour is predominantly goal-oriented, although he would say that it would be inappropriate to work with this until the second half of our life, as it is only then that we are ready to 'individuate' and develop the ability to truly introvert. Prior to this point the majority of our behaviours are designed for extroversion, focusing on career, family, growth and development.

Adlerian therapy

Adler studied with Freud at the same time as Jung did, and for a period of time was a great advocate of Freud. Adler became president of the Vienna Psychoanalytic Society and the honeymoon period of his relationship with Freud ended in 1911, as both became aware that their views were substantially different. Adler (1992) was considerably more goal-oriented than Freud and preferred to view people within a wider perspective that recognised the goal-oriented nature of the human psyche. The specific element of Adler's work that I would like to bring to mind here is his work on 'life tasks'. He identified three major life tasks – work, friendship and love – and this was added to by Dreikurs, who included 'getting on with oneself' and 'relationship to the cosmos'. In the work on values within neurolinguistic psychotherapy, and the 'wheel of life', there are parallels between these five 'life tasks' and the values areas of work/career, friends/family, intimate relationships, personal development and spirituality. As clients are enabled to work in these areas, they are encouraged to resolve 'away from' motivation within values and develop 'towards' motivation to enable fulfilment of life tasks (Lazarus, 2006; Robbins, 1991).

Humanistic influences on neurolinguistic psychotherapy

Humanistic psychotherapies consist of a range of different modalities and for the purposes of this book, I refer the reader to two specific approaches that have some parallels with neurolinguistic psychotherapy.

Transactional analysis

The first modality is that of transactional analysis (TA). TA theory accepts the notion of three drives: the 'mortido drive' or death instinct, the 'libido drive' or sexual instinct, and 'physis', the generative force that drives our behaviour towards growth and ideally towards perfection. Within this, TA considers the paranoid position of 'I'm OK, you're not OK', the depressed position of 'I'm not OK, you're OK', and the schizoid position of 'I'm not OK, you're not OK'. The purpose or goal in TA is to move to a position of 'I'm OK, you're OK' as identified by Berne (1957). This mirrors the goal of neurolinguistic psychotherapy which is aimed at achieving positive outcomes and a sense of fulfilment or integration of the client that is directed towards their goals. Within TA, the therapist works with the ego states of adult, parent and child, offering interventions at behavioural, social, historical and phenomenological levels. Each of these corresponds to one of the differing evolutionary levels within neurolinguistic psychotherapy, those of the physical, emotional, mental and spiritual bodies. It is in this concept and also the idea of working through different projected aspects of the persona that the closest links with neurolinguistic psychotherapy exist. An additional perspective within TA, which is not harnessed as fully as it could be within neurolinguistic psychotherapy, is working with projections within the therapeutic relationship – including the concept of projective transference, recognising the influence that Klein has had on TA. In this regard, Rycroft (1995, p. 173) states that 'splitting of both ego and object tends to be linked with denial and projection . . . parts of the self are disowned and attributed to objects in the environment'. Bollas (1987, p. 202) would say 'in order to find the patient we must look for him within ourselves'.

Person-centred therapy

Within person-centred therapy, Rogers' (1974) theory of personality mirrors that of neurolinguistic psychotherapy in terms of the map not being representative of the territory, and recognises that an individual's perceptual field is their reality. Person-centred therapy operates from an almost identical position to neurolinguistic psychotherapy: that the person has within them all of the necessary resources for change and self-understanding if they are encouraged in an environment that is facilitative to psychological growth. Over and above this, Rogers also operated from a position of positive regard for his clients, which, although not taken to this extent, mirrors at some level the belief in neurolinguistic psychotherapy that it is important to respect the client's model of the world. Some of the additional theoretical principles within person-centred therapy provide parallels between the idea that a client will have a series of values that they move either towards or away from, and theories within neurolinguistic psychotherapy on values and motivation direction. What is different within person-centred therapy is that the values are predetermined around a series of assumed beliefs; for example, that it is important to move the client away from living up to the expectations of others, and to move the client towards accepting and valuing himself or herself. Within neurolinguistic psychotherapy, the drivers for values are determined by the client and their subjective experience that is based much more in the now.

Behavioural modelling and relationships in cognitive and behavioural therapies

Modelling within the construct of NLP is found within the presupposition *If one person can do something then it is possible to model it and teach it to others*. To model something and be able to replicate it has applications in performance enhancement, and in a therapeutic setting would have benefits in enabling a client to model their existing unuseful strategy; by changing the mental syntax, beliefs and values, physiology or context in which they operate the behaviour, the model can then be changed. It is also possible to model how and when the client does not 'do' the problem and to replicate this behaviour across contexts. McDermott and Jago (2001, p. 54) identify the key elements that make this possible within therapy:

- rapport and attentiveness
- an attitude of curiosity and learning
- the identifying of patterns and sequences
- breaking down the patterns and sequences into their constituent parts
- modelling effective patterns.

Lawley and Tompkins (2006, p. 35) define therapeutic modelling as follows: 'The therapist uses the client's patterns of behaviour . . . to construct a model of the client's internal processes. The therapist attempts to figure out *how the structure* of the client's subjective experience so consistently gets them the results they get.'

Cognitive therapy

Beck's cognitive therapy (1976) is similar to neurolinguistic psychotherapy, and operates from three assumptions:

- the person is seen as an active agent who interacts with his or her world
- this interaction takes place through the interpretations, inferences and evaluations the person makes about his or her environment
- the results of the 'cognitive' processes are thought to be accessible to consciousness in the form of thoughts and images, and so the person has the potential to change them.

There is also recognition of the filtering mechanisms that Korzybski identified, that we distort our experience of the world through faulty and adaptive information-processing.

The main focus for cognitive therapy is to enable a client to change their negative automatic thoughts through the changing of cognitive schemata, similarly to the approaches in neurolinguistic psychotherapy that bring to consciousness modal operators of necessity, the *got to, have to* and *must* within a client's linguistic structure, that are identified as part of the process in reframing limiting or unuseful beliefs. In addition, cognitive therapy uses processes of dissociation through distancing and distraction, similar to that of dissociative processes in neurolinguistic psychotherapy, although these are more at the unconscious level within neurolinguistic psychotherapy. Strategy work also features in cognitive therapy whereby underlying assumptions and automatic thoughts are challenged, and interventions are proposed that interrupt the strategy.

There is one major conceptual difference between neurolinguistic psychotherapy and cognitive therapy that is worth keeping in mind. Whereas neurolinguistic psychotherapy focuses on goals and future-oriented processes, cognitive therapy operates more from within the client's existing reality and works towards relieving symptoms and resolution of the problem, and development of coping strategies through modification of underlying cognitive structures, such that relapse is prevented.

Behavioural therapy

If one includes the aspects of behavioural therapy developed by Skinner and Lazarus, there are similarities with the behavioural modelling components of neurolinguistic psychotherapy. The beginnings of behavioural therapy are embedded in the theory of the stimulus response, which within neurolinguistic psychotherapy is recognised as the utilisation of anchors. Lazarus (1971) was dissatisfied with this concept and encouraged behavioural therapists to consider a more eclectic approach that included the resolution of some of the internal subjective processes that drive our unuseful behaviours.

Behavioural therapy has the most correlations with the strategy, anchoring and submodality work of neurolinguistic psychotherapy. There are similarities between the 'exposure principle' and the work on fears and phobias that can be addressed through changing submodalities or working with the phobia cure. Aversion therapy and social skills training are also key components of behavioural therapy and it is at this point that the similarities with neurolinguistic psychotherapy start to disappear. Behavioural therapy is similar to cognitive therapy in that it provides a problem-oriented, structured, directive approach that is based in empirical research, whereas neurolinguistic psychotherapy offers a goal-oriented structure and approach that moves a client rapidly towards a solution state.

Rational emotive behavioural therapy

In continuing through the field of behavioural therapies, neurolinguistic psychotherapy perhaps has greater correspondences with Ellis' (1962) work on rational emotive behaviour therapy (REBT) than with cognitive and behavioural approaches. REBT accepts the idea that humans are naturally hedonistic and are programmed to pursue happiness, and they have great potential to work through any irrationality in pursuit of this happiness, mirroring the belief in neurolinguistic psychotherapy that we all have all the resources that we need. Being philosophical in approach, the neurolinguistic psychotherapy field will resonate with some of Ellis' thinking:

- that the most effective way for people to have lasting behavioural change is to change their philosophical perspective on life, the basis of reframing in neurolinguistic psychotherapy
- the testing-out of inferences and hunches about people and life is similar to the idea that we project our internal subjective processes onto our external world
- REBT is similar to neurolinguistic psychotherapy as a constructivist theory in that it places emphasis on the active role that humans play in constructing their irrational beliefs and the distorted inferences that they frequently bring to emotional episodes.

Change is achieved in REBT through a number of processes that again have parallels to neurolinguistic psychotherapy. Cognitive change is achieved by chunking down on beliefs to identify the source and evidence for these at a deep structure level. The emotive aspects are resolved through acceptance of the client's model of the world, and recognition that the therapist can act as a positive role model for the client. This is where a difference occurs with neurolinguistic psychotherapy, in that the model comes from outside the client, rather than being internally sourced. Across the three different behavioural therapies, neurolinguistic psychotherapists who prefer a behavioural modelling approach will find great affinity with the works of Ellis, Beck, Skinner and Lazarus.

Model of the mind for neurolinguistic psychotherapy

> The patient's behaviour is a part of the problem brought into the office; it constitutes the personal environment within which the therapy must take effect; it may constitute the dominant force in the local patient–doctor relationship. Since whatever the patient brings into the office is in some way both part of him and part of his problem, the patient should be viewed with a sympathetic eye appraising the totality which confronts the therapist.
>
> (Erickson, in Bandler & Grinder, 1975, p. 59)

In summarising the relationship between neurolinguistic psychotherapy and the range of modalities that exist in psychotherapy today, it is apparent that neurolinguistic psychotherapy is more than the linguistic structures that were modelled by Bandler and Grinder. As a model of mind, both the conscious and unconscious aspects are key components. The unconscious aspects are grounded in epistemological theory and it is recognised that our cognition of events is determined by the projections that we bring from our subjective reality, based on our interpretation of our life experiences as they have happened to us. Even in viewing these events as they are presented to us by a client, we cannot not be influenced by our own subjective realities as the therapist. Concurrent to this is what is known about the conscious and unconscious programmes that we run, determined by our behavioural responses that are triggered through operant conditioning, which is discussed further in Chapter 6. As a model of mind, we are neither solely conscious nor entirely unconscious; we are on a journey that for some is towards the things that make us happier, healthier or more fulfilled, and for others is away from what is deemed irrational, painful, hurtful, aggressive or just insane.

In the next chapter I consider the relationship of the conscious and unconscious processes that make up the model of the mind in neuro-linguistic psychotherapy and relate this to a range of theories that support understanding of the development of the personality.

Chapter 3

A perspective on personality

> Who am I? is the only question worth asking and the only one never answered. It is your destiny to play an infinity of roles, but these roles are not yourself. The spirit is nonlocal, but it leaves behind a fingerprint, which we call the body. A wizard does not believe himself to be a local event dreaming of a larger world. A wizard is a world dreaming of local events.
>
> (Chopra, 1995, p. 35)

This chapter focuses on the development of the personality as it was understood by Erickson, Satir and Perls. Each of the therapists had a perspective on the personality that is rooted in the impact that early childhood experiences can have on the emerging sense of self. The therapeutic process offered by each focused on the lived reality of now and by linking this with contemporary psychotherapy as it is presented by Gawler-Wright, it becomes clear that Erickson worked with neurocognitive components to facilitate rebalancing of the internal world of his clients. I consider the development of values from the work of Massey, Graves and Maslow and link this into the reinforcement of early developmental experiences through the development of metaprogrammes. An alternative perspective is given through Jung's view of the developing psyche. The chapter concludes with a consideration of the development of the self and how this can be influenced in therapy by affect regulation, which I present within a case study.

Development through the perspective of Satir, Erickson and Perls

> It will be helpful to remember that every baby who comes into this world comes only with raw materials. He has no self-concept, no experience of interacting with others, and no experience in dealing with the world around him. He learns all these things through his communication with people who are in charge of him from his birth on.
>
> (Satir, 1972, p. 31)

As one of the co-creators of the first programme in family therapy in the USA, Satir's perspective on family therapy provides grounding in systems theory for neurolinguistic psychotherapists. Satir (1972) held the view that children develop their personality by modelling the people around them as they grow up. She believed that individuals have within them a capacity for self-worth, and it is what happens inside people and between people that adds to or takes away from their 'pot' (p. 21) of self-worth. When a child is born they have no past experiences to formulate their own sense of self-worth and during the first five or six years of their life, the child relies on the messages they receive from their outside world to formulate an internal view of themselves. Once the child commences school, other influences add to this and will reinforce what has already been laid down within the personality at home.

Satir's therapy involved developing communication between the various family members, whether in reality or as constructs of the person's psychological process. Where personality attributes of family members had become part of the repertoire of behaviours that a person demonstrated as an adult, she would encourage her client to hold a 'parts party' (Satir, 1972, pp. 80–95). The client would be encouraged to act out the roles within their family unit to enable them to develop new strategies in managing these less useful aspects of their personality. This work led to what we now know as the Satir postures of blamer, placator, super-reasonable or computer, irrelevant or distracter, and leveller. She would then adopt the leveller role to break the existing patterns of behaviour (pp. 63–78). She would encourage her client to adopt a meta-perspective or 'chair person' role on these different aspects of themselves.

Haley's (1993) work on the strategic therapy of Erickson offers a different perspective to Satir's in that Erickson did not focus on opening up communication in the family dynamic, rather he would work with family members separately towards specific goals, focusing on the principle that any individual has the potential for freedom and growth. Much of Erickson's work at various different life stages cited in Haley (1993) provides examples of how Erickson utilised the belief that all behaviour is context-dependent, and that rather than it being fixed in the psyche, he could assist clients to change the context of their behaviour which then resulted in the behaviour no longer creating a problem for them. Whereas Satir used roles and analogies with individuals in therapy, Erickson used a combination of indirect suggestion and reframing to provide this different perspective.

Contemporary psychotherapist Gawler-Wright (2006), coming from both Ericksonian and systemic NLP perspectives, sees a deeper and more systematic pattern in Erickson's apparently solely behavioural approach with families, couples and individuals within family units. Erickson himself ascribed the shaping of his suggestions to his unconscious mind engaging with the unconscious (or somatic) conversation offered by the client, and he suggested that the wisdom of the unconscious used simple and natural forces to do its work. Gawler-Wright observes that Erickson reveals in his case histories a pattern of intervention that paces and stimulates an initial disorder followed by naturalistic rebalancing. This is initiated in a minimalist way within the counter-weighting of stable and unstable forces already present within the family and individual system. This model, which she calls 'continuous becoming' (p. 34), can offer up a sense of the innate and simple logic in many of Erickson's interventions, which at times can seem bizarre or random. It suggests the ever-evolving nature of the personality through a relationship of static and dynamic forces: forces within which Erickson, as a passionate naturalist, played the reverent yet provocative role of Green Man or Joker.

Perls's gestalt therapy is similar in vein to Ericksonian therapy in that therapists operate from the 'here and now' of a client's lived experience. This lived experience is based on previous events in a person's life, where an individual 'mentally metabolises' their experiences. Children literally introject their life experiences and if the experience is nutritious at a physical, emotional or mental level they will repeat the experience; if it is deemed 'toxic' they will avoid it in the future. Gestalt therapy holds within it a perception that an individual develops through effective management of boundaries between self and others: where these boundaries have been positively reinforced they will continue, and where they have been made impermeable the sense of self becomes lost, which may lead to splitting of the self.

Of the three therapists, Satir was the most concrete in her description of how the personality is formed, with Perls providing a perspective of 'towards' and 'away from' behaviours that are reinforced through the development of boundaries. Erickson was considerably less prescriptive and viewed his clients as unique individuals with unique stories and ways of presenting themselves in therapy. Erickson was a master at clearing his mind of any preconceived ideas or models as he approached each new therapeutic alliance. Gilligan, in his workshops on self-relations therapy, often recounts a story of his early learning with Erickson. He would ask Erickson what psychotherapy is, and Erickson would reply, 'I don't know.' Gilligan would persist in his questioning and finally Erickson would respond, 'Psychotherapy . . . is a process . . . whereby two people . . . sit down . . . and try to figure out . . . what the hell . . . one of them wants.'

Massey's sociological influence on the developing sense of self

Within neurolinguistic psychotherapy, Massey (1979) is referenced as providing the theoretical underpinning for the formation of the personality.

In *The People Puzzle*, sociologist Massey identified that people are shaped by the events around them and identified three different developmental phases that an individual experiences in the growth of their personality.

Imprinting

The first of these is what is referred to as the Imprint period. Massey defines the personality as being like a sponge for the first seven years of life, whereby the infant literally absorbs events in its external environment which will then shape the child's personality. Dilts (2000) considers the work of Lorenz (1935, 1970) when he defines imprinting as 'the result of an instinctive behaviour pattern by which the young within a species rapidly learn to recognize and follow a member of their own species, typically the mother. Thus, it is generally associated with the establishment of a relationship with a significant role model – such as a "mothering figure"' (p. 533).

Lorenz also considers that imprints occur at a time when neurological development is being set, and that if an infant attaches to a non-biological significant figure during the imprint period, this then becomes a permanent attachment. Bowlby (1969) continued to develop the work of Lorenz and formulated attachment theory, which has influenced the work of child psychotherapists and of psychoanalysts. Additionally we can see evidence of Lorenz's work appearing in that of object relations theorists, Klein, Winnicott, Mahler and Kohut, who emphasise the interpersonal relationship of the mother and child. The mother is the 'object' that becomes the target of the infant's feelings or attention. This past relationship with the maternal object then goes on to influence the present, supporting Lorenz's view that whatever is set during this period is then fixed and remains a permanent aspect of the individual's psyche.

Dilts (2000, p. 534) has continued this psychoanalytic perspective on the imprint process by referring to Freud's theory on transference:

> Sigmund Freud's theory on 'transference', for example, seems to point to imprint-like phenomena. The basic implication of this theory was that the therapeutic relationship was more important than any of the suggestions, techniques or behaviours which took place in the context of that relationship. Freud came to believe that the relationship between the 'doctor and the patient' was like 'the water in which they were swimming'. It surrounded them and determined much about their behaviour, yet 'escaped every effort at control'. For instance, Freud noticed that at key times in the therapeutic process the relationship between him and his patients would come strongly into focus. He observed that 'the patient, who ought to be thinking of nothing but the

solution of his own distressing conflicts, begins to develop a particular interest in the person of the physician'.

In developing the work of Lorenz, Dilts also brought in the neurological perspective of Leary (1988), who proposed that since imprinting has a neurological component, it is possible to access these biochemical states and literally re-imprint new states, thereby creating new neurological choice and behaviour. Dilts has added much to the NLP field with his work on re-imprinting, making it possible to change early neurological imprints in individuals.

Both James and Woodsmall (1988) and Bodenhamer and Hall (1999), in their respective work on 'Time Line Therapy™', and 'time lining', have taken the work of Massey and used the notion of SEE (significant emotional event – James and Woodsmall) or SEEP (significant emotional experience of pain – Bodenhamer and Hall) to enable re-imprinting by working with the gestalt of experience through time. Both approaches consider the neurological component of emotional experiences and utilise time reframing to re-imprint significant past events.

Modelling

The second stage of Massey's model is more directly related to how the imprinted aspects of the personality are then reinforced. Between the ages of 8 and 13, a child models the behaviours of those around him, both at home and at school. He will consciously and unconsciously model these behaviours as he becomes more aware of the differences between themselves and other people. It is at this age that Massey would say core values are formed. Massey believed that an individual's world at age 10 shapes their values for life.

Socialisation

Between the ages of 14 and 21, Massey refers to the socialisation period. It is at this stage in life that an individual begins to interact at a social level with other individuals, outside the immediate home and school environment. Relationship and social values are formed at this age, which tend to last a lifetime.

Development of values

Massey's work has also influenced that of the development of values according to each generation. He refers to generational values and suggests that if the value system of each generational group is examined it is possible to gain greater insight into their beliefs and behaviours. Massey divides the generations into four groupings:

- those born before 1947 are referred to as the traditionalists
- those born between 1947 and 1965 are known by Massey as nuagers and by others as boomers
- those born between 1966 and 1977 are defined by Massey as the syntech generation and by others as Generation X
- those born between 1978 and 1995 are referred to as Nxters by Massey or by others as Generation Y.

Each generation will have a direct influence on the generation following it, and it is very apparent that those born prior to 1947 are directly influenced by the two world wars and having parents who were mainly born in the Victorian era. This grouping values privacy, trust, formality and institutional leadership. Its members are less likely to seek therapy as they have been brought up to avoid 'washing their dirty linen' in public and may find it difficult to talk before a relationship of trust is built up.

The 'boomers' or 'nuagers' are sometimes known as the 'me' decade. They enjoy hard work, competition and success. They prefer working through the team and are against rules and regulations. They tend to speak in a direct style and use body language as a form of communication. As a group, they readily access therapy as a form of self-development. The 'syntech' generation are entrepreneurial in spirit and value creativity and independence. They work and play hard and will often have short spans of attention which, in therapy, means they are likely to be brief in communication and will want a quick fix to any presenting issues. 'Generation Y' groups value autonomy and have fewer issues concerning insecurity than other generations. They tend to have a positive outlook on life, will find long-term therapy tedious, and will be more attuned to self-help books and online help facilities.

Maslow (1943) also informs this work on values through his studies of psychologically healthy adults. He identified processes whereby an individual's aim in life is self-actualisation. One of his students, Graves (in Graves et al., 1965), took this work and identified that values develop in response to the environmental conditions, a dynamic process that led to the work by Beck and Cowan (1996) on *Spiral Dynamics*. Graves identified nine levels of value development. His work assumed that each of these levels of existence needed to be worked through and resolved before an individual could evolve to the next level (see Table 3.1, to be read from the bottom to the top).

Massey, Graves et al. and Maslow all provide a perspective on how values are developed and become part of the core identity of an individual.

Table 3.1 Graves' evolution of values

Level of existence	Nature of existence	Motivational system	Ethical/value system
9 Fourth being	Appreciating	Beauty	Awing
8 Third being	Comprehending	Understanding	Compassionate
7 Second being	Seeking	Information	Cognitive
6 First being	Personalistic	Esteem of self	Individualistic
5 Fifth subsistence	Socioeccentric	Belonging	Sociocratic
4 Fourth subsistence	Energetic	Mastery	Power
3 Third subsistence	Frightened	Safety	Constrictive
2 Second subsistence	Animistic	Survivalistic	Totem and taboo
1 First subsistence	Animalistic	Periodic–physiological	Amoral

This work is built on in Chapter 7, where I consider how this might be utilised in therapy.

Personality typology of Jung and metaprogrammes

> If I do not want what you want, please try not to tell me that what I want is wrong. Or if I believe other than you, at least pause before you correct my view. Or if my emotion is less than yours, or more, given the same circumstances, try not to ask me to feel more strongly or weakly. Or yet if I act, or fail to act, in the manner of your design for action, let me be. I do not, for the moment at least, ask you to understand me. That will come only when you are willing to give up changing me into a copy of you.
>
> (Keirsey & Bates, 1984, p. 1)

Jung's (1971) work on psychological types has enabled the Myers Briggs Type Inventory (MBTI) developed by Myers and Briggs (1942) to be included within the methodology of NLP, enabling personality profiling as a readily accessible tool. Jung shared his studies of Freud with Adler and, although they were contemporaries, Jung disagreed with the notion held by both Freud and Adler that individuals are all driven by the same unconscious motives. He believed that although individuals may have the same archetypes within, they are all fundamentally different. It was out of this thinking that the notion of functional preferences was derived.

Jung identified two different functions of consciousness, one rational and one non-rational. The rational aspect determines how people judge their world reality, which will be either as a thought process or through feelings. The more non-rational aspects determine how people perceive reality, which will either be through senses or through intuition. Jung's theory proposed that whichever of the traits dominated logical rational processes, the opposite would be repressed and would dominate unconscious functioning. In addition to the functions of consciousness, Jung also identified that individuals have an attitude of consciousness, which is concerned with meaning. Extroverts find meaning outside themselves and tend to focus on objects, e.g., people, places and things, whereas introverts find meaning within and therefore prefer to focus on subjects, e.g., classifications, meanings and inferences.

Although providing a useful indicator in understanding personality types, Jung's theory on psychological types does not provide indications as to how the personality develops into each of the 16 profiles identified in the MBTI. Jung (1971) suggests that although babies do adapt to the maternal influence, he would see the psychological types as being based in individual disposition rather than environmentally influenced. He argued that children born into the same family exhibit very different characteristics even from a very early age, without any apparent change in the mother's behaviour towards each child.

Charvet (1995) has captured the extensive research of the predictors of personality types, which later became known as metaprogrammes, that has been developed from Jung's work by Cameron-Bandler, Dilts and Gordon. These are a series of behavioural responses in a given context that provide clues to an individual's personality type. Metaprogrammes are programmes that individuals run that control decision-making processes. A more comprehensive and extensively researched process is evident in Lilly's (1968) work on *Programming and Metaprogramming in the Human Biocomputer*, which considers the computer-like activity of the brain in making meaning from our experiences. Lilly assumes that 'unconscious programming is used to project one's own beliefs and "presences" into and onto other persons' (p. 66) and that it is very difficult to determine precisely when this is happening, for three main reasons:

- the resemblance of one human to another
- the apparently meaningless 'noisy' signals that other persons emit in every mode
- the interlocking feedback relations between oneself and the important persons (p. 66).

Lilly goes on to say that clients will use this to create an 'evocable *proof* (false) of the *reality* (false) of their beliefs about another person' (p. 66), demonstrating at a pattern level the way a client continues to create a subjective reality.

The influence of neuroscience on the development of the personality

Since the early work of Bandler and Grinder, much has been done in the field of neuroscience that has added to theoretical understanding of the neurological components that aid the developing personality.

Damasio (1994) has challenged Descartes' view that cognition equates with existence, *I think, therefore I am,* and has brought in many aspects of neuroscience that provide a wealth of scientific research to support the evolving neuroscience theories on personality development. Descartes considered that the essence of self is fundamentally neurological, whereas Damasio assumes that the sense of self is based in neurocognitive processes. Carroll (2002), a well-respected body psychotherapist, has considered in depth the work of Damasio and connects neuroscience with object relations theory, proposing that 'the brain represents the interaction of the self and object [and] is . . . a fundamental proposition of object relations in psychotherapy' (p. 18).

Schore (2003) would support this view and presents a theory of the effect that state has on the developing psyche and the possibility through therapy to repair early trauma. He has included the work of Panksepp, Damasio, Siegel and LeDoux in his theory that fundamentally connects early emotional development to self-development later on. He proposes that 'the broader the range of emotions that a child experiences the broader will be the emotional range of the self that develops' (p. 117). Linking this to the relationship between the neurological system and the effect that intense arousal can have on the development of the individual, he suggests that 'by coordinating parallel plasticity throughout the brain, emotional states promote the development and unification of the self' (p. 117).

Schore has made great contributions to the understanding of neuroscience and its relationship to attachment theory and the development of the personality. Individuals filter the external world through the nervous system, one aspect of which is visual processing. In the first six weeks of an infant's life, he/she learns to utilise their gaze to communicate with and follow their mother. This primary object becomes a constant internal representation to the infant, with neurological links being made on a moment-to-moment basis attached to this primary object. Trevarthen (1993) has added the perspective that auditory processing also plays a role in attachment theory, with the tone of the mother's voice producing profound affects in the infant. If these are positive neurological affects, the infant will develop positive affective brain states, with the growth of the brain being dependent on these positive internal representations.

Stern (1998) has also researched extensively the brain of the developing infant, demonstrating that infant neurological functioning reorganises itself at regular intervals throughout the first two years of life, specifically social, affective, motor and cognitive capacities. He identifies four key stages of neurological development at: 2–3 months, 5–6 months, 8–12 months and 18 months. At 2–3 months, the parent has primary responsibility for any interaction with the infant's world. It is the mother's ability to adapt to the infant at this stage that will have the greatest bearing on the infant's ability to manage stress responses later in life. At 5–6 months of age, the infant's primary role is to respond to stimuli that are received from another human's face, touch, voice and movement. The infant is able to interact with these processes, and will demonstrate social and adaptive abilities at this age. Between 8 and 12 months of age, the infant is beginning to explore their world and develops relationships with objects beyond that of its mother. Both over-regulation and under-regulation of an infant's capacity to explore can have a negative impact on the developing brain, resulting in boredom or hyper stimulation. At the same age the infant is also developing attachments, which are apparent in attachment and separation responses to his/her primary carer. The infant also develops the ability to be inter-subjective at this age, whereby he/she can discern the subjectivity of his/her prime care giver's intentions. By 18 months of age, the infant is starting to develop linguistic ability which will be reinforced or limited by the parental response. Additionally the child develops an ability to move around, which increases his/her capacity to experience stress responses through falling, bumping into things or being constrained by his/her parents.

Plutchik (1983, p. 243) sources Piaget as being the first to identify that 'with the development of the cognitive ability to represent the self and external causation, affects such as shame, defiance, and negativism appear'. Research by Amsterdam (1972), Amsterdam and Levitt (1980) and Lewis (1982) has supported this view that shame and self-consciousness appear at the time of separation and individuation, when an infant develops the ability to stand up and move around on their own. It is at this age that Mahler (1980, p. 7) suggests that when a child is becoming 'intoxicated with his own faculties and with the greatness of his world . . . he is exhilarated by his capacities'. If this is handled in a way that does not develop appropriate boundaries for the child, he/she may continue in his/her narcissistic world, or if it is constrained too much, the child may not develop a strong sense of self.

Neuroscience and emotional dysfunction

It is the effective management of stress responses as an infant that enables an adequate stress response as the person becomes a functioning adult. This is highlighted in Chapter 5. Over-protective parenting sets the child up for inadequate stress responses as the neurology has not become immunised to these responses; for example, the child may develop a heightened sense of insecurity when left alone if they have not learnt to separate from their parent, yet on the other hand, if a child experiences too much stress it can create neurological deficit in the developing brain and they may seek higher levels of risk and associated excitement to activate stress responses.

The right side of the brain is the neurological basis for attachment functions. Devinsky (2000) proposes that it is the effective development of this side of the brain that leads to the ability to develop a unified sense of self. Schore (2003) has added to this work and identified that where neurological impairments have been created through trauma, usually through poor attachment histories, this has a neurobiological effect on the developing nervous system, both in terms of being able to regulate internal states and interpret neurological messages that are received and also with regard to accurate reading and response to external communication. At an emotional level the individual experiences difficulty in managing intense feelings of rage, disgust, etc., or indeed positive feelings of joy, happiness and excitement. Where the deficit is marked, more complex problems such as personality disorders may arise. Evidence of this level of deficit is apparent in clients who find it difficult to form effective bonds with others and often have dysfunctional relationships. These clients have experienced a 'collapse of internalised representations of the external world' resulting in 'the patient regressing from whole to part object relationships' (p. 347). Schore suggests that this is indicative of the potential for the development of personality disorders later. Additionally, clients may present with borderline personality and other dissociative disorders that may be represented through self-harming activities.

Schore (2003, p. 372) considers Basch's (1995) view that would argue that the role of the therapist is to work with affect-regulating mechanisms as part of the therapeutic process:

> The more I know about how we are designed to function – what neurophysiology, infant research, affect theory, cognitive psychology, semantics, information theory, evolutionary biology, and other pertinent disciplines can tell me about human development – the better I am prepared to be empathic with a patient's communication at a particular time in his or her treatment.

Even in considering one of the most basic premises of NLP, that of rapport, it is important to recognise that the process of mirroring, particularly facial expression, will trigger high levels of endorphins, creating an optimum environment for repair and development of right brain processes (Hoffman, 1987; Panksepp, Siviy & Normansell, 1985).

Cybernetics of the self system

There are many competing aspects of the developing self, from the imprints that are developed through the nurture of the child by its prime carers to the innate attributes of the personality defined by Jung. If these are combined with the neurological components presented within recent neuroscientific research, all of this has considerable implications on the self system, i.e., the neurological, emotional, somatic and cognitive aspects that make up the self.

Bateson's cybernetic theory suggests that the system is designed for adaptation and there will sometimes occur pathological splitting within a system to enable optimum functioning of the individual. This is supported by Dilts's (2000) perspective on schismogenesis, which he defines as the splitting of parts of the personality that are dependent on positive feedback loops. Where certain attributes of a personality do not generate productive responses in the person's environment, they then become 'split off' or excluded from the rest of the functioning psyche. This splitting process becomes essential for survival and eventually, if left unchecked, can create conflict or imbalance in the psyche, resulting in severe psychological disturbance such as schizophrenia. The complexities and implications of this are discussed in greater depth in Chapter 8.

Satir (1972) provides a simplistic yet very meaningful interpretation of this, where she identifies that the family rules only allow the expression of justified feeling: 'You shouldn't feel that way' (p. 101). Her view is that 'if you make a distinction between acting your feelings and telling your feelings, it might be easier to give up the rule, "Thou shalt have only justified feelings"' (p. 101). She recognised this very early in her work and recommended to the families that she worked with that they could develop a set of rules that 'whatever feeling you have is human and therefore acceptable, the self can grow' (p. 101). She discussed with families the option of generating different courses of action for certain feelings as an alternative to continuing old and unacceptable patterns of behaviour.

Rossi (in Erickson & Rossi, 1989) provides considerable insight into Erickson's approach to working with the self system through his use of age regression techniques to heal past traumas in his work *February Man*. Rossi asks Erickson to expand on the development of a child, particularly the very early defence mechanisms that an individual develops: 'one of the first important discriminations for a newborn infant is to say no by turning its head away from the breast when it has had enough'. Rossi recognises within this process that an individual will 'frequently use these very primitive defense mechanisms of denial against others as well as against the new in ourselves' (p. 141).

Neurolinguistic psychotherapy has a fundamental role in developing effective regulation of the self system. By using the components of neuroscience identified by Schore (2003) we are able to facilitate, within the therapeutic relationship, the principal components that enable effective repair of the self. Neuroscientific theory has identified that the right brain continues to grow throughout a lifetime, therefore there is the potential to develop this through 'effective, affectively focused psychoanalytic treatment'. The role of the therapist is to create a series of 'ongoing external and internal affectively charged relational experiences', which in turn will add to the auto-regulatory flexibility of an individual, resulting in 'the generation of more complex psychobiological states and higher levels of self-reflective consciousness' (p. 248).

By combining the potential for brain growth throughout the life of a client and bringing into the therapeutic space the potential for developmental work, including the repair of the neurological deficits, neurolinguistic psychotherapy presents a model of therapy that can span the in-depth psychodynamic processes of developing relationships available within analytic traditions and the cognitive application of classical conditioning to repair the neurology. In the following case study is a demonstration of how it is possible to hold both aspects within one therapeutic relationship.

D presented at age 58, with a history of weight problems for his entire life, a lack of confidence and a desire to be a 'new me'. He recognised that he was a comfort eater and since the age of 16 had tried 'every diet in the book'. His relationship with food was one where 'a shovel is good enough'. He had experienced one episode of anorexia in his mid-thirties. He was finding that as he got older he was becoming less tolerant of other people, with increasing levels of aggression. He used food to control his anger and then when he had eaten everything available would feel even more angry. If he did not feed his anger he would fall into an 'empty, hollow darkness'.

His history was one of predominantly female carers, having been brought up by his maternal grandparents and his aunts. He recalls food as a central focus of his early life: 'apple pie and custard, ice-cream, and rice pudding'. His father had left the family home when he was a baby, and he only reconnected with him when D was 43. His mother was deaf – 'she only ever heard half a story and made the rest up' – therefore he had needed to be loud to get her attention when he was a child. The only significant male in his life was his grandfather, and he recalled being beaten by him with a leather belt.

Psychobiologically, D had a poor self-regulating system and from a very early age had used food as a way of dealing with his internal distress resulting from insecure attachment.

His relationship with his wife was one of her bullying him for being overweight, and mealtimes were a constant battleground of him eating as much as he could and her articulating her disgust towards him.

D had continued his early defence mechanism into his adult relationships and by the time he came to therapy, although he recognised that he needed to change his behaviour, he did not have the flexibility within his right brain functioning to respond from a different affective state.

> My first impression of this client was one of a very large and loud man. There was only space in the consulting room for him, and I found his presence very overbearing.

From a neurological perspective he was operating within a constant state of arousal and had a need to make himself 'known' to his external world, which had the opposite effect of pushing people away from him.

> He found it very difficult to get in touch with and express in an articulate way his inner world. He regularly tried to shape the therapy and was unable to acknowledge that he was trying to control our relationship. After a few weeks in therapy I was finding it increasingly difficult to stay in the room with him and considered how I might use a metaphor to enable him to gain some insight into his needs that resulted in his overbearing personality.
>
> We discussed how we might share a meal together; I asked him what kind of meal this could be. He described which restaurant he would take me to, what he would order for me and the kind of wines that I might drink. He had no awareness of my own needs other than what he thought they might be. There was no space for my own decision-making at all in the process. This came as a shock to him and we spent a few weeks enabling him to acknowledge his 'massive hunger for my mother'. Over a period of two months, he found his emotions towards me almost unbearable – 'You are the teacher, I can't fall in love with the teacher'. Acknowledging his emotions with an Other created even more conflict for D, and he started to experience an escalation in his levels of anger – 'I can't let anyone in to share it with me, it absorbs everything, it is shite'. He was aware that underpinning this emotion was a 'rampant energy, I think I use food because no one would want to have sex with me'. We continued to work on his feelings in therapy and over the subsequent six months he started to acknowledge his sexual identity as a man which then created problems in his marriage.

Psychodynamically, he was starting to develop a positive affect in his relationship to me, and it was important at this stage for me to continue the therapeutic process to enable continuing development of his own internal affect-regulating process and gradually move him from relying on myself as the therapist to manage this for him.

A breakthrough occurred one year into the therapy, with me having operated from within the maternal role in the transferential relationship. He attended for therapy in a very low state, could not see the point of continuing and became increasingly distressed as the session went on. He eventually broke down into a primal state of distress and after some time emerged into consciousness to share the experience that he had 'literally given birth to myself'. We reviewed what had occurred and shared our respective experiences of what he had been through. I voiced that I had found it so very hard not to pick him up and nurse him while he was so distressed, and he said that my not doing this was probably the most empowering thing I could have done. He recognised that he needed to become his own mother and learn how to soothe himself.

He continued to see me for a further nine months, and he finally discharged himself after two years in therapy.

In summary, his time in therapy combined the 'externally and internally charged relational experiences' through his transferential relationship with me, while at the same time it enabled development of new neurological links in his psychobiology.

In the following chapter, I continue with an in-depth elucidation of neuroscience and include recent research that will have considerable influence on the work of the neurolinguistic psychotherapist.

Chapter 4

Neurological processes

> The overall function of the brain is to be well informed about what goes
> on in the rest of the body, the body proper; about what goes on in itself;
> and about the environment surrounding the organism, so that suitable
> survivable accommodations can be achieved between the organism and
> the environment.
>
> (Damasio, 1994, p. 90)

In this chapter, I link the known components of neurological processing
that are core to NLP with some of the existing theories in neuroscience.
This could fill a volume on its own, and rather than attempt to provide a
full exposition of existing theories, I will provide the reader with indicative
references to encourage greater exploration of the various texts in full. I will
consider how neurological processing influences the development of the
individual which has been considered in Chapter 3 and the pertinence of
linking what is now known about neuroscience with attachment theory and
development of the self.

Neurological components of NLP

Korzybski's (1933) work *Science and Sanity* set the stage for much of the
developmental studies that later became included in NLP. He expanded on
Aristotelian thinking that assumed duality and developed his own theory of
'general semantics' to include a wider range of possibilities than that
presented by duality theorists.

> Many issues are not so sharp, and therefore a system which posits the
> general sharpness of 'either-or', and so objectifies 'kind', is unduly
> limited; it must be revised and made more flexible in terms of 'degree'.
> This requires a physic-mathematical 'way of thinking' which a non-
> Aristotelian system supplies.
>
> (p. xxi)

His work on general semantics (1933) came out of his view that a theory of
meaning was impossible and a theory of evaluation was more pertinent in

understanding evolutionary processes. Within this theory he recognised that individuals are not separate from their 'neuro-linguistic and neuro-semantic environments' (p. xxii).

Bandler and Grinder used this principle of the neurolinguistic relationship that an individual has to their environment to underpin much of their early modelling work. Within the wider field of NLP additional factors are considered that directly influence a person's responses within their environment. Neurolinguistic psychotherapy builds on this by attempting to hold the space between neuroscience and the work of theorists such as Damasio, Edelman, Panksepp and Pert, and that of constructivists who would prefer that a person can change their reactions if they change their perceptions. Huxley (1954) in *The Doors of Perception* refers to the brain as a reducing valve, whereby sensing through the cerebral cortex is filtered along a nervous system that is rich in neuropeptides, each of which is programmed for different emotional responses, which will inevitably result in individuals being selective in what is given attention at a basic neurological level. Yet if I bring in the constructivist view presented by Von Foerster (2003), who considered that the nervous system cannot absolutely distinguish between a perception and a hallucination, since both are patterns of neural excitement, the distance between the schools of thought is not so great.

Within the basic neurological aspects of NLP, it is recognised that individuals receive information from an external reality via one or a combination of the five senses. These are visual, auditory, kinaesthetic, gustatory and olfactory. What NLP omits from its theory is the relationship between the more complex aspects of the nervous system and unconscious processing. Pert (1997) has identified that where the nervous system connects to the external world through one of the five senses, there is a high concentration of neuropeptide receptors, and it is the quantity and quality of the sensory receptors at these points that determine what an individual pays attention to, i.e., the basis of filtering.

NLP continues its journey through the neurological system by bringing in 'operant conditioning' through anchored responses, particularly in relation to creating new behavioural choices by 'collapsing' unuseful triggered responses, or creating new state-dependent resources by bringing these from the past into now. Utilising neurological responses is also an inherent part of strategy work, particularly the triggers for strategy activation and also biofeedback mechanisms which mean that wherever there is a change in the physiological state this will always be accompanied by a change in the emotional state, which may be conscious or unconscious – and vice versa.

The nervous system in its entirety

The human nervous system is made up of over 30 billion connections, and structurally consists of the brain, spinal cord, nerve cells, synapses,

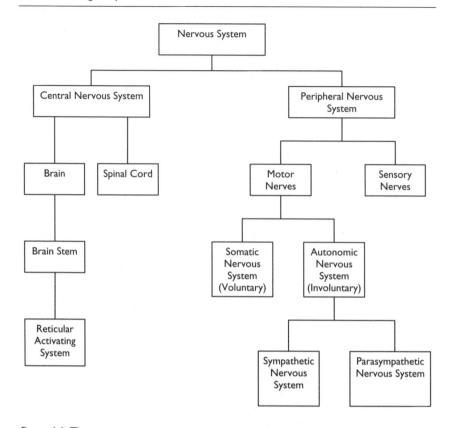

Figure 4.1 The nervous system

dendrites, axons, soma and the various biochemical components that enable the transmission of impulses along the neural pathways.

The nervous system (Figure 4.1) is subdivided into the central nervous system (CNS), which consists of the brain and spinal cord, and the peripheral nervous system (PNS). The CNS controls and coordinates all physiological activity within the body. The primary function of the PNS is to send nervous impulses to and from the CNS from external stimuli and the organs of the body. The PNS is divided into the somatic nervous system (SNS), which is responsible for sending messages from the body to the CNS and for coordination of musculoskeletal movement, and the autonomic nervous system (ANS), which is the one that most concerns the neuro-linguistic psychotherapist.

The ANS as a self-regulating mechanism does not require conscious communication to function and has responsibility for maintaining homeostasis of the bodily functions. The ANS has two different neural branches, the *sympathetic* and *parasympathetic*. The sympathetic nervous system governs our arousal responses, such as the flight, fright, fight mechanisms, and the parasympathetic nervous system has the opposite effect in controlling relaxation, our digestive system and our ability to return to homeostasis.

Another aspect of the nervous system that is directly utilised in the work of neurolinguistic psychotherapy is the reticular activating system (RAS). This is the part of the brain responsible for arousal and motivation, as well as circadian rhythm and basic functions of respiration and cardiac rhythms, and is situated in the core of the brain stem.

The developing brain of an infant and implications for neurolinguistic psychotherapy

Trevarthen and Aitken (2001) have identified that during pregnancy the foundations of the nervous system are laid down, including the development of interneuronal activity that enables regulation of the developing foetus within the support system of the maternal nervous system and bodily processes. These structures are built upon by intrauterine stimuli and when a baby is born, it is the most primitive aspects of the brain – the brainstem and sensory motor cortex – that are the most highly developed, enabling the baby to function in an 'acceptable' state of arousal according to the chemical and electrical messages received from the nervous system. In Schore's (2003) research he highlights how this functional development continues into early infancy, where the infant's right hemispheric functions are 'psychobiologically attuned to the output of the mother's right hemisphere' (p. 12).

During the first two years of life the social brain is then developed in direct response to the factors present in the external environment of the infant. Damasio (1994, p. 128) says that there is an absolute correlation between the emotions of the individual and the core regulatory processes: 'Nature appears to have built the apparatus of rationality not just on top of the apparatus of biological regulations, but also *from* it and *with* it'.

Goleman (1996) defines the aspects of brain functioning that are relevant to the emotional development of an individual as follows.

- The emotional or social brain consists of the forebrain and the cerebellum.
- This is subdivided into the areas of the hippocampus, hypothalamus, cerebral cortex, anterior cingulate gyrus, the prefrontal cortex and the orbitofrontal cortex.
- The hippocampus is developed over time and holds the basis of memories, particularly in enabling the holding of memories until they become generalised experiences.
- The hypothalamus provides the basis for reticular formation and is responsible for circadian rhythm, neuroendocrine outputs and homeostasis.

- The thinking parts of the emotional brain are the anterior cingulate gyrus and the prefrontal cortex.
- The anterior cingulate gyrus renders new memories permanent aspects of the psyche and also enables the experience of anticipation that has an element of reward attached to it.
- The prefrontal cortex adds to decision-making processes by creating emotional linkages to the deeper aspects of the brain within the sympathetic nervous system and the RAS, tying the emotions of pleasure, joy, pain, anger and panic to the flight, fright, fight responses.
- Both these aspects of the brain are used to inform decision-making and consider alternative choices when faced with emotional or survival-based responses.
- The orbitofrontal cortex has links to the sensory aspect of the nervous system via the cerebral cortex and enables the regulation of behaviour associated with reward and punishment.
- This part of the brain also regulates decision-making processes, including social relationships.
- It is these three parts (anterior cingulate gyrus, prefrontal cortex and orbitofrontal cortex) of the brain that are thought to be the basis of emotional intelligence.

Chugani, Behen, Muzik, Juhasz, Nagy and Chugani (2001) identified that as these parts of the brain are activated, a set of neural synapses are triggered into action, which, if activated on more than one occasion, will start to form patterns. It is these patterns of neurological activity that then form the basis of generalised behaviour, ensuring that social intelligence is developed predominantly between the ages of 6 and 18 months.

A clinical example of the effect that this can have on the developing brain is apparent in the case of the young man with Tourette's syndrome in Chapter 1.

> In therapy, he discussed his early childhood experiences and can recall quite clearly being looked after by 'Granny' in the village from the age of six months (a local lady who had no blood relationship to him). He distinctly remembered being bored when he stayed with her as she had very few toys and did not encourage him to play much. He recalled that he used to amuse himself by learning to make different noises, with his mother noting that the tics first emerged when his sister was born and he again was cared for by 'Granny'.

The neural synapses that had been activated at this time then became part of his behavioural repertoire and the pattern would emerge if he accessed the generalised response of being bored or frustrated with himself, resulting in a diagnosis of Tourette's syndrome.

During the first two years of an infant's life, the environment and immediate social relationships directly influence how the rest of the brain and the neural synapse patterns are developed and how norms for arousal and regulation are managed. Babies who experience an environment that is responsive, caring and 'good enough' will find that the world is responsive to their feelings and their nervous system is able to return to a state of equilibrium relatively quickly after sympathetic arousal. Babies whose environment is less sensitive may experience prolonged activation of the stress response and an increase in levels of the neuropeptide cortisol.

In the early days of life, an infant learns to regulate her external environment solely through her nervous system and the emotional responses that this generates. Her nervous system will react towards positive stimuli and she will seek this out, giving 'towards' based behaviour, or generate 'away from' behaviours in response to painful or unpleasant stimuli that are seen within NLP values work. She may also develop a process of dissociation or 'freezing' if the sympathetic arousal remains prolonged. This will result in a forced parasympathetic response where the infant adopts a non-response reaction to the environment. This is discussed further in Chapter 7.

Gerhardt (2004) considers the development of the right brain in her work on the developing child and demonstrates research that shows that right brain dominance continues throughout the first two years of life, and it is only when the orbitofrontal cortex is developed that there is a shift towards development of the left brain. This is apparent in the development of speech production, linguistic ability and sequential processing. Once this appears there is less plasticity in the right brain, and growth continues in the left brain with development of the anterior cingulate which enables awareness of internal states and feelings. The prefrontal cortex also continues to develop, forming the dorsolateral prefrontal cortex which is where thoughts about feelings are first developed and where a 'working memory' for them becomes part of a person's internal dialogue.

In terms of the complexities of neurological development and functioning, how the client presents in therapy will be representative of their own neurological development. Carroll (2002) proposes that if an individual has experienced 'good enough' parenting resulting in optimum development of their social brain, as an adult they will have mechanisms that enable self-regulation of emotions, an awareness of others' emotional states and an ability to manage the effects of stress. The client brings to the therapeutic process an emotionally sound psychoneurology and the therapy offered by the core aspects of neurolinguistic psychotherapy is likely to be successful.

Where a client has experienced prolonged stress responses and hyper-arousal in infancy, their neurological processing will have developed a mechanism whereby they have learnt to communicate their distress directly into another human being. This can be immediately accessed by the therapist, and may occur unwittingly. There is a resonance between Schore's view and that of Freud (1957, 1958) and Buck (1994), that the infant becomes psychobiologically attuned to the mother's right hemispheric functioning as a natural process. This process becomes neurologically triggered during rapport whereby communication occurs directly from the unconscious of the client to the unconscious of the therapist and vice versa, *without* going through the conscious of either person. This then has implications for the neurolinguistic psychotherapist, whether it be to influence and inform her own practice regarding unconscious communication between client and therapist, or her own therapeutic process in discovering and working through unconscious material, with a willingness in supervision to explore and acknowledge her own unconscious process and how it might directly affect her work with clients.

If a client has experienced neurological deficit or delay in early infancy, the role of the therapist in the therapeutic relationship becomes essential to successful therapy. Where the deficit or delay has occurred in very early infancy, with right hemispheric developmental delay, and where associated hyperarousal or elevated stress responses have continued over a prolonged period of time, Schore (2003) suggests that dissociative and personality disorders are likely to be present and comments that 'early traumatic attachments are therefore a powerful source generator of the most severe deficits described in self psychology' (p. 137).

As Chugani *et al.* (2001) have identified, the social brain is developed between the ages of 6 and 18 months. Schore (2003) describes the effect that deficit or delay can have on the development of this area of the brain, with the adult client likely to present with difficulty in social relationships, or socioemotional stress responses, which may result in autism, mania, phobic states, alcoholism and drug addiction.

The psychotherapeutic process in each of these cases where developmental delay has occurred is essential to successful therapeutic outcome. The therapeutic role becomes one of working with the projections of the client, utilising projective identifications and accessing resources within the therapeutic relationship to enable resourcing and learning for the client while at the same time containing the process in a way that is safe and ecological for the client and therapist. The therapist is required to work at relational level with the client to facilitate neurological re-patterning through the therapeutic relationship. This re-patterning or re-programming of the client at a neurological level is likely to require prolonged periods in therapy as the developmental delays are addressed. This then calls into question the appropriateness of neurolinguistic psychotherapy with its inherent brevity. Where a neurolinguistic psychotherapist is familiar with attachment disorders and has sufficient behavioural flexibility to work psychodynamically with a client, the potential that a psychodynamic generative approach combined with the processes that enable neurological change affords will facilitate a considerable degree of potential for the client.

Neurological re-patterning in therapy

> M first presented at the age of 23, he had a four-year history of cocaine use and this was now interfering with his work and rela- tionships because of his increasing levels of paranoia. For the first year or so of therapy he was unable to relate verbally to me as the therapist; he would ask to lie on the floor and would drift off to a world of his own while I 'tried' a range of hypnotherapeutic processes to assist him. He would leave therapy, saying very little, and would always turn up for his next session.

Neurologically, this client was unable to formulate positive social attach- ments, mirroring Schore's theory of a socioemotional stress response. M had used cocaine as a way of accessing a sociable, confident state whenever he needed to communicate with others in a social environment. Thera- peutically, M was unable to communicate his internal world yet he did demonstrate a degree of insight and willingness to stay with the relationship that he had developed with me.

> After this first year, we moved to a more dialogical relationship and he would talk about his 'perfect' relationships with his parents, and would blame his relationship with his partner for his anger, paranoia and drug taking. I experienced his unspoken frustration and anger towards his parents as a projection and whenever I challenged this or offered it back to him in a way that I thought he could process usefully, he would regress and either not turn up for therapy, or would want to return to lying on the floor. I adapted what I was doing in the therapeutic relationship and reverted to working in a very accepting way of wherever he was during the sessions with me. This continued for a further year and by now he had been in therapy on and off for about four years.

The therapy relationship enabled M to transfer his unuseful and unresolved anger to myself as the therapist through projective identification. The role of the therapist in this situation is to develop a secure and contained environment through becoming a secure attachment figure. This then enables the client to access internal resources and develop new neuro- psychological processes to effect change.

One day something changed and he started to ask my advice about his relationship with his mother. He cared about her deeply, but felt she needed too much from him and he was feeling smothered. We talked about how he could manage this and he said he felt like he was six years old and all he wanted to do was to be free of her demands of him. We both accepted that he needed permission to be a free child and talked about the kind of things he wanted to do when he was six. He then moved out of therapy for about nine months, as he wanted to go away and enjoy being six and all that this entailed. (By now he was free from his drug problem.)

I had worked with M for some time as his secure attachment figure, and he was now beginning to explore his own boundaries and begin a process of individuation. He communicated this to me by talking to me about his mother. I used the opportunity afforded within the therapy relationship to assist him to find ways to move out of the therapy and become a self-regulating individual.

I didn't see him again for almost two years, and he returned to therapy quite recently. He had met someone that he loved and had married her. He had felt some of the old pressures returning to him, reverting to using cocaine again as a way of escaping his worldly responsibilities, although infrequently. He had recognised that he was now being expected to be an adult and wanted to respond to this, his new wife was quite demanding and he was finding this difficult to be with, wanted to go back to being free again and was using cocaine as a way of enabling this to happen.

Neurologically, M had developed an alternative pattern of behaviour, and although he recognised that some of the previous neurological patterning existed, he was now able to access a more resourceful behavioural response from his adult self.

His return to therapy was much briefer this time, and was mainly spent looking at resourcing his adult self, modelling adult behaviours and developing coping strategies to ensure that he could manage in the relationship while at the same time finding ways to enjoy 'freedom' in a way that was ecological for his sense of identity.

My role as therapist in this relationship over a seven-year period was initially to soothe and enable him to bring into his neurological processing an adaptive response that was built on 'good enough' care. Whenever I tried to make demands of him in therapy, by following tried and trusted processes, he would regress, and I would return to soothing. This took some considerable time and developmentally matched the period of time that would have been required for his own neurological development as an infant. The therapy then moved to a place where he could experience socioemotional stress and bring this into the relationship. Where I was able to contain it, he was able to move on in therapy; where I became demanding and offered his projections back to him this would then trigger him to regress. As his neurology developed he was slowly able to contain and manage more and more of his own emotional responses until he could get to a developmental age where he could verbalise the conflict within his internal world. At this point he required me and him to let go of the relationship, something that he had been unable to do as a child with his mother. In doing this, he was then able to move our relationship to one that was much more of societal equals, where he could return willingly and seek advice and support for an 'adult-based' issue.

Theories in neuroscience

There exists a wider body of knowledge within the associated field of neuroscience that can also enhance the work of the neurolinguistic psychotherapist. Beginning with Darwin's theory of evolution, this has been developed by Edelman (1987) and utilised by therapists in developing a greater understanding of the relationship between attachment theory and neuroscience.

Darwin (1998) developed a number of theories in neuroscience as part of his work on evolution. In *Expression of the Emotions in Man and Animals* he identified that people have facial expressions that represent specific emotions and some of these are shared with animals. He particularly refers to the musculature used by a wolf baring its fangs as being identical to the musculature used by man when he is angry or threatened. Out of this came his theory of neurology that proposed that where a group of neurons are activated simultaneously and therefore strengthened, they will then remain 'wired' together, and that where collections of synapses are unused, these will weaken and be 'pruned' to form efficient neural pathways.

Edelman (1987) has built on the work of Darwin and has coined the term 'neural Darwinism' to expound on the theory created by Darwin of 'survival of the fittest'. At birth the human brain rapidly creates synaptic connections which reach a peak in number by eight months. It is at this point that 'pruning' begins, and by the age of ten, a child will have only half the number of neural synapses that it had at age eight months, having kept only the most useful synapses.

It is from this basis that Edelman offers the view that to consider the mind as a digital computer is an untenable position, and that all learning and memory is dependent on synaptic strength. He proposes that all neural development is unique to each individual and it is impossible to know where particular connections in a nervous system have come from. Each person's mind is so unique that there will always be fluctuations in brain patterns, and each person's map will be dependent on the availability of input. What he does propose is that individuals develop extensive generalisations in object recognition, which supports the concept of generalisations found in NLP. He also holds the view that the brain is constructive and will be sensitive to specific contexts, which will enable perceptual categorisation, i.e., that neurological reactions will only occur in a given context. An example of this would be when we find we only experience feelings of loss for a loved one when a particular piece of music is played. It requires the neurological pathway that begins in our auditory system to be activated, and to follow a series of other pathways before the emotion-bearing neuropeptides are released, enabling one to feel loss.

Panksepp (1998) has considered the work of Darwin and recognised that as mammals, we have common 'emotional operating systems'. He identifies seven neurobiological systems that have specific neural circuitry which directly impacts on our behavioural responses. He describes these as instinctual in nature and they are an inherent aspect of the intrinsic potential of the nervous system. The seven systems are referred to as:

- the seeking system – responsible for governing curiosity, searching and meaning making
- the rage system – triggered when we experience frustration
- the fear system – which is linked directly to the sympathetic nervous system responses of flight, fright and fight
- the panic system – which is triggered by separation distress
- the lust system – found in sexualised behaviour
- the care system – which enables maternal behaviour
- the play system – which enables play activities.

Other developmental theorists such as Gerhardt (2004) highlight how affection shapes the development of a baby's brain, bringing Darwinian theory into line with attachment theory. As I have alluded to in Chapter 3, an infant requires positive looks as the stimulus that enables the brain to grow into one that is socially and emotionally intelligent. As a baby receives a positive look from a parent, his nervous system responds in a state of positive arousal; this then causes neuropeptides to be released which go directly to the orbitofrontal region of the brain, and dopamine to go directly to the prefrontal cortex, enabling both areas to grow. Gerhardt also identified that the prenatal period of a child's life will be indicative of the development of a socially and emotionally intelligent brain. Where an infant's mother has experienced high levels of cortisol from increased stress in pregnancy this will be passed on directly to the baby, who will then have a sensitised stress response.

Developmental studies have shown that babies whose mothers smoked or drank during pregnancy are more likely to demonstrate antisocial behaviour. Trevarthen and Aitken (2001) support this theory and consider that interneuronal activity first occurs in the womb and later enables adaptive processes as a human response. If intrauterine stimulus is provided, the foetus develops the neural pathways to the forebrain and cerebellum that are later enabled by the intuitive responses of the parents. It is this very early development that enables purposeful consciousness and an ability to cooperate with others and learn from these interactions.

The role of the psychotherapist is brought into a new light through the implications of working with psychoneuroimmunology. Validating the client's model of the world and negative feelings, the therapist enables the neurotransmitters associated with the negative state to be released from the subcortex and the existing neural networks activated. This results in the release of the stress hormone cortisol which then floods the brain, setting up an appropriate environment for the development of new neural pathways. When the client is in this state it is important that the therapist works with the client to reflect on their old feelings, and consider how to respond differently. In this consideration of new behavioural choices, the cortisol-flooded brain has in place the necessary elements for growth of new neural pathways in response to the subcortical signals generated in response to the newly considered choices.

Applying NLP to neurological theory

It is important to consider the links between neuroscientific theory and the role of the neurolinguistic psychotherapist. All the behavioural and emotional issues that a person presents with in a therapy setting will have direct links to their own neurobiological make-up. In addition, neurolinguistic psychotherapy as an outcome-oriented therapy provides the optimum conditions to enable lasting neurological change.

It is the RAS that NLP techniques such as anchoring and goal-setting utilise to facilitate goal achievement and positive state actualisation. When a client visualises actualisation of a goal this results in neuropeptides being released and blood and oxygen flow to the part of the body directly responsible for achievement of the goal. Pert (1997) refers to Erickson's demonstration of this in his experimental work with women who had flat chests and were keen to have treatment to enlarge their breasts. He suggested to them 'that their breasts would become warm and tingly and would start to grow' (p. 147). The increased blood supply to their breasts as a direct result of Erickson's hypnotic communication to them enabled the breast tissue to be stimulated and grow.

Additional to this are the theories of Pavlovian conditioning or anchored responses by Pavlov (1927), developed by Adler (1992) to influence the work of psychoneuroimmunology, and Pert (1997) who recognised that we have a process inherent in our bodies referred to as 'state dependent recall', inferring that a person is more likely to recall positive emotional experiences when in a good state and negative emotional experiences when in a bad state. Pavlov took the work of Twitmeyer (1902) and developed 'classical conditioning', which later became known as anchoring in NLP. He was particularly interested in hypnosis, identifying that hypnosis creates an inhibitive state in the brain which is related to sleep in that it inhibits motor impulses by affecting the amount of uptake of sensory stimuli. He studied laboratory animals and utilised the theory of applying sensory stimuli to develop a theory on classical conditioning. Classical conditioning or anchoring requires pairing of a known stimulus with a new conditioned stimulus to create a conditioned response. Damasio (1994) took anchoring to a deeper level, and identified that anchoring works by excitation of the neurons which causes an electrical current to be sent from the nerve cell down the axon and into the synapse. A response is then triggered within the synapse that releases neurotransmitters that have a direct effect on nerve receptors. If the next neuron that is fired through its own nerve receptors also has an action potential, in other words a neural memory in response to the impulse, it too will release neurotransmitters and the neurological chain will continue. Where no neural memory exists, the anchoring process cannot work.

A therapist may use anchoring processes with volition through creating collapsing or chaining anchors. Even greater potential exists if anchoring and the development of neurological chains are used within the context of the outcome-oriented aspects of therapeutic work. By facilitating a client to find their own internal resources, positive states and times when they don't 'do' the problem, they are encouraging neural networks to be stimulated that are more aligned with solution state than problem state. As each of these states is accessed consistently in therapy, the client finds it more difficult to do the old problem state and easier to move to the solution state.

Ader and Cohen (1982) were also inspired by Pavlov's work, and experimented with mice to demonstrate that when mice that had lupus were given a saccharine solution to drink at the same time as being injected with cyclophosphamide, a specific response would be observed in the immune system. When the mice were then given just the saccharine solution, the immune system reacted as if it had been given cyclophosphamide. This groundbreaking work of Ader and Cohen, later termed psychoneuroimmunology, demonstrated that the immune system could be conditioned and was directly under the influence of the brain.

Pert (1997) developed Ader and Cohen's work and identified *molecules of emotion*, whereby the endocrine system is flooded with neuropeptides when positive emotions are experienced, resulting in neurotransmitter activation. The opposite of this also applies, in that neuropeptides are released when pain or negative emotions are experienced, which are regulated by the limbic areas of the brain. She identified that neuropeptides are present throughout the body and particularly around the spinal column and gut; therefore feelings are experienced by both the body and the brain. Chopra (1989), an advocate of Pert's, commented 'If being happy, sad, thoughtful, excited and so on all require the production of neuropeptides – and neuro-transmitters in our brain cells – then the immune cells must also be happy, sad, thoughtful, excited, too' (p. 67). Pert (1997) expanded on her original work on neuropeptides and started to make relationships to the storage of emotionally based memories at a psychosomatic level. Building on the work of Kandell, she comments that:

> Memories are stored not only in the brain, but in a *psychosomatic network* extending into the body, particularly in the ubiquitous recep-tors between nerves and bundles of cell bodies called ganglia, which are distributed not just in and near the spinal cord, but all the way out along pathways to internal organs and the very surface of our skin.
>
> (p. 143)

Neuropsychotherapy in action

K presented with a 40-year history of depressive illness. There was no reactionary cause to the commencement of his depressive tendencies and his profile represented classical endogenous depression. His initial history was unremarkable and apart from being depressed about being depressed, he lacked motivation to change, did not really believe change was possible and was looking for assistance in dealing with his current symptoms sufficiently to enable him to return to work. As his history was so benign, we agreed to move towards future-oriented work, rather than consider all that had gone on in the past and the many things that he had tried and failed at. During the early sessions I worked with him persistently utilising the linguistic patterns in brief solution-oriented therapy with the aim of enabling new neural networks to be developed.

Particular linguistic patterns that solution-oriented therapy offers include that of the 'miracle question': 'if you were to go to bed tonight, and a miracle were to occur overnight (and you didn't know it had happened), what would be different in the morning, such that you knew a miracle had happened?'. This pattern enables the client to act as if the problem had been resolved, and the solution state was already present. It is different from the 'as if' question of neurolinguistic psychotherapy, in that it offers absolute potential for change to happen by creating a 'miracle'. As soon as the client accesses the future-oriented state, the neurological potential is then created for change to happen. Solution-oriented therapy also asks the client to identify as many things as possible that will be different, ensuring that the client fires the neurological pathway a number of times in therapy, making it easier to re-access once the session has ended. Additionally, solution-focused therapy encourages the client to focus on times when they haven't done the problem state during the previous week. This process reinforces the 'not problem' state, again reinforcing positive neurological patterning.

Although this was difficult and he initially kept reverting to an old pattern of neurological, psychological and linguistic impotence, we persisted in the therapy and he agreed to return the following week. At this next session, we both noted that he could more easily move towards future-oriented thinking, that the resistance was not as great and that he could track himself to future scenarios where his depressive stance had changed considerably.

This was evidence that the neurological re-patterning that we had done the previous week had started to work and he was now accessing this preferred state spontaneously.

When he returned the following week, he appeared very different at a physiological level. His skin appeared younger, lighter and more elastic, he had a light in his eyes that had not been present previously and he was both walking and talking differently. He explained that he did not know what had happened, but it was almost as if his brain was working differently. The depressive fog that had been present for 40 years had gone, as had the butterflies in his stomach. He was reacting differently and rather than struggling to get up in the morning, he kept finding himself waking before the alarm and getting up immediately and looking forward to the day.

His progress continued and what is apparent in the work with this client is the power of working with the development of new neural pathways towards a future-oriented state, rather than working to resolve underlying old patterns of behaviour.

Potential for neurological re-patterning in therapy

There exists an enormous potential for linking research and theories in neuroscience to the existing theories in psychotherapy. Panksepp and Carroll are bringing this into the general arena of psychotherapy and over the next few years we will inevitably see further evidence of the potential afforded through psychotherapy to literally rewire a client's neurology such that past traumas remain in the past and are disconnected from a client's now and future. Mollon (2004) has already begun this in his comparative work linking psychoanalysis with Eye Movement Desensitization and Reprocessing, and I would anticipate that neurolinguistic psychotherapists will become actively involved in this debate, and will include the linguistic representation of neurologically held traumas in this work.

Chapter 5

The psychology of language

> In any work, you are going to use words to influence the psychological life of an individual today; you are going to use words to influence his organic life today, you are going to use words to influence his organic life twenty years from today.
>
> So you had better know what you are saying.
>
> You had better be willing to reflect upon the words you use, to wonder what the meanings are, and to seek out and understand their many associations.
>
> (Erickson, 1985, p. 32)

This chapter considers the linguistic components that support neurolinguistic psychotherapy. Chomsky's work on transformational grammar considers that a person will present a representation of their lived experience at surface structure, which is often considerably disconnected from how it has been experienced within the deeper structures of the psyche. Neurolinguistic psychotherapy uses the processes of the 'Milton Model' and the 'Meta Model' from Erickson and Satir to enable a client to access the deeper structure of their internal constructs. As this work progresses, therapists may find that clients access dissociated, disowned, split or fragmented aspects of their personality, and by using the processes within quantum linguistics it is possible to work with a client to facilitate a process of ownership and integration of these aspects. The chapter concludes with the client's search for meaning being at the centre of the therapeutic relationship.

Transformational grammar

Chomsky's work (1957) on transformational grammar is often quoted as providing the theoretical underpinnings of the linguistic components of neurolinguistic psychotherapy and is supported by two concepts. His first theorem is that the structure of human language is innate in all human beings, with a baby only needing to learn the vocabulary and parameters of language to enable communication; this hypothesises that all languages have the same basic rule structure. This first aspect is what we linguistically represent at a conscious level. Watzlawick (1978, pp. 14–15) describes this as follows: 'The one, in which for instance this sentence itself is expressed, is objective, definitional, cerebral, logical, analytic; it is the language of reason, of science, explanation, and interpretation, and therefore the language of most schools of psychotherapy'.

Chomsky's second theorem proposed that sentence structure is made up of two aspects – deep structure and surface structure – and a series of rules or transformations that connect these two levels. Within the surface structure of language, the sounds and words used are important to the individual, and fundamental differences between individuals will apply at this level, whereas at deep structure level the meaning of the words as they are represented is found, alongside a corresponding commonality of experience. He proposed that we move from deep structure to surface structure through the rules or transformations, with the transformation occurring via a process that takes the input and changes it in some way to create a surface structure representation. It is at this level of surface structure that differences occur between an original or primary experience (deep structure) and how it is represented at a linguistic level (surface structure).

Piaget's (1968) epistemological and psychological perspective challenged Chomsky's view of transformational grammar. He acknowledged the opposite perspectives of Chomsky, who considered that language is based in reason, and the contrary view that logic is a linguistic convention, preferring his own view: 'there is a whole selection of possible solutions, and the choice among these solutions must be made on the basis of fact, that is, on the basis of psychological research' (p. 5). This was supported by Watzlawick (1978, p. 15) whose perspective that directed thought follows 'linguistic logic . . . grammar, syntax and semantics' and undirected thought consists of 'dreams, fantasies, and other experiences of our inner world' (p. 15) later informed the co-developers of NLP.

By the 1990s Chomsky had reinterpreted his work on deep structure and surface structure and began to reflect the more epistemological stance of Piaget. He developed the concept of minimalism, which assumes that an economy of derivation occurs to ensure that a transformation will only happen if we receive input that is non-interpretable, based on our life experiences. In other words, a client will reduce concepts to understandable levels of meaning if they are unable to make logical sense of the experience. He proposed that an individual will distort information to make it interpretable, making meaning of events that may bear no relationship to reality, and create internal constructs that may result in emotional or psychological disturbance. If this distortion connects with an internal rule or transformation, a generalisation is set up to respond to the distortion and a pattern of behavioural response is then created. By listening to the linguistic structure of these patterns, often held at belief level, it is possible to work with the client to assist change by interrupting the pattern of behaviour.

Watzlawick (1978, pp. 104–105) provides an example of how Bandler and Grinder reported on this process in a group therapy session with a client who presented with an inability to say 'No'.

> Not surprisingly, this inability was the cause of stereotypical problems, from material exploitation all the way into the sexual area. But in her world image the act of denying was associated with far worse consequences than these. She claimed that as a child she had once refused to stay home with her father and upon her return had found him dead. Since then she was terrified of the magical consequences of any denial and avoided it. In front of the group the therapist imposed a double bind by asking her to say 'no' about something to every member of the group. She reacted strongly and refused to carry out the task. 'No! It's impossible for me to say "no" to people! You can't expect me to do it just because you ask me to' (Sluzki & Ranson, 1976). After several minutes of this agitated refusal and only after the therapist pointed out to her that she had been saying 'no' to him all this time did she realize that she had indeed been denying something without any dire consequences.

Pinker's (1994) work on the acquisition of language has added to the findings of Chomsky. He describes the notion that the use of language is an innate human ability and that far from being connected to the human's ability to reason, it is developed genetically. He has identified through research that rather than there being learned rules for language it is a neurological ability centred in the left hemisphere. Where aspects of the left hemisphere are damaged, certain types of aphasia or loss of speech, including interpretation of language, can occur, demonstrating the neurological aspects that make up an individual's ability to utilise language. Although Pinker proposes that the development of language is innate, he acknowledges that there are some factors that influence the ongoing development of linguistic ability that have implications for the therapy context. He identifies these as three external influences:

- positive evidence, whereby a parent will reinforce the use of positive and grammatically correct language
- the context in which the language is learnt, which enables us to make meaning of the language as it is used
- the prosody, which includes the rhythm and inflections that are used to infer meaning.

The clues to a client's inner world therefore exist in the linguistic presuppositions, i.e., what is presupposed in their language. If the linguistic structure does not follow a grammatical rule such as a negation or dissociative language, it is therefore created by an external event at some point in the client's life and is an accurate representation of the client's reality in a given moment. A client may refer to themselves as being dead in relationships, and as they describe the relationship they refer to themselves as *you*, e.g., *you find it very hard to not love someone when you feel dead inside*. This does not follow a grammatical rule in two instances. The client is dissociating from themselves, by referring to *you* rather than *I*. Additionally, they negate their love of someone by using the word 'not', when what they are looking for is to love someone, which will enable them to feel alive. The deeper structure of the client's experience is one of *deadness* which would have been created in their past experiences through not being loved. The role of the therapist in this instance is to unglue the double bind, and I discuss this process further in this chapter.

The meta-model of Satir

Kostere and Malatesta (1990) identified that we use symbolic representation to make sense of our world: 'It is through the process of modelling that the infinite variety of experience is organised into a form that can be interpreted, understood, and utilised. Modelling is an integral part of our daily lives and is the way by which we transform the chaotic into the structured' (pp. 1–2). Bandler and Grinder (1975) recognised this in their modelling of Satir and developed a linguistic model for challenging the distortions, deletions and generalisations that occur in everyday language that is known as the meta-model. This supports the views of Piaget and Watzlawick, of utilising the conscious representation of a presenting issue in therapy to access the deep structure of the unconscious and often illogical root cause.

Through the meta-model, it is possible to facilitate the client towards an understanding of the transformations they have made within their own linguistic constructs that have deleted, distorted or generalised an experience held at deep structure level. Although readily used by the therapist to assist their understanding of the client's internal constructs, enhanced levels of change can occur with a client who is enabled to recognise their own linguistic deletions, distortions and generalisations, thereby assisting the client to reframe their experience. Watzlawick (1978) had already identified this process which Satir utilised in her therapy work, where one of her aims was to reconnect her client's conscious perception of their world with their unconscious resources and facilitate resolution of the problem state. He refers to the client already knowing the solution: 'what now remains to be done is to find the way by which I have arrived at it' (p. 33). The therapeutic process facilitates integration of the solution held within the right hemisphere with the left hemisphere, that through its 'specialization for detailed, stepwise investigation' will 'supply the proof' to the person that the change has occurred (p. 31).

A client presented to me with a history of having difficulties in relationships. He had been in a series of relationships and referred to always looking for 'that elusive intimacy'. His current relationship had just ended and he recognised that he was being pulled back into it and felt split between wanting to stay and wanting to go.

Linguistically he immediately presented a double bind between his conscious desired state and unconscious existing state. Grammatically it is not possible to have 'elusive intimacy', they are mutually exclusive value sets or descriptors of a state of being. He also describes his split between his conscious and unconscious drives as being split between wanting to stay and wanting to go.

As a child his perception of his mother was that of a self-centred woman, his father distanced himself from the home and the parental relationship had been one of violence interspersed with overt sexuality. His own role was one of, 'I became very good at reading her [mother's] moods and learning to keep my head down. I had to protect my sister.' His early life was spent abroad and his recall of his relationship with his father was of going fishing and shooting together; he also recalled how his father would go for a drink and leave him in the care of local prostitutes.

His history of relationships with women began with his sister and they formed an early sexual bond – 'I felt like she was in control – it was fascinating and exciting.' He expressed horror and disgust at what had occurred between them. He was aware of being 'very' interested in girls from the age of 11, and all subsequent relationships were with women that he perceived as 'manipulative, controlling or domineering'. He viewed his own success according to how effectively he could satisfy women sexually – 'I need to please my lady' – and his current relationship was one where his partner 'used sex to control our relationship'.

His very early history suggests a considerable level of trauma that he had then articulated into his adult relationships as being 'manipulative, controlling and domineering'. Yet he measured this negative relationship with women through his own ability to please them sexually. The surface structure of his relationships was rooted in controlling sexual processes, which mirrored to some degree his early years where he was sexually controlled by his sister, yet he felt the need to protect her. He was not able to articulate to me linguistically the impact of his early years spent with prostitutes, or the impact of his father's drinking on his own developing personality.

> The overarching pattern to his history was one of using seductive processes to avoid intimacy, creating a double bind for himself. At a conscious level he recognised that he had formed a distorted view of his role in relationship to women at a very early age. This led him to rapidly recognise at a deep structure level that he was split between the 'euphoria and ecstasy' of each sexual encounter and the desire to 'end it, it's over and done and I can at least get the hell out of there'.

This is another example of the double bind that he had created for himself. He needed the sexual experience to create a positive feeling, yet as soon as he had this, he wanted to leave the relationship as fast as possible.

> The therapeutic process was one of enabling this client to reconnect with his own early experiences through the challenging of his deletions, distortions and generalisations, and recognise how they had influenced his later choices in relationships.

Linguistically, the client articulated distortions about his view of women that were contradictory, e.g., *I want sex when things go wrong, I measure my success through someone else's pleasure then I feel bad about myself.* Through therapy he was able to reconnect with a split-off part of his personality that felt as if *I am nothing.* Once this was integrated, he was able to gain a more realistic view of himself in future relationships and move on in his life.

The client wrote to me a week after he had finished in therapy. Below is a direct transcript of his communication to me.

> Two days of wanting to contact her with all my being, real yearning. I did not contact her. I left on Wednesday calm and stable. The grief for my childhood and how it affected me hit me the next day and eased off on Sunday night. A lot of tears shed. Sometimes I find myself crying and not sure what about.

Neurologically he still had a connection to his former partner, yet rather than being dissociated from this loss, which was his previous pattern of behaviour, he was able to acknowledge his loss and provide his own comfort rather than look outside of himself.

> After Wednesday one childhood habit was not there anymore. There are a number of other changes and behaviours that are different or I can choose how I want to react. Being even more in contact with my feelings is challenging. There is no place to hide or pretend about feelings. I have to deal with acceptance. It just is.

He acknowledges his reconnected sense of self and is aware that this is a new place for him to be. Previously he would have operated from a dissociated position, and now he accepts the feelings that are a natural part of life and is learning to deal with these.

> My feelings for X [former partner] are becoming less clear. I was clear that I loved her, a week later I don't know. That's not being inconsistent; it's a shift to a more adult place.

There is evidence of his having integrated his dissociated younger self and moved to a more adult functioning place.

> I do not feel a constant loss for her and because I don't miss her, because I need my own space, does not diminish the bond that I still feel is there, it just feels much healthier. Being away from her has given me the space to heal. The more I have learnt about her the greater my appreciation of her own internal turmoil and the greater my sadness has become. In my current and future I'm okay, I am more able to focus on my own wants that, when I was with X, were subsumed by her wants and her neediness.

He now has to take responsibility for his part in the relationship and rather than absorbing his partner's projections, his emerging sense of self has enabled him to focus on a future based on his own values.

> I am increasingly calm and centred. The word that is coming back from friends, family and colleagues is 'positive'. There are a lot of good things happening in my life and I had the most positive feedback from an initial job interview I have.

The client has continued to progress and has now formed a strong relationship with a new partner whom he views as equal to him and who does not take him back into old patterns of behaviour.

Ericksonian linguistic influences on neurolinguistic psychotherapy

Within core NLP teaching, there is a strong emphasis on the Milton Model (Bandler & Grinder, 1975a, 1977) as the predominant linguistic structure modelled from Erickson. The Milton Model deliberately uses generalised language structures to move a client from surface structure to deep structure by creating distortions, deletions and generalisations. The model goes some way towards elucidating how Erickson used language to facilitate a client to access unconscious resources held within their inner world. Other therapists, such as Haley, Rossi, Rosen, Zeig and O'Hanlon have brought a wider perspective of Erickson's work to neurolinguistic psychotherapy that go beyond the Milton Model. This work has focused on Erickson's ability to utilise all that a client presented with towards a positive outcome frame; his utmost respect for and ability to enter the client's model of the world; his unwillingness to engage in therapeutic diagnosis or medicalisation of their problem; and his utilisation of resistance within the client to enable them to access their own internal resources. He also fundamentally believed that all clients could enter trance and use the unconscious process to facilitate change.

Similarly to Satir, Erickson recognised that clients represent a subjective reality of their experience in therapy, and there is evidence of his ability to work with the subjective reality through the use of metaphor in Rosen's work, *My Voice Will Go With You* (1982), and his own referencing to this in *The February Man* (Erickson & Rossi, 1989, p. 105):

> The multiple meanings of words lead each person to draw different levels of confidence about the inferences, implications, frames of reference and belief systems he or she creates as a function of his or her particular life experience with these words. Thus one person's reasonable inference can be ludicrous to another. This is the basic problem in all efforts at creating consensual belief systems as well as consensual psychotherapeutic approaches.

Erickson's preference for future-oriented work is apparent in the outcome-oriented nature of neurolinguistic psychotherapy and particularly the use of the well-formed outcome. O'Connor (2001) highlights the benefits of this outcome orientation process within NLP work and identifies that by setting an outcome and being specific about the future desired state, 'you become proactive, take ownership of the problem and start to move towards a solution' (p. 11).

If I return to the client mentioned above with relationship difficulties, there are strong parallels with Haley's (1993) summary of Erickson's perception of his work and the use of outcome-based language in working with clients to develop a future-oriented state. Rather than focus on a past trauma, Erickson preferred to 'see the problem more as one of arranging a situation where a person can make use of what he has learned and have the opportunity to learn more of what he must know to enjoy himself sexually' (p. 109).

Haley (1993) highlights further evidence of the subtlety by which Erickson used outcome orientation whereby he recognised that if he were to be too outcome-oriented in his language, this in itself could create resistance. Instead, he developed a process where he facilitated change towards an outcome by directly accepting the patient as he is. Erickson would focus initially on the negative attributes of a particular situation or problem to enable the client to 'feel himself in the right, even when he is wrong, and a therapist needs to join the patient on this'. He would work with the client, validating their current state and wait for 'the patient to correct his mistake' so that the client and himself could 'do this jointly and so the therapy is a more cooperative endeavour' (p. 129).

Erickson and Rossi (1989) utilised active dissociation within trance states as a way of assisting resolution of problems. In this work, Erickson's embedded commands towards a future orientation enable his client to dissociate from her past trauma and successfully resolve a current phobia. Erickson was fascinated with 'the separation or dissociation of thinking, feeling and doing, whereby a patient could calmly receive insights into the repressed traumatic situation (thinking) without the disturbing affects that accompanied it (feeling and doing)' (p. 55). As his work with this client continues, it is also apparent how Erickson uses linguistic reframing to change the client's interpretation of her experience. Bandler and Grinder (1975a) recognised the importance of Erickson's use of dissociative processes and highlighted his work in assisting clients to make changes in one aspect of their consciousness while other aspects of their consciousness remained unaware of the processes that had occurred.

O'Hanlon in particular, has developed Erickson's work and brought this into the therapy field in his solution-oriented hypnosis, which he later developed into solution-oriented brief therapy or possibility therapy (*A Brief Guide to Brief Therapy*; *A Guide to Inclusive Therapy*; *A Guide to Possibility Land*; *Even From a Broken Web*; *In Search of Solutions*; *Love is a Verb*; *Rewriting Love Stories*; *Solution Oriented Hypnosis*; *Taproots*). I have summarised the main focuses of Erickson's solution-oriented hypnosis within O'Hanlon's work. They demonstrate a series of key aspects that are used conjunctively within his therapeutic approach, as follows:

- The use of presuppositions in hypnosis, which includes the creation of options to lead in a desired direction, that may presume that something is about to happen, or has happened, or is happening, and bringing this into the client's consciousness. There are parallels of these aspects occurring within the Milton Model language patterns, which may be the creation of alternatives that suggest an element of choice and result in a client moving towards their future direction.

- The matching of non-verbal and verbal communication, considered as a fundamental aspect of rapport, and expanded on by what O'Hanlon refers to as 'descriptive matching', i.e., the use of an analogy to bring to the client's awareness their current state and behaviour, thereby creating 'truisms', while at the same time narrowing the client's focus of attention, which in itself will induce trance.

- The use of permissive and empowering words, which, by moving into the realm of abstract thinking, moves the client away from concrete representations of their problem state and into vague notions that create the opportunity for possibilities to be created, leaving the client at choice as to how they fill in the gaps for themselves, and encouraging activation and utilisation of internal resources. O'Hanlon builds on the use of permission by creating the concept of 'nots' or the opposite polarity. The effect of this is to create a sense of ambiguity and choice in the client's unconscious, while at the same time ensuring that all options are covered, which will reduce the likelihood of client resistance within the therapy.

- Tag questions that are used at the end of sentences to turn statements into questions, again creating an element of choice for the client, enabling displacement of any resistance.

- Splitting provides an opportunity for the therapist to create a perception of separation between elements that have hitherto been perceived as intrinsically linked. Erickson initially used splitting to separate the conscious and unconscious mind, using his voice and body movements to indicate which aspect of the person's thinking he was referring to. Through this process he was able to direct his client's attention either to their internal world, and induce trance states, or to their external world, bringing them to a more conscious state. This splitting is also used to create a split between the current problem as it is in the now and the past, and the future orientation of the solution through the use of time-based language.

- Linking is the opposite process of splitting whereby Erickson used linking processes to connect two apparently disconnected concepts to facilitate a client towards a solution orientation. This process may be done verbally or non-verbally, by providing linguistic links of cause and effect, such as 'if you listen to me, then you will find yourself feeling more relaxed', and also by linking through complex equivalences. This enables a link to be made between an external event and an internal state, or a presenting problem and a resultant solution.

- The interspersal of linguistic commands during a sentence that structurally holds one level of meaning for the conscious mind and a second level of meaning for the unconscious mind. It was this multi-level of communication that is apparent in Erickson's work as it is portrayed in Rosen (1992).

The binding constraints of language

> How does myth think?
> Myth thinks by providing 'a logical model capable of overcoming a contradiction.' Since this is an impossible achievement, myth grows spiral-wise until the intellectual impulse which has produced it is exhausted.
>
> (Strauss, 1963)

Bateson (1972) has provided considerable insight into the world of double binds, the catch-22, or 'damned if you do, damned if you don't' constructs that exist in the world of those experiencing conflict. Dilts (1999, p. 231) refers to double binds as 'conflicts that are at the root of both creativity and psychosis (depending on whether one is able to transcend the double bind or stays caught inside of it)'.

He identifies the prerequisites for the creation of double binds as:

- the involvement of two or more persons, one of whom will play the role of 'victim'
- repeated experiences of the situation
- a primary injunction that is negative, and often based in a punishment that involves the withdrawing of love, expression of hate and anger, or abandonment by the authority figure who is helpless
- a secondary injunction that conflicts with the primary injunction and is at a higher or more abstract level
- a potential tertiary injunction that prevents the victim from escaping their dilemma
- finally, the complete set of requirements becomes unnecessary when the victim perceives their world through a set of double binds.

There are a number of models within neurolinguistic psychotherapy that enable the resolution of the double binds, i.e., reframing through 'sleight of mouth' patterns (Dilts, 1999), quantum linguistics (Chen, 2002; James, 1996) and symbolic modelling (Lawley & Tompkins, 2005).

Within a double bind a client holds a logical paradox that results in a paradoxical conclusion; for example, the client with relationship difficulties mentioned earlier in the chapter is caught between the self-referencing experience of the *euphoria and ecstasy* of each sexual encounter and the paradoxical conclusion of acting this out that resulted in his desire to *end it, it's over and done and I can at least get the hell out of there.*

He had a series of double binds within his linguistic structure that I represent here to demonstrate the complexity of his paradoxical world:

- people are very honest in who they are which creates so many masks, shields and pretence
- wanting trust while not wanting an intimate relationship
- if I ask for what I need or want it is built on lies
- saying who I am is pretending to be who I am not
- being open means not being who I am
- to meet my partner as an equal means that I get bloody lonely
- having freedom means that I will go away and hide
- I want to know her well which means I get drawn into another relationship with all the crap and baggage that comes with it.

In unbinding this series of double binds through the use of a variety of sleight of mouth patterns and quantum linguistics, he finally connected with the ultimate double bind of wanting the intimacy while at the same time wanting to get out of the relationship. This then enabled him to access a deeply held core belief that he was able to finally resolve.

Schrödinger (1958) states that *Every man's world picture is and always remains a construct of his mind and cannot be proved to have any other existence.* Quantum linguistics provides a methodology that facilitates the undoing of the constructs of the mind by utilising the theory of quantum physics and rules regarding motion within a linguistic structure. The process as it is taught within neurolinguistic psychotherapy enables the unpacking of double binds through a process of linguistic binding and double binding to 'unglue' the subjective nature of a core belief structure. Chen's (2002) use of quantum linguistics holds within its theory a number of postulates, as follows.

- Language is the result of neural activities in the brain and nothing else. This provides an antidualist position and accepts that both verbal and non-verbal language is a product of neural activity. Therefore if a client rewires their neural activity they will have a different neurological, verbal and non-verbal response to a given situation.
- The brain is a quantum mechanical system with quasi-classical memories. This assumes that the brain is a measuring device and that memories are stable objects, therefore if the memory is changed in some way, through reframing, additional learning or dissociation, the measurement of the memory changes.

- The 'reality' in the brain is a quantum mechanical experimental set-up arranged by the brain and consists of the subject matter of thought. Memories are held within the nervous system and the 'reality' held within the brain is based on the nervous impulses as they are received. By changing the nervous input to the brain, it is possible to change the lived reality.
- Language understanding is a quantum measurement performed by the language user. Experiences need to be measured before meaning can be applied to them. The brain has duality at its core, therefore something cannot 'be' and 'not be' at the same time; as soon as a person creates a non-duality the concept that they hold no longer exists.
- Language understanding and language formation do not commute. Whenever a person tries to understand something that currently they do not understand they create a different interpretation of the thing they are trying to understand. They change it to make meaning of it, and never copy exactly the original input. It is this non-commuteness that causes the wave form of the client's current reality to collapse and therefore no longer hold the problem in their neurology. Hence, when a client gets to a place of *I don't know, I can't compute that, I don't understand,* or *Can you say that again?* – the therapist is creating an interruption in the wave formation of the construct of the problem enabling it to be freed from their neurology.

Lawley and Tompkins' (2005, p. 187) work on symbolic modelling adopts an alternative approach to the resolution of double binds. 'In Symbolic Modelling it is not your job to resolve the client's binds. Rather your function is to facilitate the client to model their metaphors so that the organisation of their binding pattern becomes clearer and clearer to them. As a result, the conditions for transformation arise.' The approach within symbolic modelling assumes five steps to assist the client to transform their construct.

- When the client identifies two or more symbols whose intention or function cannot be enacted or satisfied, facilitate them to model the pattern preventing resolution and then to identify a metaphor for the primary bind.
- Use the six approaches to facilitate the client to explore the primary bind's inherent logic until either:
    - a secondary bind appears, or
    - it spontaneously changes.
- Facilitate the client to self-model the pattern of the secondary bind and its relationship to the primary bind, and identify a metaphor for the double bind.

- Use the six approaches to facilitate the client to explore the inherent logic of the double bind, until either:

  - a tertiary bind appears (in which case continue modelling the whole organisation), or
  - it spontaneously changes.

- Mature all changes as they occur until either:

  - the binding pattern *translates* and repeats in a different form, or
  - the binding pattern *transforms*.

A search for meaning

One of the fundamental principles of NLP as a methodology is that all meaning is context-dependent, and that if we take the meaning and place it in a different context, the meaning itself will change – the basis of reframing within NLP. The aim of making meaning of the world is such that a person can identify the meaning of events in relation to the sense of self. Schore (2003), in his work on the development of the self, considers the relationship between attachment and the developing sense of self. He argues that regulating mechanisms are used either to add to an increasing sense of self or to avoid the negative consequences of unuseful attachment relationships. Moore (1998) builds on this notion in his interpretation of the human experience of the world as being one that is non-linear and of multiple causes where people tend to simplify experiences to enable effective functioning. We therefore make meaning of our experiences outside our linguistic representation. Kovelman (1998) links this to the work of Jung and his perspective on synchronicity, presenting an additional perspective that supports the view that meaning is influenced by processes that are beyond consciousness. She considers that all individuals share common archetypes and that these are communicated through 'a psychological unified field in which all things are inter-connected and non-local'. She proposes that through synchronicity an individual psyche will 'seed three or four *co-incidents* into an individual's world of space-time, in order to dramatically gain Ego Self's attention and bring about desired change' (p. 22).

The role then of the neurolinguistic psychotherapist is to enable a client to develop a more effective relationship between themselves and the external world through altering the client's perception of meaning. This is enabled through the dialogical process of therapy, enabling integration of unconscious and conscious processes.

In attempting to bring this alive within a therapy setting, I present here a case with a client whose search for meaning had taken him through a number of therapy relationships and medication to deal with his lifelong depressive tendencies.

> He had approached me for therapy to 'have my brain rewired'. He had exhausted all other attempts at either self-help or therapy, and was finding that medication was not helping him alter his melancholic approach to life. He was in an unfulfilled marriage, his wife had long-term disabling health conditions, his children had reached adulthood and had left home and he faced a future of working in a depressing job until his retirement a few years away. He could see nothing in life to live for and viewed this as a final attempt to see if there was any light at the end of the tunnel.

His initial presentation was a depressed position. His archetypical meaning in life meant that he created negative projections all around himself. As we reviewed each of the areas of his life, each one had a melancholic theme to it, and he was unable to represent it linguistically in any way that did not look bleary, depressed and hopeless.

> My therapy work with him was very much of accepting him for who he was and working within his constrained way of thinking. He was resistant to my usual therapeutic repertoire and much of our time was spent discussing the meaning of life with him challenging my somewhat esoteric and non-linear thinking. He had an interest in Jungian archetypes and we discussed how his MBTI (Myers, 1962) profile of ISTJ viewed life differently from my own profile of INFJ, yet we were both naturally introverted in nature.

As he was a scientist by nature, I found that when offered a model that was grounded in theory he was able to reflect on his personal relationship to this. He found it difficult to consider abstract concepts and in reading Jung's work he was able to develop a reference structure for his own experiences.

> We argued about our very different perspectives on life, and I often questioned my role in benefiting him as a therapist as I viewed the relationship as one of two acquaintances arguing about different philosophical perspectives rather than providing what I perceived to be a therapeutic alliance centred on his internal world. During his time in therapy, he appeared to be improving, evidenced by the care he was taking in his appearance, he shaved his beard off, having had one since being a teenager, his mood improved and he started to develop interests outside his work and responsibilities for his wife.

Because we were communicating in a similar language, and he was able to make meaning of his experience, and also find a rationale for why he felt the way that he did, this validated his experience and he started to recognise that he was not completely alone, and that there were other people in life who were very similar to him.

After therapy ended, he wanted to continue the relationship on to a more social footing, which I declined. I agreed to continue to dialogue with him by email as he wanted to know that I was still available to talk to if he 'slipped backwards'. This continued for a short time and he then moved on with his life. I later received a book from him, Steppenwolf by Hesse (1965).

During therapy, he had told me that a previous therapist had suggested that he read this book, and although he had attempted to, he had been unable to progress beyond the first couple of chapters. In his letter to me, he said that I had inspired him to pick the book up again. The book tells of the story of one man's search for meaning and addresses his inner fears through a fantasy world. He highlighted four passages for me to read.

The first passage refers to Harry's meeting of Hermine for the first time, where he very clearly elucidates the double bind that he faced between life and death (Hesse, 1965, p. 123). This strongly resonated with the client's current state when he first consulted me for therapy. The passage opens as follows:

The importance of my relationship to this unknown girl had become alarmingly clear to me. I thought of nothing but her. I expected everything from her. I was ready to lay everything at her feet. I was not in the least in love with her. Yet I had only to imagine that she might fail to keep the appointment, or forget it, to see where I stood. Then the world would be a desert once more, one day as dreary and worthless as the last, and the deathly stillness and wretchedness would surround me once more on all sides with no way out from this hell of silence except the razor.

This passage highlights the torment that he was experiencing when he first consulted me for therapy. He frequently discussed death and seemed ambiguous about suicidal thoughts, yet within this passage he was finally able to articulate to me the terror that he had felt concerning his own internal thought processes. Next there is a reference to his suicidal thought process and the role that I as the therapist had played in this very difficult emotional state that he was experiencing (Hesse, 1965, p. 124).

> I realised that it was the unendurable tension between inability to live and inability to die that made the unknown girl, the pretty dancer of the Black Eagle, so important to me. She was the one window, the one tiny crack of light in my black hole of dread. She was my release and my way to freedom. She had to teach me to live or teach me to die. She had to touch my deadened heart with her firm and pretty hand, and at the touch of life it would either leap again to flame or subside in the ashes.

He then chooses a second passage that refers to Hermine and Harry's initial conversation at this meeting and he recognises the transferential process within the therapeutic relationship. In the dialogue between Hermine and Harry, Harry asks 'How did you manage to look like a boy and make me guess your name?'. She says that 'I am a kind of looking-glass for you, because there's something in me that answers you and understands you' (p. 127). This is a reference to our sharing of the insights from Jung's work and our protracted discussions about our introverted nature, including how each of us could react so differently even though we were inherently the same. The dialogue continues and Harry highlights the fact that he is completely opposite to Hermine, at which point 'a dark cloud of seriousness spread over her face. It was indeed like a magic mirror to me. Of a sudden her face bespoke seriousness and tragedy and it looked as fathomless as the hollow eyes of a mask' (p. 128).

The story then moves to Hermine and Harry dancing and listening to music and the client appears to have selected this paragraph to mirror the similarities in our respective psyches, and the transferential process as learning points for himself. Hermine responds to his acknowledgement of her positive attributes by reminding him of the transference between them. 'Think of that evening when you came broken from your despair and loneliness, to cross my path and be my comrade. Why was it, do you think, I was able to recognise you and understand you?' (p. 147). During the therapy with the client, I had used disclosure at key points in the therapy as a way of enabling the client to recognise that all people experience distress, unhappiness and loss in their lives, and that we all have a choice about how we react to it. The client chooses the following (Hesse, 1965, p. 148) to acknowledge that he has recognised this.

> I don't despair. As to suffering – oh, yes. I know all about that! You are surprised that I should be unhappy when I can dance and am so sure of myself in the superficial things of life. And I, my friend, am surprised that you are so disillusioned with life when you are at home with the deepest and most beautiful things, with spirit, art, and thought! That is why we are drawn to one another and why we are brother and sister. I am going to teach you to dance and play and smile, and still not be

happy. And you are going to teach me to think and to know and yet not be happy. Do you know that we are both children of the devil?'

Towards the end of the story, Harry enters the theatre that he had been afraid to enter earlier in the story: the point when the client moves on with his life. In this final episode the client acknowledges the work that he has done in recognising and accepting his personality for what it is (Hesse, 1965, pp. 205–206).

> This little theatre of mine has as many doors into as many boxes as you please, ten or a hundred or a thousand, and behind each door exactly what you seek awaits you. It is a pretty cabinet of pictures, my dear friend; but it would be quite useless for you to go through it as you are. You would be checked and blinded at every turn by what you are pleased to call your personality. You have no doubt guessed long since that the conquest of time and the escape from reality, or however else it may be that you choose to describe your longing, means simply the wish to be relieved of your so-called personality. That is the prison where you lie. And if you were to enter the theatre as you are, you would see everything through the eyes of Harry and the old spectacles of the Steppenwolf. You are therefore requested to lay those spectacles aside and to be so kind as to leave your highly esteemed personality here in the cloak-room where you will find it again when you wish. The pleasant dance from which you have just come, the treatise on the Steppenwolf, and the little stimulant that we have only this moment partaken of may have sufficiently prepared you. You, Harry, after having left behind your valuable personality, will have the left side of the theatre at your disposal, Hermine the right. Once inside, you can meet each other as you please.

Inside the book was a note from the client where he acknowledges the learning that he has made and also recognises that the therapeutic process was part of his journey, and that the time has come for him to move on in his life.

> This book means a great deal to me and I hope we can share it.
>
> When I first read it, it turned quickly from a story into something that touched my soul. Each time I have had therapy, I have tried to read it again but always stopped when Harry enters the magic theatre . . . it was too painful. When therapists tried to get me to read it, I just broke down. Now, I have been able not only to re-read it, but re-read it avidly, seeing not a soul-destroying sorrow but an opportunity for the future.

> Finally, you will read that Hermine has to disappear from Harry's life, which gives him sorrow and pain, but also release. When you read this, remember that Hermine is Lisa the therapist. Lisa the friend is who I have given the book to and Lisa will never disappear even if we never meet again.

Meaning within therapy

By working with the linguistic components of a client's inner world it is possible to gain a comprehensive map of how the client has constructed their reality. The search for meaning is a process that can be enabled through sensitive and respectful work as a therapist. It is the responsibility of the client to make meaning of their experiences: both those that have brought them to therapy and those that they create within the therapeutic relationship. Neurolinguistic psychotherapy offers a range of linguistic techniques that enable understanding of the deeper linguistic structures of a client's experience, yet this can only be done if the client is willing to consider this within a supportive and containing environment. This then creates the opportunity for growth that so far has eluded the client.

Chapter 6

Patterns of programming

> The patient's behaviour is a part of the problem brought into the office; it constitutes the personal environment within which the therapy must take effect; it may constitute the dominant force in the local patient–doctor relationship. Since whatever the patient brings into the office is in some way both part of him and part of his problem, the patient should be viewed with a sympathetic eye appraising the totality which confronts the therapist.
>
> (Erickson, in Bandler & Grinder, 1975a, p. 59)

In the previous two chapters I have considered the relationship of neurological processes from the development of the frontal brain through to how deficits in early development can lead to unuseful patterns of behaviour later in life, and then connected this to the way an individual makes sense of their experience through language. The combination of the neurological and linguistic constructed reality of a client is what is presented in therapy. When these become consistent and persistent patterns of behaviour they then become part of the programmed reality of a client's world. The final element of NLP that I want to consider in this chapter is the *programming* aspects. As I have already identified, Bandler and Grinder modelled the programmatic linguistic aspects of Erickson, Satir and Perls; they then added to the model operant conditioning and the theories of Pavlov and the work on strategy formation by Galanter and his colleague Miller, who theorised that a person can only consciously process 7 plus/minus 2 chunks of information at a time.

In this chapter, I continue beyond these components and include the work of neuroscientist and Nobel Prize winner Edelman, who determined that *where neurons are fired together, they will stay wired together*. I present a case study that demonstrates the relative ease by which a therapist can assist neurological re-patterning through metaphor, enabling a client to access neurological resources in one context and transfer them to another context to aid problem resolution. Within behaviourist theories, classical conditioning provides a wider understanding, beyond that presented by Pavlov, of the potential of including this work in relational therapy to aid psychological repair. Systemic patterning is also considered within the work of Dilts and his theories on logical and neurological levels of change. Dilts proposes that our system is self-organising, and I use a case example to demonstrate how a client can make a change in one area of their life, at a high neurological level, that then assists change in a number of other areas. The chapter concludes with a consideration of the goal-oriented nature of neurolinguistic psychotherapy and how this is merged with Ericksonian approaches in a case example.

The brain as a computer?

The notion of programming in NLP emerges out of the sciences of Artificial Intelligence and Information Theory, having been developed in the early 1970s in California at the same time as the personal computer. Dilts and Delozier (2000) refer to these two processes as being parallel occurrences to each other. I have been unable to find evidence to support the more recent unsubstantiated sources quoting Bandler as a student of maths and computers at the time that NLP was being developed.

The models of 'artificial intelligence' and 'information theory' have influenced the more programmatic aspects of NLP, with the most obvious parallels being the major programming elements of modelling and strategies. The three key mechanisms of artificial intelligence – receiving input from the environment, then determining the action or response, and finally delivering the output to the environment – can be seen in the modelling of Erickson and Satir by Bandler and Grinder. This has been developed with the addition of Miller, Galanter and Pribram's (1960) work of the 'TOTE' (Test–Operate–Test–Exit) model and strategy formation.

Dilts and Delozier (2000) state that information theory provides the basis for the development of modelling and is the study of how information is generated, coded, stored and transmitted. Similar to TOTE in its focus on data processing, the programming aspects of the 'state operator and result' (SOAR) model focuses more acutely on the feedback loop mechanism of the system. The SOAR model is grounded in the principle of heuristic learning, that of an 'expert system that is continually learning, updating and enriching its map of a problem space' (p. 1255).

This use of a programmatic approach to the therapy setting provides an underpinning knowledge base for therapists who welcome a structured way of working. However, this approach in itself presents limitations if viewed in isolation. If the views of scientists Pribram, Edelman, Sheldrake and Wolf and the psychological perspective of Jung are included then accepting a simplistic model that assumes a computerised modelling of the human brain would be reductionistic and would move therapists further away from

Erickson's aim of viewing the totality of the client as they seek support through psychotherapy.

Kovelman (1998, p. 23) refers to Sheldrake and Wolf's perspective that individuals intentionally create new 'least action pathways', i.e., that the more times a pattern of behaviour is used the easier it is to manifest, and it is out of this process that order is created. 'It is meaningful to consider each person as an event or process occurring over a particular space-time coordinate, rather than as a *discrete*, individual being. Indeed, physicists have posited the existence of invisible fields, forms, and patterns that lie beneath the physical world and organize matter into systems and wholes' (emphasis in original). This view is supported by Pribram (cited in Fields, Taylor, Weyler & Ingrasci, 1984) who suggests 'we must conclude either that our science is a huge mirage, a construct of the emergence of our convoluted brains, or that indeed, as proclaimed by all great religious convictions, a unity characterizes this emergence and the basic order of the universe' (p. 210). O'Connor (1985, p. 17) again links this back to Jung's more psychological stance and says that 'there are as many archetypes as there are typical situations in life'. He goes on to say that this is caused through a process of repetition and that will then cause the experiences to be 'engraved . . . into our psychic constitution . . . as forms without content representing merely the possibility of a certain type of perception or action'.

Edelman's (2004) most recent developments in neuroscience align more closely with Dilts's acknowledgement of the SOAR model; Edelman (p. 29) proposes that:

> The control of neural connectivity and fate becomes epigenetic; that is, it is not prespecified as 'hardwiring,' but rather is guided by patterns of neural activity. Neurons that fire together wire together. While at earlier stages, patterned cell movement and programmed cell death determine anatomical structure, the movement and death of individual neurons are nonetheless statistically variable or stochastic. The same holds for which particular neurons connect to each other at later stages. The result is a pattern of constancy and variation leading to highly individual networks in each animal. This is no way to build a computer, which must execute input algorithms or effective procedures according to a precise prearranged program and with no error in wiring.

Edelman (2004, p. 39) then goes on to reiterate his view that the brain cannot be viewed as a computer. His research has included in-depth studies of the anatomy of the brain, and demonstrates sufficient evidence that even when individuals carry out the same task they are not responding 'in the way a computer does – using formal rules governed by explicit, unambiguous instructions or input signals. Once more, with feeling: the brain is not a computer, and the world is not a piece of tape.'

A stronger parallel to Dilts and Edelman is being developed within the systemic field through the work of Bateson. Gerhardt (2004) refers to Bateson's development of the work of Wiener, who first identified the importance of feedback in maintaining systems. Bateson continued this from an anthropological perspective and it was his work on human systems theory that proposed that systems managed to stay stable only by constantly adapting to ever-changing conditions. This gave rise to the NLP presupposition of 'the law of requisite variety', that 'To **want** control is the pathology! Not that the person can get control, because of course you never do . . . Man is only a part of larger systems, and that part can never control the whole' (Bateson, 2006, p. 2; emphasis in original).

In considering the implications of this for therapy, neurolinguistic psychotherapy provides a methodology that facilitates new neurological patterning by changing the different aspects of internal process, internal state or external behaviour. O'Hanlon (1992) builds on Erickson's recognition of the infinitely various ways that the brain could utilise neurological connections to assist behavioural change, as evidenced in his metaphorical work *My Voice Will Go With You* (Rosen, 1992). O'Hanlon uses Ericksonian therapy to assist clients to make change by working at the level of class of problem and class of solution. He assumes that the brain, with its infinite variety of neurological choice, will already have the solution in place, and it is just a question of connecting this to the behavioural response requiring change.

A young girl of 12 consulted me (with her mother) with a history of bedwetting. She had experienced very few dry nights in her life, and despite her mother lifting her each night, having medical investigations for the cause, medication and mattress alarms, she continued to wet the bed.

At a neurological level the girl had not yet developed voluntary muscle control of her bladder sphincter. O'Hanlon would propose that if a therapist chunks this up to find the class of problem, then it is possible to find the opposing class of solution and generate a solution response to be mapped across by the unconscious mind. The class of problem existed within the somatic elements of her peripheral nervous system, therefore the solution would need to be generated from an alternative somatic aspect of her peripheral nervous system where she did have effective control.

In talking with the girl, I discovered that she was passionate about horse riding and was due to go on a trekking holiday in a few months.

Horse riding, and particularly moving from walking to trotting, cantering and galloping required her to have excellent somatic control within her nervous system, and most importantly within her pelvic region.

> She was worried about camping overnight and whether she would be able to be dry. We talked about her upcoming riding holiday and during light-level trance, I used a metaphor to provide a graphic description of the muscle control that was required for each of the different riding positions of walking, trotting, cantering and galloping.

This process enabled her unconscious mind to access an existing resource and map it into her current presenting state.

> At no time did I refer to the bedwetting and one week later her mother contacted me to report that she had experienced only two wet nights in seven and a feeling that we had resolved the problem. She continued in therapy for a further two sessions with me using a similar metaphor to embed unconscious commands, and her problem resolved.

Behaviourist theory

One of the core components of NLP is the utilisation of Pavlov's (1927) work on classical conditioning, which enables the resolution of negative patterning created through classical conditioning. Through the methodology of anchoring, it is possible to alter conditioned responses, facilitate a more useful response and create links between current states and desired states.

The notion of classical conditioning is much older than this. Aristotle's law of contiguity states that when two things commonly occur together, the appearance of one will bring the other to mind. Pavlov assumed that there are two main conditioned responses – a positive conditioning that is linked to anticipation and satisfaction, and a negative response linked to fear – within which there are parallels to the notion of 'towards' and 'away from' values (Lazarus, 2006, pp. 78–82; Robbins, 1991, pp. 347–357). Schore (2003, p. 153) states that 'the earliest expressions of affect are automatic responses described as varying along a singular pleasure–unpleasure continuum, but later this is followed by an "expansion in the affect array"'.

Within the behavioural psychology field, classical conditioning underpins a range of therapies that include 'aversion therapy' and 'systematic desensitisation', both of which are models utilised within cognitive behavioural therapy. Two additional approaches within classical conditioning are used less frequently, and are recognised as being controversial mainly because of the negative physiological response that can occur, i.e., 'flooding' and 'implosion therapy'. Lazarus and Abramovitz (1962) further expanded Pavlov's work through the development of a model that utilised emotion-arousing situations to induce an anxiety-inhibiting response rather than the more traditional approach of teaching a client to relax when stressed. Within this model, they identified that emotions have a direct effect on the autonomic nervous system; therefore if a positive emotion is used at the same time as a stressor is introduced, the nervous system will override the negative conditioning, the theoretical basis of collapsing anchors.

The use of programmed behavioural responses is to be found across a range of psychotherapies. Bolstad (2002) provides a comprehensive reference to these in his work. He refers to the transference and countertransference as being anchored responses in psychoanalysis and suggests that 'the therapeutic relationship re-creates stimuli (anchors) that were present in the client's early significant relationships, accessing those neural networks and enabling the therapist to explore and modify what happens there'. He proposes that the psychodynamic process of reparenting collapses 'the positive anchor of the therapist support with a previous problem state' (p. 49).

Systemic patterns

Bateson's (2006) systemic perspective has had a considerable influence on neurolinguistic psychotherapy. He operated from a theoretical framework based on a simple model of self-organising pattern-recognition processes: 'There is something called learning at a rather small level of organisation. At a much higher gestalt level, learning is called **evolution**' (p. 3; emphasis in original). Kostere and Malatesta (1990) refer to this differentiation as first-order change versus second-order change. They define first-order change as 'change that is made within a system or reference structure', whereas they see second-order change as occurring within the systemic structure which 'allows the client to create a new reference structure, regarding the identified problem or symptom' (p. 70). This view is rooted in a number of philosophical perspectives including that of Descartes (1991), who assumed the notion that primary qualities are more real than secondary qualities and that we will always extrapolate on our experience to create a more highly evolved notion or experience. Piaget (1968) refers to these as levels of abstraction, and states that a person will move across levels of abstraction to reorganise their thought processes.

Dilts (1990, p. 209) refers to three systemic models of change: 'logical levels of change', which he attributes to Bateson's perspective that 'in the processes of learning, change and communication there were natural hierarchies of classification'; logical levels in NLP; and 'neurological levels'.

Table 6.1 Logical and neurological levels

	Spiritual concept	Transmission	Holographic	Nervous system as a whole
A	Who I am Identity (who)	Mission	Immune system and endocrine system	Deep life-sustaining functions
B	My belief system Values, criteria (why)	Permission and motivation	Autonomic nervous system (heart rate, pupil dilation, etc.)	Unconscious responses
C	My capabilities States, strategies (how)	Direction	Cortical systems	Semiconscious actions (eye movements, posture, etc.)
D	What I do Specific behaviours (what)	Actions	Motor system (pyramidal and cerebellum)	Conscious actions
E	My environment External context (where, when)	Reactions	Peripheral nervous system	Sensations and reflex reactions

Logical levels are psychological levels of processing and operate at six different levels, as shown in Table 6.1.

Dilts (1990, p. 209) identified that working at each of these levels and incorporating elements of conscious and unconscious patterning would bring deeper levels of neurological 'circuitry' into action. In the example given above of the young girl with a history of bedwetting, I utilised a metaphor that involved her capabilities within riding, which enabled activation at a deeper neurological level of her semi-conscious movements, i.e., those of pelvic floor muscle control.

Lawley and Tompkins (2005, pp. 29–31) provide an alternative perspective to Dilts whereby they consider each person as a self-organising system. In introducing the work of Wilbur, they highlight a number of common features that will exist across these systems.

- Self-organising systems are organised into *levels*. These determine what the system can and cannot do, its capacity to conserve and to transform itself, and its evolutionary direction.
- Each level of organisation is simultaneously a whole/part. Whether a symbol, a relationship or a pattern is perceived as part of a whole or as a whole compromising parts is simply a matter of different ways of punctuating experience.
- A self-organising system simultaneously *self-preserves* and *self-adapts*. At the same time as it seeks to preserve its own recognisable pattern, wholeness and identity, it adapts to maintain relationships with other

systems and the environment, and to express its 'partness' of something larger.

- Each level exhibits its own *emergent properties*. These are not properties of any individual component and they do not exist at other levels. For example, 'salty' is not a property of either sodium or chlorine, both of which are poisonous. Neither is it a property of the compound sodium chloride. 'Salty' only emerges from the relationship between salt, taste buds and the nervous system – a higher level of organisation than its components.
- Each lower level is nested within a hierarchy of higher levels and each higher level 'transcends and includes' all lower levels.

Lawley and Tompkins (2005, pp. 29–31) go on to describe the process by which symbolic modelling can assist in changing unuseful patterns of behaviour. Inherent within this work is the identification of elements that need to be present for a pattern to exist. The model goes to on to describe how working with the symbolic landscape of a client makes it possible for the client to achieve transformation beyond their presenting problem.

- Patterns are made up of 'parts' or components that constitute the raw material out of which the pattern is fashioned.
- There is an 'arrangement' such that the parts are in relation to one another.
- The arrangement 'repeats or corresponds' so there is some continuity, some non-randomness, some predictability.
- There has to be *someone* to notice the pattern's existence.
- This someone must process the sensory input in a certain way, one that requires identification of similarities and differences through comparative and contrastive analysis.
- Just as a painter requires a canvas on which to paint, the process of perceiving a pattern requires a medium (such as time, space or form) over which the regularity can manifest.

There is a strong similarity between Lawley and Tompkins' work and Erickson and Rossi's (1989) approach to working with patterns. Erickson refers to this as the 'domino theory of psychological problems and growth: When you deal with one issue successfully, other related problems tend to fall in line and cure themselves'. He suggests that 'we are able to be objective and matter-of-fact about past emotional issues when we have made a genuine, growth-maturing jump beyond them'. In his work with his client, he is assisting her to resolve a fear of water. When he checks out an event previous to one the client originally sought assistance for, he notices that she has experienced a 'spontaneous resolution of another of her important, early, traumatic experiences' (p. 240).

To highlight how working with patterns and the domino theory operates in neurolinguistic psychotherapy, I have summarised a case.

> J presented in her thirties with a history of failed relationships, a poor relationship with her child, periods of feeling down, and seeing the world as a dark place. She found it very difficult when people let her down, which resulted in her feeling abandoned. Her current relationship was very difficult and she experienced this as one where he would not take responsibility for the relationship and wanted her to deal with her emotions. The relationship was constantly on/off and there were frequent rows.

Her presenting issue was one of difficulty in her existing relationship, yet she very quickly referred to how this had been a repeating pattern in all her adult relationships.

> She described her parents as having a happy marriage. Her father was placid and compassionate and her mother she described as a 'tornado'; she was 'volatile, outspoken, judgemental and critical'. She had a very close relationship with her sister. She had been brought up in a typical Asian family and it was expected that she would have an arranged marriage. Suitors were brought to the house from when she was very young. She recalls her childhood as being very conservative and recounts how her brother was violent towards herself and her mother. She described her brother holding a knife to her throat. Following a childhood accident, she had spent a long period of time in hospital.

Her early history suggested poor relationships in the family home and although she refers to her parents as having a happy marriage, she experienced her mother and her brother as having either verbally or physically violent tendencies, both of which would have impacted on her during the imprint period of her development. Her hospitalisation at a young age also created a trauma for her.

> At the age of 18, she ran away from the family home and describes her father as being very upset as she had disgraced the family. She was successful in her career, was financially secure, and had continued her good relationship with her sister.
>
> We began the therapy by looking at the pattern of her previous relationships. Prior to this relationship she had three significant long-

term relationships. Her first significant relationship had been with her husband. Her parents had not approved of him; he had been violent throughout their marriage and they had split up on a number of occasions, with her becoming emotionally distant as a way of protecting herself. She had become pregnant early in the marriage and she described instances where he would hold the child in one arm and beat her with the other.

Using Erickson's domino theory, it is apparent here how she recreated her own early years within her marriage and used a pattern of distancing as a way of protecting her core self.

Since their separation she had been in therapy for a period of time, to enable her to deal with the loss of two of her children, one through cot death and one who had been removed from her and sent away to school. She viewed her relationship with her remaining child as very close.

Again this is a repeat of her own pattern of being separated from the family home as a child.

She described her second relationship as happy and joyful. He wanted to marry her and for them to have children. She was not ready for this, and they soon split. Her third relationship, prior to her current one, was with someone that she described as the antithesis to her husband. He wanted to marry her, and although she cared about him she found him to be emotionally cold.

Even when she is presented with an opportunity to enter into a relationship that would have been the opposite of the one she had modelled as a child, she is unable to enter it, yet in her third relationship she was able to recognise an ineffective potential relationship.

We discussed other social and work relationships and she described a former boss who had been abusive to her.

This provides evidence of her continuing the pattern across contexts, moving from her intimate relationships into her work life.

We then spent some time considering her values (Robbins, 1991, pp. 341–368) in the context of her family as this seemed to be where most of the conflict in her life occurred. She identified the following values as being important to her:

- *the family as a deep part of who she is*, which was underpinned by a belief structure that without this she would not 'be'
- *a sense of equilibrium* that kept her centred; although this value was motivated in a 'towards' pattern, it was dissociated
- *support from the family* that was built on solid foundations
- *the family to be the giver* that protected her
- *the family as symbolising her ancient roots*, and that if she were without this she would not be able to 'be'
- *to be healed from the past* which was concerned with repairing her damaged inner child, and provided an opportunity for a new beginning.

Her values were predominantly 'away from', moving her away from her childhood experiences as an ingrained behavioural response.

Once she was aware of these values, we discussed how they were supporting her sense of identity within the family and she quickly accessed a victim role that she had played for most of her life.

The start of her recognising her own 'domino' effect was as follows.

This then led her to recall her distressed and subsequent dissociated state while in hospital and she voiced the belief that she was dead. She found this metaphorical description of her state while she was in hospital as a very young child both distressing to acknowledge and at the same time enlightening. She voiced her perception that in reality she had 'played dead' in all her relationships to avoid pain and that this pattern had first commenced when she had been hospitalised; she recalls hearing her mother being told that she might not live. She also connected with a transgenerational belief structure around whether or not she deserved to live and her healing work involved integration and resolution of these two areas.

Neurologically, she has now connected with her first experience of dissociation to avoid pain and she quickly connects this pattern to her subsequent relationship. Once her conscious mind recognises this, she is able to rationalise her past and disconnect this neurological chain.

Subsequent to her working through these, her values realigned and she moved to a place where her most important values in the context of her family relationships were:

- *closeness*, which enabled the sharing of love and affection
- *unconditional support*, which symbolised wholeness
- *a richer and deeper relationship with her sister* which she viewed as a happy and joyful experience
- *happiness*, which she recognised she needed to use as an internal calibration to measure her relationship with her mother; she recognised that she was unable to change her mother, and could decide whether she would let her mother have a negative impact on her
- *healed relationships*, which enabled her to make peace with herself
- *wholeness*
- *love of her family* including her ability to love herself
- *the light* giving her liberty, success, energy, growth, love, joy and peace.

We reconnected a month after her therapy with me ended. She had learnt to take things more slowly and had spent some time connecting with her inner child that had dissociated so clearly when she had been hospitalised. She had gained integration between her ambitious working self and her self that wanted a relationship. She finally split with her partner, recognising that the relationship was not serving her, and she was now seeking a future relationship based on equality.

The domino effect enabled her to realign her values within her relationship and she was able to resolve a series of traumas that she had initially considered as unconnected. She had also changed her experience in a work context and was able to align fully with her sense of success in her career.

Goal orientation as a pattern of therapy

What do you want? This is the definitive question in NLP. An outcome is what you want – a desired state, something you don't have in your present state. Outcomes 'come out' when we achieve them, hence the name, and the first step towards achieving them is to think them through carefully. Why you want your outcome and whether you would want it are questions that need an answer. NLP outcomes are different from targets, goals and objectives because they have been carefully considered and meet certain conditions that make them realistic, motivating and achievable.

(O'Connor, 2001, p. 11)

McDermott and Jago (2001, p. 11) describe NLP as a brief, outcome-oriented model of therapy, 'a therapy of what is possible: it opens for client and therapist a voyage which is genuinely into the unknown'. Neurolinguistic psychotherapy assumes that *a client has all the resources that they need to be effective*, that *there is no failure, only feedback*, and that *every behaviour has a positive intention*, each of these presuppositions supporting the outcome-oriented nature of the therapy. Additionally it assumes that the brain has an amazing capacity for learning, and neurolinguistic psychotherapy uses this assumption to assist change through effective utilisation of generalised learning. The role of the neurolinguistic psychotherapist is to facilitate change in the client of the current state or problem and to enable learning across contexts that can assist the client to achieve their outcome. If change is made without the conscious mind taking the opportunity to learn from the experience, then the client is less likely to transfer the change into other contexts.

Neurolinguistic psychotherapy has some parallels to cognitive behavioural therapy, in that it assists clients to develop greater behavioural choice, and also to Hargaden and Sills' (2002, p. 32) description of transactional analysis, which stresses that 'it is important that the therapist and client have a shared idea of why they are in the consulting room together. They can articulate the problem and the goal they are aiming for. They have agreement about how the therapy will proceed.' McDermott and Jago (2001, p. 11) highlight an additional aspect of neurolinguistic therapy: a 'fundamental assumption in NLP is that a client should always leave the therapist's room with more choice than they came in with'.

One of the fundamental differences between neurolinguistic psychotherapy and other models of therapy is that the former utilises an outcome frame to assist clients to move from a stuck or problem-oriented state to one that is goal-oriented. The outcome-oriented nature of NLP emerged out of Erickson and Rossi's (1989) work *February Man* in which they utilised pseudo-orientation in time to assist a client to make a change towards a future orientation. Erickson quickly moves his client from her current time frame into one in the future where he asks her to 'tell me about swimming, what you did about it, and how you did it' (p. 209). O'Hanlon (2003, p. 17) refers to this as de Shayzer's 'crystal ball technique'. This has strong parallels to the use of future pace in therapy, whereby a client is asked to imagine that they have created the solution and describe in all sensory modalities the achievement of the goal.

This approach to developing a future-oriented frame for the client mirrors the work of de Shayzer (1988) and the creation of the 'miracle question' in solution-focused brief therapy: 'Suppose that one night, while you were asleep, there was a miracle and this problem was solved. How would you know? What would be different?' Outcome frame questions identified by McDermott and Jago (2001, p. 45) that are commonly utilised within neurolinguistic psychotherapy are:

- what do you want?
- how can I help you?
- what would that do for you?
- what is your greatest ambition?
- what would make life better for you?

If an outcome orientation is applied in therapy and linked to the subjectivity of a client's experience, through the filters of time and space the client will come some way towards recognising Kovelman's (1998, p. 126) intricate links between subjectivity, future orientation and the use of time-based language. 'Each singular event, when viewed from other dimensions, is seen as an aspect of a still larger pattern. This pattern is a field of endless potential; it includes every conceivable variation of form this same event might assume under different circumstances. Hence, every particle and event exists first in potential, within the World of Formation, until chosen for actualization in our world.' Edelman (2004) also recognises the neurological components of our natural inclination towards a goal orientation, which he links to the work of William James, considering that consciousness is a continuous process and that the only thing that changes is 'intentionality'. He links this directly to where a person places their conscious attention and suggests that attention will 'modulate conscious states and directs them to some extent' (p. 126).

Freud (1959) also used the notion of working with the affective state of goal orientation in therapy, suggesting that affect can cause neuronal excitation that will facilitate achievement of a goal. Further experiments on this have been led by Kosslyn, Ganis and Thompson (2001, p. 641) who confirm that 'visualising an object has much the same effect as seeing the object . . . imagery can engage neural structures that are also engaged in perception, and these neural structures can, in turn, affect events in the body itself'.

Erickson (in Erickson & Rossi, 1989, p. 242) embeds future-oriented neurological patterning: 'So she learns step by step, with active inner rehearsals before she actively does it. In a similar manner, hypnosis does not involve passive fantasy but an active grappling and changing of one's inner experience to activate one's potentials.' O'Hanlon continues this in his therapeutic work and refers to the 'Viktor Frankl strategy': Frankl collapsed while in the death camps of Nazi Germany; he dissociated from himself and imagined a future time when he would give a lecture about his experiences in the death camps and receive a standing ovation. O'Hanlon (2003, pp. 87–88) summarises this story with the following comments: 'He had created the future he had imagined. Such is the power of a future with meaning. It can pull us forward, out of the terrible present and into a better life.'

Utilising resistance as a way of facilitating goals

Erickson's approach was very much one of goal orientation: Haley (1993, p. 31) demonstrated how Erickson was cautious in assuming that a client might improve too quickly, and often deliberately created resistance in the client to ensure that when the goal was achieved it could bypass any conscious resistance.

> Erickson often deals with such a situation by using a challenge that is a directive rather than an interpretation. If a patient is too cooperative and seems to be recovering too rapidly, he is likely to relapse and express disappointment with the therapy. To avoid this, Erickson will accept the improvement but direct the patient to have a relapse. The only way the patient can resist is by not relapsing, but continuing to improve. With this approach, Erickson uses different explanations to make it reasonable to the patient. One of his more graceful procedures is to say to him, 'I want you to go back and feel as badly as you did when you first came in with the problem, because I want you to see if there is anything from that time that you wish to recover and salvage.' When done effectively, the directive to relapse prevents a relapse, just as the challenge enforces a hypnotic response.

Although the use of resistance in therapy is not one that is common in all neurolinguistic psychotherapists, when used cautiously and with sufficient rapport with a client it can have profound effects. I utilised this approach along with Erickson's model of making it harder for the client to keep the problem than to give it up.

> A young girl consulted me for therapy for her feelings of very low self-worth and poor relationships with her family. Her appearance was somewhat striking in that she wore very shabby clothes, her hair was coloured a lurid shade of purple and was spiked upwards, and her jacket had obscene writing on the back referring to her identity.

Her appearance suggested a resistance to societal norms, therefore it was important that I continued this within the therapy. I decided to stay in her model of the world and avoided becoming like her parents and offering judgements or suggestions as to how she might get on better if she tried to fit in with others. On this basis I spent much of the time with her discussing possible futures.

She was a very pleasant person to speak with and we progressed rapidly through therapy using predominantly a future-oriented time frame. She was pleased with her progress and after a few sessions felt that she was ready to end the therapy. I was anxious that her external appearance had not changed and she still continued to refer to herself in negative ways, although she described her mood as considerably improved. We discussed her living arrangements and she said she hated living there. I suggested to her that she could spend some time thinking about all the things that she hated about herself, and write these on the walls of her flat in paint as I was aware that her need to externally validate her negative self-perception remained high, despite her mood change.

As part of this discussion, I suggested a range of expletives that I had heard her use during her therapy sessions which validated her current experience and also ensured that her neurological affect state as it had developed was included in the tasking process.

She returned to therapy two weeks later, with her hair styled and dyed black with purple highlights. She was dressed all in black, and had discarded her jacket. In explaining how she had progressed over the preceding weeks, she said that she had done as I had suggested and bought some bright pink paint and started to daub the walls of her flat with a range of descriptive expletives about herself. Part way through this, she took a phone call and on returning to the room that she had been painting she had been shocked by what she had written. She immediately went out and purchased some purple paint and had decorated her flat with the one colour. She had then gone on to purchase new curtains, candles and a rug, and now wanted to invite friends round. This had spurred her on to 'ritually burn' her jacket and expand her limited wardrobe. She told me that she did not need to be in therapy any more and was planning to return to college later that year.

I used patterns of neural excitation with this client and moved her current state into a future-oriented time frame. This had two effects: firstly her neurology was activated from her past state into the present, so that as she moved into the future the neurological patterning would be interrupted. The second process was to take her internal constructs and project these into an external reality. This had the effect of enabling her to dissociate from her reality and see this from a third-person perspective – something that her parents had unsuccessfully tried to do, and which she had rejected. By her acknowledging the pattern herself, she was able to take control of it and change it in a way that was meaningful for her.

Re-patterning as an effective therapeutic process

In this chapter I have reviewed the opportunities for change at pattern level that neurolinguistic psychotherapy offers to clients. As more is discovered about the neurological components that are required for successful therapy, it would be naïve to consider a solely programmatic therapeutic approach. Neurologically it is essential that a client's affective state is accessed as part of the therapeutic process, while a future-oriented state is facilitated at the same time. To provide each in isolation is unlikely to facilitate lasting change for the client. Similarly, to focus only on the conscious mind will mean that the potential for unconscious change is lost, whereas if therapy focuses only on unconscious processes, the conscious self cannot rationalise past experiences and achieve the 'domino effect' of carrying their learning across contexts.

Chapter 7

Reframing internal belief structures

> There are indeed potions in our own bodies and brains, capable of forcing on us behaviours that we may or may not be unable to suppress by strong resolution.
>
> (Damasio, 1994, p. 121)

Neurolinguistic psychotherapy offers a model of brief therapeutic change that can be respectful, ecological and effective. In this chapter I review the basis of emotional constructs and their relationship to neuroscience. Chapter 3 has presented some ideas on the development of the personality and I continue this dialogue with respect to core personality structures and their relationship to personality types and neuroscience. As an individual forms their sense of self, trauma can have a direct impact on the regulating system and negative effects can be portrayed as disabling belief structures, dissociative states or the development of splitting within the personality, resulting in the development of parts. By understanding these internal structures it is possible to repair the self through temporal reframing, or alignment of disintegrated or fragmented aspects of the self. Parallel to this is the possibility created through neurolinguistic psychotherapy to repair developmental deficits, and I consider the relationship of core belief structures or prime concerns to attachment disorders. I conclude with a summary of the key points that could be considered as the therapy is progressed as a practice into the subsequent chapter.

Within neurolinguistic psychotherapy there are some fundamental programmatic models that assist therapeutic change. These models consist of 'linguistic reframing', discussed in Chapter 4, Cameron-Bandler, Gordon and LeBeau's (1985) work on 'metaprogrammes', 'time reframing' (Bodenhamer & Hall, 1999; James, 2003), 'parts reframing' to resolve internal conflict and splitting within the personality (Gilligan, 1997; James, 2003; O'Hanlon & Bertolino, 1988), the use of motivation patterns through the values and belief change work developed by Dilts (1990), and elicitation and reframing of 'prime concerns' (Dilts, 1990; James, 1996).

The basis of emotional constructs

James's (1884) essay 'What is an Emotion?' suggests that emotions are visceral and that there is no brain centre for emotional expression. Pert (1997) expands on this and explains that James held the view that a body will register a sensation in response to neurological reactions that occur as it adapts to the environment, and that it is these sensations that are labelled as emotions. Damasio (1994) supports this and suggests that *somatic markers* are formed or 'feelings generated from secondary emotions' to enable the course of action to be determined as a visceral response to an external stimulus. Positive somatic markers act as a 'beacon of incentive' whereas negative somatic markers when linked to a particular outcome will act as 'an alarm bell' (p. 174).

Pert (1999) expands the theory presented here and demonstrates that the autonomic nervous system cannot react quickly enough to cause the emotional response that individuals feel in given circumstances; neither do other aspects of the nervous system react when one particular stimulus is applied to recreate the visceral changes observed in emotional responses. It was Pert's realisation that 'in fact, it's both *and* neither! It's *simultaneous* – a two-way street' (p. 137) that led her to continue her research into emotion-carrying neuropeptides. This work is reinforced by that of Edelman (2004), who identifies that there are specific areas of the brain that neurologically give rise to emotions such as fear. Rothschild (2000, pp. 20–21) supports this view and goes further than Edelman in explaining the role of the amygdala in storing and processing the emotions and reactions to emotionally charged events. She suggests that because the early developing brain, notably the hippocampus, is not yet formed, a process referred to as *infantile amnesia* occurs and 'the resulting memory of an infantile experience includes emotion and physical sensations without context and sequence. This is the probable explanation for why, in later life, infantile experiences cannot be accessed as what we usually call "memories".' Erickson (in Erickson & Rossi, 1989, p. 225) uses this process to therapeutic advantage as he works with his client: 'I want you to keep this knowledge in your unconscious and not to discover it until later this summer. Do you understand? Just as you repressed and forgot painful things in the past.' Rothschild suggests that the more intense an emotional experience, the more likely it is that it will be stored, which provides the basis for reframing the gestalts of negative emotional responses in time reframing, or the use of positive emotions in anchoring. Satir and Baldwin (1983) recognise that it is normal for individuals to experience emotions of sadness, fear, etc., and that these are the consequences of being human. It is rather how the individual deals with emotions that can create problems, and the concealing of feelings is identified as the major cause for low self-esteem.

A notion that is held in some schools of NLP, and taught as part of a time reframing process, is that all negative emotions should be resolved and 'let go of'. This runs counter to normal neurological patterning. Damasio (1994, p. 53) raises questions about removing all sources of emotion: 'Reduction in emotion may constitute an equally important source of irrational behaviour'. Pert's (1997) work has identified that we need all emotions to 'unite the mind and the body' (p. 192). She suggests that it is the repression of these emotions that causes 'dis-integrity' in the mind–body system, which will then lead to disease at a cellular level; 'All honest emotions are positive emotions' (p. 193) and it is the role of the therapist to assist clients to reframe their emotions and any limiting belief structures that deny the acknowledgement or expression of emotions. In neuro-linguistic psychotherapy, the role of the therapist is to enable a client to reframe their emotions such that they can be usefully accessed by the client and that appropriate and ecological choices occur in response to the emotional charge. In considering the use of time reframing to assist the resolution of emotionally held constructs, it is important that this enables a client to deal with the repressed aspects of their emotional experiences, rather than the healthy aspects. The first evidence of time reframing as a philosophical underpinning for neurolinguistic psychotherapy work is presented in the hypothesis of Descartes (1991), who suggested that space and time are needed to create dreams. The purpose of time reframing is to literally change the meaning of internal dreams that make up the client's reality. The NLP methodologies of 'changing belief systems' (Dilts 1990), 'Time Line Therapy®' (James, 2003; James & Woodsmall, 1988), 'time lining' (Bodenhamer & Hall, 1999), and Rothschild (2000) in her work on post-traumatic stress disorder and trauma resolution, present a series of alternative perspectives on how time reframing may be used to assist resolution of repressed negative emotions. Rothschild supports the view of Satir and has reinforced my own thinking that the 'goal of trauma therapy is to relegate the trauma to its rightful place in the client's past' (p. 155). Each of the techniques mentioned above enables accessing of past experiences through a linear process of time and the purpose of any trauma therapy is to ensure that 'explicit memory processes must be engaged to secure the context of the event in time and space. Usually separation of past and present is an automatic result of any good trauma therapy; it does not usually need to be addressed head-on' (p. 155). The processes of time reframing provide an effective technology to place emotions in the past and this dissociation from the emotional experience, rather than repression, is thought to occur for three different reasons. James (2003, p. 24) suggests that the first reason is based in the work of Korzybski (1933) and Cameron-Bandler and LeBeau (1987) and the notion that 'emotions require time to express their meaning, so a switch in the temporal perspective reframes the emotion'. The second rationale is based in metaphysics, and is that emotion is an illusion.

Foundation for Inner Peace (1972) suggests that there is only one real emotion on the planet – love – and that any negative emotion is a derivative of fear and therefore an illusion. James proposes that the shift in temporal perspective will show the emotion to be an illusion and the emotion will then disappear. The third aspect of James's perspective on emotional reframing through time coding is to provide 'a multidimensional neurological opposite of "now". What happens is that this position acts like anti-matter, and the neurological boundaries of the emotion in the body get blown out – they disappear' (2003, p. 24).

Programmes of personality

The notion of different personality types appeared as early as the fifth century BCE with Hippocrates' definition of four temperaments that determine human moods and behaviour: choleric or irritable, phlegmatic or calm, melancholic or depressed, and sanguine or optimistic. By 1907, Adickes had also observed four distinct world views: dogmatic, agnostic, traditional and innovative. His work is continued in that of three psychologists and behaviourists:

- Adler, who observed that individuals pursue mistaken goals when they are upset, and are driven by the need for recognition, power, service or revenge
- Kretschmer and his notion that individuals are hyperaesthetic (too sensitive), anaesthetic (too insensitive), melancholic (too serious), or hypomanic (too excitable)
- Springer, who identified four predominant human values – religious, theoretic, economic and artistic (Keirsey & Bates, 1984, p. 3).

Jung continued this work to formulate a theory of personality that is summarised in Chapter 3. Neurolinguistic psychotherapy uses Jung's types to assist clients to gain greater choice within their lives. Bolstad (2002, p. 153) suggests four main neurolinguistic methodologies that can be directly linked to the Jungian temperaments and enable the development of skills in clients for more successful lives: dissociation, association, chunking up and chunking down.

- *Thinker*. Assists a client to dissociate and distance themselves from experiences and feelings, and to see themselves from the outside, which is useful for negative experiences.
- *Feeler*. Encourages clients to associate and step into experiences and feel them from the inside, which is useful for positive experiences.
- *Intuitor*. Teaching a client to chunk up and move to the bigger picture will enable them to move beyond conflict and find alternative solutions to their existing patterns of behaviour.

- *Sensor*. Connecting with sensory-specific aspects of their experience and reconnecting them to the source of their deletions, distortions and generalisations through chunking down.

Neurolinguistic psychotherapy has within it a further developed model of the personality known as metaprogrammes: the programmes of behaviour that run above the conscious known self. Among the work that informed the early pioneers of NLP was that of Lilly (1968) who drew parallels between the brain and computers and identified that there are a series of programmes that the brain runs that can be likened to computer programmes. These metaprogrammes were further developed by Cameron-Bandler, and were originally observed as 'patterns of coherency' by Bandler. Dilts and Delozier (2000) and Cameron-Bandler, Gordon and LeBeau (1985) continued research into this area and developed a way of coding programmes that 'code and direct other thought processes' (Dilts & Delozier, 2000, p. 756). Subsequent to Cameron-Bandler's work, two of her students, Bailey and Steward, developed the 13 categories that were later developed by a student of Rodgers, Charvet (1995), into the Language and Behaviour Profile.

Erickson used an individual's pattern of personality to facilitate change, rather than trying to impress on them the need to change their personality. He used internal programmed patterns of personality in a number of stories in *My Voice Will Go With You* (Rosen, 1982). In 'competition' he utilises his patient's internal programmed competitiveness, which Jung might identify as 'judger' typology, to assist his client to develop a way of dealing with tension headaches. In 'autohypnosis' he assists his client to continue to operate from within her introverted frame of reference to resolve her problem of neurosis. He also successfully utilises the motivation pattern of 'towards'/'away from' to facilitate a client to lose weight in 'reduce–gain–reduce'.

Bolstad (2002, p. 168) describes Erickson's work with schizophrenics in using the programmed patterns of behaviour apparent within the diagnosis. He suggests that someone with schizophrenia will think in 'chunked up and very dissociated' ways. This was Erickson's natural style of communication, therefore he suggests that this enabled him to 'assist them to avoid halluci- nated "dangers" and [in] helping clients work towards goals that most therapists would have rejected as unrealistic'.

Patterns of identity

It appears that to find and to 'know our Self,' we have to first repress and hide parts of ourselves. Only after we form an 'I', a 'me', and a personal identity, can we complete the rest of our psychological and spiritual growth. Our psychic journey propels us onward toward the rediscovery and reclaiming of these inner cast-off, disowned, split off portions of ourselves, personally and collectively. In order to mature and grow, each of us is obliged to assume responsibility for our projections, feelings, ideas, and acts, so that we might reclaim, heal and integrate these aspects of our psyches and once again become whole and unified.

(Kovelman, 1998, pp. 55–56)

Erickson, Satir and Perls all directly referred to parts or splitting aspects of the personality. Satir (1972) recognised that people repress aspects of themselves that they consider unacceptable, and proposed that 'If you try to hide or bridle your tendencies, however, you won't be able to do this very well. They will be waiting for the chance to escape and act up behind your back' (p. 87).

Perls (1969) identified that unacceptable aspects of the personality were disowned by the individual: 'There are many of these kinds of ways to remain intact, but always only at the cost of disowning many, many valuable parts of ourselves . . . You do not allow yourself – or you are not allowed – to be totally yourself. We all have a number of different parts, each with expectations of fulfilment. These parts often find it difficult to get along with each other and may have inhibitory influences on one another' (pp. 86–95).

Erickson (in Erickson & Rossi, 1989, p. 74) encourages an understanding of how parts are created:

But she does not want to remember either trauma. This is a peculiar dissociation: she has a grasp of the connections between the two incidents, yet she does not want to remember them because her mother says she should only remember 'nice things'. Such is the hypnotic repressive power of a mother's suggestion on a child troubled by fears and guilts she does not know how to handle.

O'Hanlon's (1998) work on solution-oriented therapy for sexual abuse and trauma provides insight into how identities are formed in response to patterns experienced in early life. He identifies that individuals will usually have an integrated sense of self, but 'when people subject to trauma split internally and develop rigid boundaries, the sense of integrated self is lost', resulting in a self that has disidentified, devalued or dissociated aspects. This then develops into a pattern of behaviour that is recognised through the language of 'should's, can'ts and don'ts' (p. 7).

Bandler and Grinder (1979, pp. 139–140) first refer to parts of the personality, 'part of you that makes you X – even though you don't like that consciously – is doing something on your behalf, something that benefits you in some way', which later became the basis of the six-step reframe. This was developed by Dilts, Hallbom and Smith (1990) into parts integration and more recently into alignment therapy. Lawley and Tompkins (2006) refer to 'multiple perceivers' and highlight the evidence of splitting within the personality demonstrated within linguistic dissociation.

James (2003) has developed a series of assumptions about parts within the field of NLP, including a model for understanding how parts are created. This model provides a limited insight into the development of splitting aspects of the self within the personality. I have expanded on this model and included Bateson's (1972) theory on schismogenesis, noting James's theory in italics, as follows.

- *Parts are non-integrated fragments of the whole, unconscious mind with their own purpose/intention and function/behaviour. They put boundaries (or blocks) on the wholeness of the unconscious mind.* Bateson (1972) provides a more comprehensive insight into the development of fragmentation within the unconscious and proposes that four basic premises need to be met to result in unconscious double bind formation: the child's relationship to the mother is one of vital dependency, thereby making it essential that the child can accurately assess the maternal communication; the child receives contradictory or incompatible information from the mother, e.g., the child is told that he is loved after being smacked; the child is unable to clarify or understand the incoherence of the communication; the child cannot leave the relationship/environment. Bateson proposes that when each of these factors is present, severe psychopathological disturbance will arise through the distortion of the inner and outer reality of the child.

- *Parts are functionally detached from the rest of unconscious mind (non-integrated).* This assumes that the conscious mind is unaware of these aspects of the personality that are split off, disconnected or in some other way fragmented. Bateson (1972) provides an alternative perspective to this and considers two types of schismogenesis, complementary and symmetrical. Within complementary schismogenesis, the two aspects of the psyche complement each other which results in a class struggle, with one behaviour eliciting or triggering a complementary behaviour from a different aspect of the psyche; for example, a client may binge to get rid of a feeling of self-hatred, which then results in an increased feeling of self-hatred. Symmetrical schismogenesis elicits similar behaviour in the alternative aspect of the psyche; for example, a client may buy a new handbag to reward herself after a difficult time at work, which then triggers a compulsive spending behaviour from the repressed aspect of the psyche.

- *Often parts represent minor personalities or significant others (modelled, imprinted) which impose arbitrary boundaries.* James's model assumes that these will be self-generated personalities rather than alter egos or schizoid aspects of the self; for example, they may be a self at a very young age or on occasions may be an early representation of the mother or other family member. Bateson (1972), however, would challenge this perspective and proposes that this development of a psychological double bind will, if left unchecked, lead to schizophrenia because of the mutually competing demands of the different aspects of the psyche.

- *Parts have an intelligence of their own and usually have their own values and belief systems.* They are neurologically detached from the rest of the system.

- *Parts are thought to be in charge of the maintenance of the system.* Because they have been created out of a trauma and are repressed, the unconscious mind will keep them repressed as a protection mechanism. This protection process becomes important for the maintenance of the rest of the system. Bateson's theory suggests an alternative perspective: that they are in fact co-dependent and that neither can exist in isolation.

- *Parts are frequently born or created from significant emotional events (wholly associated intense events), usually with others that result in conflict and incongruity, and therefore a boundary is created.* In most instances the part is a younger self that lacks rational thought and therefore the unconscious mind creates a boundary to repress this aspect of the personality such that it stays repressed and does not carry the trauma across contexts as the personality develops.

- *Parts protect and continue a non-integrated, and in many cases repressed, behaviour.* This happens only in some instances; in other situations the splitting may result in a compensatory process being developed, which is then relayed to the outer world, e.g., narcissism. There may also be a resultant fixation and exploitation of particular aspects of the outer world because of the distortion process that has occurred; for example, compulsive patterns of behaviour, alcoholism, drug addiction.

- *Parts are a source of incongruency in the individual because the behaviour of the part is incongruent with the behaviours of the adult.* The part has stayed functionally regressed and, because it is also neurologically detached from the rest of the unconscious, it will not be aligned to the adult functioning behaviours. Where the distortion has become ingrained into the adult functioning, this may result in a personality that operates through narcissistic tendencies, or is apathetic in relationships.

- *The incongruency of parts is generally in the difference between the purpose/intention and the function/behaviour. The highest purpose/intention is not congruent with the function/behaviour. Since it is non-integrated, this results in inner conflict.* The function of the part may be to play dead in a person who chose this as a defence mechanism during a traumatic event; its purpose may be protection so that it can live, mirroring the complementary schismogenesis. Alternatively conflict may arise because of escalating patterns of behaviour where symmetrical schismogenesis exists.

- *A part presupposes an opposite part for balance. It usually has its opposite number, an alter ego, or a 'flip side of the coin'.* In the example given in the previous point, the opposite side might be to grow up and love others. Bateson (1972) considers that symmetrical schismogenesis towards a positive support of each aspect of the psyche through the development of rules and agreements is an effective way of resolving dysfunctional splitting. This mirrors the work of O'Hanlon (1988) and Gilligan (1997), who consider validation and sponsoring of all aspects of the psyche as being integral to repair of the self.
- *These two parts will have the same highest purpose/intention. This is a function of chunking and will, therefore, be stated as a nominalization.*
- *These two parts were also once a part of a larger whole.* This assumes a greater whole and may even include the spiritual aspects of an individual.
- *Reintegration is possible on this basis and will be long term. If not, the integration will be short term and could be negated in one to three months.* If the integration occurs without recognition of a greater whole, there is unlikely to be unconscious integration. The recognition of a greater whole accesses a neurological state that is beyond that of the two opposing parts; integration into the entire neurological circuitry is possible at this point and the part no longer remains dissociated. This can be achieved through dialogical processes and assisting the client to recognise and validate the less functional aspects of their own processes.
- *Fewer parts are always better than more parts.* Neurologically, if a client has aspects of their personality that are functionally detached from their unconscious processing, this results in continued fragmentation and disconnect for the individual. The client will not be able to access all aspects of their personality and may find that their conscious desires and drives are not matched by their unconscious patterns of behaviour. In the case of the client in Chapter 5 who was seeking intimacy, his disconnected part believed that he was nothing, which meant that he felt as if he was not really present in relationships, even though he wanted that 'elusive intimacy'.

Rothschild (2000) provides a useful perspective on some of the dissociative processes that are available within NLP, and considers Janet's hypothesis 'that consciousness was comprised of varying levels, some of which could be held outside of awareness' (p. 66). Rothschild suggests that dissociation is a 'neurobiological phenomenon that occurs under extreme stress . . . It is possible that dissociation is the mind's attempt to flee when flight is not possible' (p. 66). Schore (2003, p. 62) adds to this view that dissociation is a deficit of the right brain and suggests that 'Dissociation is a very early appearing survival mechanism for coping with traumatic affects, and it plays a crucial role in the mechanism of projective identification' (p. 62). He describes projective identification as a process that occurs if the child does not have their immediate trauma responded to by a positive maternal figure: the child then moves into a 'dissociative strategy to counterregulate the hyperarousal, [which] is expressed by staring into space' (p. 68) and represents the mechanism that drives what Klein (1946) described as an 'evacuation of the self'. Schore (2003, p. 62) suggests that these different aspects of the personality 'that are associated with the patient's past traumatic relationships are . . . projected onto the therapist, so that these affects are also experienced by the therapist'. This directly mirrors Bateson's (1972) four premises that must exist for splitting to occur.

Carroll (2002, p. 17) brings to mind Damasio's work and the notion 'that potent unconscious representations of the self derive from older, more primitive parts of the brain; and that the self's most basic foundations are in systems that represent the body'. Damasio (1994, p. xvi) refers to the dissociative process as equally damaging as that of an associated trauma. His view that 'it is thus even more surprising and novel that the *absence* of emotion and feeling is no less damaging, no less capable of compromising the rationality that makes us distinctively human and allows us to decide in consonance with a sense of personal future, social convention, and moral principle' connects with the one I have given above concerning the absence of emotions.

There are strong parallels between parts theory of neurolinguistic psychotherapy and that of a number of other modalities. Freud (1933), Winnicott (1958), Klein (1960), Kernberg (1976), Kohut (1984) and Mollon (2001) in psychoanalytic and psychodynamic theory, Mearns and Cooper (2005) in person-centred therapy, Stewart and Joines (1987) in transactional analysis, Moreno (1977) in drama therapy, Lowen (1972) in body psychotherapy, and Layden et al (1993) in cognitive behavioural therapy all recognise the development of split-off parts of the personality as defence mechanisms to trauma. Mollon (2001, p. 128) refers to dissociation, depersonalisation and derealisation as forms of detachment that occur as reactions to trauma: 'If childhood trauma or abuse is repeated, and if the abuser is a caregiver, so that the child has *nowhere to run and no-one to turn to*, then internal escape is resorted to – the child learns to dissociate more easily and in a more organized way' (emphasis added). He goes on to highlight that the personality will preserve parts of itself by 'sequestering or sealing off, the area of damage'.

Repair of the self

Repair of the self within neurolinguistic psychotherapy is possible through a number of different approaches, ranging from the structured processes of 'Time Line Therapy™', 'time lining', 'parts integration', 'alignment therapy', 'change personal history' and 're-imprinting' through to the more relational and dialogical therapy that is apparent in Erickson's work and schismogenesis as it is carried forward in the work of O'Hanlon and Gilligan. Both Erickson and Satir enabled an internal perceptual positioning that has been expanded on by Gilligan (1997). Gilligan's self-relations model recognises and validates internal aspects of the self, assisting the client to develop unconscious communication and relationship to their inner world which is an inherent part of being.

Dilts (1990) also provides an opportunity through neurological levels to assist the client to reframe their internal reality. In the case summary of K in Chapter 1, her initial 'problem' was held at identity level and it was as she started to acknowledge and validate this aspect of herself that she could consider the behaviour at a different neurological level, and it became an accepted part of her behavioural repertoire.

At a more programmatic level, time code interventions provide an opportunity for temporal reframing of an experience, collection of experiences or gestalt. Korzybski (1933, p. xx) identified that it was possible for humans to learn from their experiences in a way that animals could not, precisely because each generation has the ability to use the learnings from previous generations:

> The origin of this work was a new functional definition of 'man', as formulated in 1921, based on an analysis of human *potentialities*; namely, that each generation may begin where the former left off. This characteristic I called the 'time-binding' capacity. Here the reactions of humans are not split verbally and elementalistically into separate 'body', 'mind', 'emotions', 'intellect', 'intuitions', etc., but are treated from an organism-as-a-whole-in-an-environment (external and *internal*) point of view. This parallels the Einstein–Minkowski space–time integration in physics, and both are necessitated by the modern evolution of sciences. (emphasis in original)

Time reframing utilises the unique characteristics of the right brain to assist resolution of complex constructs that cannot be resolved through left brain cognitive understanding, hence neurolinguistic psychotherapy can result in faster change than more cognitive outcome-oriented approaches to therapy such as CBT. Watzlawick (1978, p. 22) refers to the holographic nature of the right brain, proposing that the 'right hemisphere not only masters the perception of a *Gestalt* from the most diverse angles and consequent relative distortions . . . but that it may manage to perceive and recognise the totality from a very small portion of the latter'. This results in the client connecting with one small portion of their experience through their unconscious processing, and their unconscious mind carrying any learning associated with this one portion across all contexts associated with the gestalt.

James (2003) summarises many of the underlying principles of the unconscious aspects of Ericksonian therapy as the 'prime directives of the unconscious mind'. These provide a useful insight into the basic functions of unconscious processing that enable the therapist to provide appropriate direction and insight for the client in the therapeutic relationship:

- stores memories – temporal and atemporal
- makes associations and learns quickly
- organises all memories
- represses memories with unresolved negative emotion
- presents repressed memories for resolution
- may keep the repressed emotions repressed for protection
- runs the body and has a blueprint of the body now and in perfect health
- preserves the body, maintaining its integrity
- is the domain of the emotions
- is a highly moral being, guiding from the morality that was taught and accepted by the developing person
- enjoys serving and needs clear orders to follow
- controls and maintains all perceptions, both regular and telepathic, and will receive and transmit these to the conscious mind
- generates, stores, distributes and transmits energy
- maintains instincts and generates habits
- needs repetition until a habit is installed
- is programmed to continually seek more and more
- functions best as a whole integrated unit
- uses and responds to symbols
- takes everything personally
- works on the principle of least effort and will follow the path of least resistance
- does not process negatives directly.

A range of approaches using time reframing are available to the neurolinguistic psychotherapist, all of which are supported by the principles outlined above. 'Time Line Therapy®' (James, 2003) provides a structured hypnotic programmatic approach to change that can be effective when used ecologically. The same applies to time lining (1999) developed by Bodenhamer and Hall, who note that 'The strength of Time Lining lies in its ability to direct the participant in reframing old and no longer useful thinking patterns' (p. 353). Dilts's (1990) work on re-imprinting provides a conversational and less programmatic approach to time reframing and brings in a more dialogical approach to enabling the client to access their own internal resources.

Parts integration (Bodenhamer & Hall, 1990; Bolstad, 2002; Dilts, Hallbom & Smith, 1990) and alignment therapy are both core skills taught at the more advanced levels of NLP. Both approaches provide a process whereby the client is assisted to first identify and then dissociate from the split part of their unconscious. The part is then encouraged to recognise internal resources and learnings that are present in its behaviour. A process of chunking up then occurs that moves the client into abstract concepts and greater unconscious communication, which facilitates resolution and integration between the split-off part and the rest of the person's unconscious self.

All the above techniques provide a methodological structured approach for assisting integration of the self. Although effective in principle, they do not always provide the most appropriate form of therapeutic intervention for clients who are unable to verbalise their early experiences and make sense of them. They also make an assumption that the client has 'problems' that they need to resolve or 'let go of'. What is missing is the potential for mind–body communication between client and therapist, particularly where there is early childhood trauma and developmental deficit. One of the fundamental aspects of NLP, the use of rapport in the therapeutic setting, sets up a relationship with the client whereby a process of responsiveness occurs between therapist and client at the level of the unconscious. If one stays cognitive and methodological in the therapeutic process, the chance is missed to facilitate deep levels of change through what Schore (2003, p. 80) refers to as Kohut's (1984) 'archaic bond' with the therapist, and thereby facilitates the revival of the early phases at which his psychological development has been arrested. Schore goes on to highlight the need for this space to be created such that the therapist can experience what is described as the somatic marker, described earlier in this chapter by Damasio. If the therapist remains in a detached 'third position' space, as is highlighted in the few books on neurolinguistic psychotherapy, the client misses out on the possibility of developing a relationship of attunement with the therapist, what Sands (1995) observes as: 'The patient and I succeeded in co-creating in me a state in which I could "get" something viscerally about the pathogenic interactions of his childhood that he unconsciously needed me to understand'.

To highlight the process as it occurs in therapy, I return to the case of D discussed in Chapter 3.

As I have described, his history was one of separation from both his mother and father at a very young age, and being cared for by grandparents and aunts. The therapeutic work was underpinned with the philosophy and principles of neurolinguistic psychotherapy, yet the methodology of working with patterns and associative and dissociative processes proved to be ineffective. After only a few weeks in therapy I recognised that D's presenting problem was not being resolved, nor was he moving closer towards his outcome. He was unable to articulate his internal world, other than feeling angry and finding that eating large quantities momentarily eased this feeling [Bateson's complementary schismogenesis]. I discussed this with D and we considered the option of revisiting the therapeutic contract to move to a more relational approach. This process involved both of us being willing to work with the transferential relationship and assist D to gain alternative perspectives to his inner reality.

Over time this enabled him to repair the developmental deficits highlighted in Schore's work before he could begin to relate to me as his maternal object. This later enabled him to articulate his somatised distress, and develop an internal sense of self such that he could repair and soothe his inner child.

Schore's perspective on working with the regulatory aspects of the self is more closely aligned to that of Gilligan's (1997) self relations, which is underpinned by three main principles, the first being what he refers to as the 'Erickson function'. Gilligan recognises that it was the client's unconscious in relation to Erickson that assisted his success with clients rather than Erickson being viewed as the observer of a client's internal process. Gilligan has built on this and encouraged a model of therapy where the client learns to relate to his own unconscious in the same way that Erickson would have done. The second principle is that of the embodiment of the unconscious, where Gilligan encourages the client to bring to consciousness the somatic experience of their internal state and processes, the somatic markers referred to by Damasio. This enables the client to develop a somatised sense of self that they can reconnect to when faced with challenging situations and they are also encouraged to use somatic markers to identify centres of disturbance, which are enabled through sponsorship of the unconscious to recognise the positive contribution they make to the person. The final aspect of Gilligan's work is the notion of using trance that is more connected to the world and the 'now' of a person's reality, rather than the traditional utilisation of trance to move further away from the external world.

Core belief structures or prime concerns

Cogito, ergo sum
(I think therefore I am)
(Descartes, 1991)

Descartes' perspective that because one has the ability to think, one must therefore exist is frequently called into question by clients who express core belief structures of *I'm dead; I don't exist; I am nothing*. The philosophical basis of constructivist thinking is rooted in the notion that when a client has knowledge or beliefs about a particular subject, he will extrapolate this to all other aspects of the same class or type. Therefore, when he brings doubt into existence concerning one item in a class, the doubt will generalise across all other aspects held in the same class or type. This then becomes the basis for the generalising of core beliefs, which are sometimes referred to as 'prime concerns'. If a client experiences being hurt or abandoned in one relationship, the ability to generalise will mean that they expect the same thing to happen in all subsequent relationships. Watzlawick (1978, p. 41) identifies with Aristotle's definition of core beliefs – 'things are true and primary which command belief through themselves and not through anything else . . . generally accepted opinions, on the other hand, are those which commend themselves to all or to the majority or to the wise – and suggests that the purpose of psychotherapy is to assist individuals: 'where the world cannot be changed, he can adapt his image to the unalterable facts'.

There is a strong relationship between core belief structures and the developing brain of the infant, particularly in relation to stress responses. An infant who has her stress levels managed for her is unlikely to produce high levels of cortisol and is therefore less likely to develop negative internal core belief structures. Infants who are left to cry for prolonged periods of time have high levels of cortisol flooding the developing brain; this is thought to cause a level of toxicity which, if left unchecked, can mean that an individual has problems in reading social cues and adapting their behaviour accordingly later in life. Gerhardt (2004) suggests that infants who are handled sensitively and frequently in early life, particularly when distressed, have greater ability to cope with stress later in life. Infants of depressed or absent mothers often experience 'dead periods' in their own development which results in cellular death in the infant brain. Schore (2003, p. 126) describes this as the child finally detaching and becoming silent to match the mother's state: 'this state switch from a regulatory strategy of intense struggling into the dissociative immobilized state mimicking death is ultimately experienced as a "dead spot" in this child's subjective experience'.

There are parallels between Schore's notion of the 'dead spot' and the object relations theory of Klein (1946) and Bion (1984). Kristeva (2001, p. 179) suggests there is the presumption of an 'innate preconception' within the infant of a breast, and that when this need is not met, the infant moves from a 'thought as no thing . . . replaced by the *non-realisation of the breast*' (emphasis in original). She refers to Klein's idea of how this initial non-response from the mother can result in a traumatised response in the infant at the separation: 'Some babies are unable to tolerate such separation; they experience it as a "projective explosion" of urine, gas, feces, saliva, and other substances that are linked to the absent nipple, which forces the infant to confront a terrifying world that is no more than a "black hole"' (Kristeva, 2001, p. 182).

Neurolinguistic psychotherapy provides methodologies that enable the resolution of core belief structures through Dilts's (1990) work on belief systems and core beliefs and James's (1996) prime concern. Dilts recognises the difficulty in identifying core beliefs as opposed to other belief structures, and suggests that clients use a number of processes to conceal their core beliefs from themselves, as well as the therapist. It is important to note that concealing of beliefs is a protective mechanism of the unconscious mind, is dissociative in nature and reflects an avoidance of Klein's description of the 'black hole'. Processes that clients use to conceal their beliefs may include a smokescreen, which may be represented through vague language from the client, a blank response or the therapist getting lost. The client may also present with a red herring or false clue, whose purpose is to lead the therapist in the wrong direction as a protection mechanism. This leads to Dilts's third assumption of concealing processes, that of the 'fish in the dreams'. A client may accept suggestions made by the therapist of processes that are not present in their own neurology, as way of cooperating with the therapist and avoiding addressing their core belief structures. When the client is involved in this collusive process, there is a high level of risk that the therapist may install a belief structure that was not there previously. The final point that Dilts makes is that of critical mass: the more times the belief is reached, the more likely it is that a chain reaction will eventually occur and the belief structure will break down, which is the basis of James's work on quantum linguistics and prime concern elicitation.

James's process works on the principle of utilising quantum linguistics to break down the neurological structure of the belief as it is held in the 'now' of the client's subjective reality. He has identified a form of questioning that facilitates elicitation of the core belief structure and taps into a client's sense of self at the level of 'being', 'doing', or 'having'. The earlier work of Schore, Klein, Bion and Freud suggests that clients who have 'being' level core beliefs often believe *I don't exist* or *I am nothing*. This resonates with Bion's notion of nothingness that exists before the notion of the innate breast as an object, and is likely to stem from unfulfilled very early attachment needs. Clients who present with 'doing' level beliefs, such as *I am bad, I am evil, I am wrong*, are likely to have experienced trauma slightly later in their development when they were able to differentiate between the notions of good and bad, based on the principle that the judging subject cannot exist without a lost object. Clients who present with 'having' level beliefs often represent beliefs around their own worth, such as *I am worthless, I don't deserve to live*; they have experienced trauma within their differentiated self sometime after the age of 17–21 months, when they are able to make a symbolic linguistic representation of their relationship to their external world.

Whichever process is used to assist in the resolution of core beliefs, it is important that this is done with ecology, rapport, and sensitivity for the client's internal state and willingness to explore their own internal world.

Constructing patterns that then define the therapeutic process

In summary, neurolinguistic psychotherapy offers a process of change at identity level that can resolve some of the underlying deficits in development through the understanding of the linguistic representation of the inner world, the distortions that the client has developed in their subjective reality and the neurological components that facilitate an outcome frame. In addition, in understanding the relationship between core belief structures or prime concerns and psychoanalytic theory of attachment disorders, it is possible to create the potential for change at a neuroscientific level, the key elements of this being:

- to define the emotional constructs and the somatic representation of these through the work of Gilligan
- to facilitate internal communication, validation and sponsorship of the various aspects of the psyche
- the use of time reframing to change the meaning of experience and facilitate a healthy relationship with previously repressed emotions
- to consider the identified personality type and utilise the processes afforded by neurolinguistic psychotherapy to gain a different perspective
- to integrate, validate, sponsor and name dissociated, disowned or fragmented aspects of the self
- to facilitate integration and/or healing of prime concerns through alignment of the self
- to develop an effective therapeutic relationship such that re-patterning can occur within the therapy setting.

In the next chapter I provide two case examples of how I use aspects of each of these within a therapy setting.

Chapter 8

Therapy in practice

I am often asked about my psychotherapeutic method.

I cannot reply unequivocally to the question, therapy is different in every case.

When a doctor tells me that he adheres strictly to this or that method, I have my doubts about his therapeutic effect.

So much is said in the literature about the resistance of the patient that it would almost seem as if the doctor were trying to put something over on him, whereas the cure ought to grow naturally out of the patient himself . . . I treat every patient as individually as possible, because the solution of the problem is always an individual one

(Jung, 1961, p. 152)

There are a number of aims and constructs within neurolinguistic psychotherapy that set it apart from other modalities, yet as the quote above demonstrates there are strong parallels between neurolinguistic psychotherapy and the analytic approach of Jung. Both approaches support the constructivist principle that each client lives in their own subjective reality and that the solution will be inherent within their psychological make-up. In this chapter I present two further case histories to demonstrate the potential breadth and diversity of neurolinguistic psychotherapy in practice. One of the case histories involves work with a client with a complex psychological history that demonstrates an Ericksonian approach to facilitate neurological re-patterning where there are obvious developmental deficits, combined with a psychodynamic process. The second case history is less complex and involves a more structured programmatic approach that enabled the client to regain control of her projections and her life.

McDermott and Jago (2001, pp. 18–19) list the aims of neurolinguistic psychotherapy as being:

• to reorganise existing patterns of learnt behaviour/feeling (e.g., by changing sequences and strategies)

- to shift perspective (e.g., through personal position shifts, representational system changes, taking a meta position)
- to become less involved, or more fully involved in specific experiences (e.g., through association/dissociation, changing representational systems and modifying sub-modalities)
- to recognise and manage emotional/behavioural states, reclaim ideas and experiences that have been reified and are therefore felt to be fixed, factual, outside the client's ability to control, and re-establish them as active and therefore manageable processes (through denominalising)
- to use a variety of linguistic and experiential means to scramble existing dysfunctional body–mind (neurological) codings of experience so that more enabling patterns can be established
- to reclassify items as part of larger, or smaller, categorisations in order to re-contextualise their meaning (e.g., by chunking up or down).

As a neurolinguistic psychotherapist I operate from within the presuppositions of NLP, discussed in Chapter 2, and I also consider a number of assumptions from O'Hanlon's (1997) 'possibility therapy' as I work with each client.

- 'Here is a perfect place to start from' – this is what Edelman (2004, p. 8) refers to as the 'remembered present', where all the client's past experiences formulate their reality as it is presented in the 'now'. Kostere and Malatesta (1990, p. 21) propose that 'the therapist and the client co-create a consensual world view which includes within it both the presenting problem and the resources needed to implement the desired change'.
- 'Nothing is taken away' – Haley (1993, p. 125) identified that Erickson did not want people to change; rather he suggested to his patients that any change he suggested was in fact just an extension of what they were already doing.
- 'The client realises they are more than their problem' – Problems start to be reframed as states, strategies or belief structures rather than at identity level. By working with Schore's (2003) affective states of a client and assisting change in these it is possible to facilitate a client to have a more useful relationship to their sense of self. 'It is not the past we seek but the logic of the patient's own state regulating strategies' (p. 262).
- 'As the client gains greater clarity about their strategies of behaviour, they stop being as reactive and start to be proactive.'
- 'It is hard to maintain the myth that "I'm a victim"' – Perls et al. (1973) held the view that clients should be encouraged to own their projections and begin to take responsibility for them as part of the therapeutic process.

- 'You work with the client's goal' – By focusing on the client's goal rather than their problem, an immediate shift in the neurology occurs such that the neuronal circuitry attached to the achievement of the goal is activated. This neuronal circuit is then flooded with neuropeptides which results in physiological changes in the mind–body system that would be necessary to achieve the goal.
- 'Once is enough' – the client has already suffered and the therapy should not reiterate this. Accessing the problem state results in continuation of the stress response and the client finds it more difficult to get out of the negative feedback loop that has caused the continuation of the problem.
- 'The client gets a sense of wonder and renewal of curiosity about themselves and others and learns to dream a bigger dream.'
- 'The client gets to know how their brain works.' This includes conscious awareness of strategies that they are using to continue the existing pattern of behaviour, and also greater awareness of their emotional, physical and spiritual experiences. As the client learns how their brain works, they are then able to transfer their learnings to other contexts and other people.

Central to neurolinguistic psychotherapy is the principle of rapport, which sets up a process of responsiveness in communication and can be aided through matching and mirroring a client's physiology. Beyond this, rapport also enables communication between the client and therapist's unconscious minds; Schore (2003) suggests that this directly influences the right amygdala, which 'acts as a sensor of unconscious affective communications, since this structure is known to act as "a dynamic emotional stimulus detection system"' (Wright *et al.*, 2001). The use of rapport in the therapeutic relationship assists the client to hold the experience of therapy within their memory system, which it is thought affects change in the synaptic connections particularly with regard to bonding and attachment. Therefore a client who has previously experienced problems concerning relationships and attachment may be enabled to develop a useful bond with the therapist that can be transferred as an unconscious learning to other contexts. Rosen (1982, p. 31) refers to Erickson's use of 'reparenting', to 'replace "parental" injunctions with new ideas, which he instilled by means of posthypnotic suggestions'. Schore (2003, p. 264) suggests that 'a critical role of the psychotherapist is to act as an affect regulator of the patient's dysregulated states and to provide a growth-facilitating environment for the patient's immature affect regulating structures'. Within this process, sensory acuity plays an essential role in enabling the therapist to calibrate negative psychobiological states and to adapt their own role in the therapeutic process accordingly.

Neurolinguistic psychotherapy, reparenting and obsessive-compulsive disorder (OCD)

The first case history that I present would normally be considered a contraindication of working with the more unconscious patterns of neuro-linguistic psychotherapy as OCD involves the client creating conscious distraction strategies to protect themselves from accessing trauma held within the unconscious. In accepting the client for therapy, I recognised that it would be necessary to work both psychodynamically and through neurolinguistic processes to assist the client to move towards her outcome.

> A presented at the age of 27 with a four-year history of depression and a 12-year history of OCD. She described herself as very obsessive: each shower would take her four hours to complete; she slept on the floor on a mattress, which seemed to be a contradiction to her phobia of dirt and germs that could be picked up from the floor. She recognised the contradiction but could not rationalise it to herself, other than the fact that when she was clean she felt OK as long as she did not touch anything, and when she was dirty she felt contaminated and could not touch anything either.

Her initial history indicated a high level of conscious control and recognition of her irrational behaviour and thought processes, a strong indicator of clinical OCD as defined through DSM–IV.

> Her behaviour had improved since commencing Fluoxetine, but now found that she slept for up to 20 hours a day. She had seen a therapist previously and had also been under the care of a psychiatrist, but found their approaches unuseful so had stopped attending for therapy.

She had found that CBT had helped her in the short term in managing her symptoms, but she felt that it had not addressed the underlying cause and she always reverted to her old condition within a few months.

> She was married, but had returned home to live with her parents as she found that her living arrangements with her husband exacerbated her OCD. She explained that she loved her husband, he was her soul mate, she felt totally reliant on him, but found his poor personal

hygiene and messy habits intolerable. This had happened in a previous relationship, with her again escaping to her family home as she had been unable to cope with the demands of the relationship. She said it seemed that the happier she was in her relationships with both of these partners, the worse her OCD symptoms became.

She was able to recognise the patterns that she had created and that escape to home was her default position, yet at the same time she recognised that this was not an effective way of dealing with things.

At her first appointment, A was dressed in shabby clothes and looked unkempt. She explained that she could cope with her depression, but was finding her OCD and her weight gain out of control. She was able to identify clearly her outcomes for therapy, which were to be confident in herself and her appearance and to stop her current binging. She wanted to stop 'mulling over things that have happened', to be OCD-free and to lead a more normal life. She hated taking her medication as it made her sleepy, but was scared to come off it as she had experienced suicidal thoughts in the past. She described three suicidal episodes where she felt that 'I had to leave myself and escape to another world'. She knew that she needed to develop a wider circle of friends and move away from what she identified as her overly strong attachment to her mother, and a father who was 'too familiar with her', but she was terrified of going out and meeting people.

She was able to access a solution state, and neurologically could associate into the potential of this for short periods during therapy. During this exploration of her history, she would move between being agitated, through to distancing herself, to then return to the therapeutic process and become very sweet and compliant with the process.

Her rationale for seeking a neurolinguistic psychotherapist was that she had heard that this type of therapy was about the future, not the past. She said she could not look at the past, and did whatever she could to avoid looking back on things.

She had a high level of expectation for the therapy and was very clear that she did not want to explore past related issues. Working from constructivist principles, it was relatively easy to stay with her in the current and future and appreciate and value her for all that she brought to therapy, rather than her past experiences.

> At this initial session, I was concerned about accepting A as a client. I knew that working purely with NLP methodologies would not help her OCD; she appeared to have a co-dependent relationship with her mother, and I was not sure that she was ready to commit to the therapeutic process and be willing to make the necessary changes in her life. I spent some time with her considering any secondary benefits of her keeping her problems, and between us we identified that she had the potential to be a 'really happy brilliant person', but she was not sure if she could live a life outside the shell of her parents' protection. The idea of doing this frightened her, and at the same time she had considerable insight that she had the potential for change; she voiced this as 'I've discovered that I can be a lot more forgiving and understanding. I can jump into people's shoes more easily – *they* don't realise what words can do to another person.'

During this first session, beyond ensuring that I undertook a risk assessment of her psychological state, I stayed within a space of creating rapport with the client and enabling her to share and have validated as much of her experience as she chose to share with me. I clearly heard her comment '*they* don't realise what words can do to another person' and kept my own communication from my world to a minimum and non-directive.

> A returned a week later for a second session of therapy. She had spent some time thinking about her relationships with her family. She described her father as controlling and a bit of a bully. She recognised that her relationship with her mother was exclusive, and explained that her mother had suffered from depression for most of her adult life, was socially isolated and would frequently have panic attacks when left alone. A recalled this as being present for as long as she could remember, but did not want to talk about it any more as it upset her. Whenever I tried to encourage A to talk more about her previous experiences, her past or her relationships within the family, she would become distressed and have a panic attack. I stayed within her model of the world and agreed to talk only about the future. I asked her to consider what outcomes she would like to achieve within the next six weeks as a result of attending therapy. She identified five key areas, and I asked her to scale each of these for where she was

now and where she wanted to be, which she was able to do. At the same time I asked her to complete some homework for me in the intervening week, which was to identify what moved her emotionally in a positive way.

Although the client presented her own experience of her past, she was unable to allow the therapeutic process to explore this and if I at any point attempted to move the therapy beyond where she wanted to go, she would regress and experience an exacerbation of her symptoms. She was comfortable with future-oriented work and I used this as part of her tasking such that she could begin to develop awareness of her emotional self outside of the therapy session. I considered that it was important that this was non-directive and enabling rather than specific and potentially regressive for her.

At the following session she said that she had found it quite difficult to find something that moved her, but had experienced a recurring dream that she used to have as a child. She described the dream to me; it had only one central character, a camel. This camel would be used to carry tents and provisions across the desert for a nomadic tribe, and because it could cope for a long time without food and water, it was never taken care of. It was beaten by its owners but was so used to this that it did not react to the beatings and would just stand and take them. She explained that the camel must now be quite old as she had been having the dream for as long as she could remember and that it still did not show any emotion in response to the beatings. She then changed the subject and started to tell me about her dog. She explained that he was the only 'person' in her life that she did not 'do OCD with'. He could climb on to her bed after a long walk and put paw marks on her covers and she never minded. Her parents did not approve of the dog sleeping with her, and she had been unable to take it with her when she married.

We talked for some time about her dog, and we shared stories about the role of dogs in people's lives and how they developed personalities very similar to their owners. The client had communicated her own internal world through her dream of the camel, and to focus on this at this stage in therapy would have been unhelpful, therefore I validated her story by listening to it, and metaphorically worked to encourage her to develop an understanding of her own process through our joint tales about dogs. Within this I used a series of hypnotic suggestions and embedded commands with the primary purpose of enabling her to explore her inner world in a way that was safe and generative.

> At her third session of therapy, I continued to stay within an Ericksonian process of finding out more about A and what her interests and passions were. She explained that she loved to make jewellery, and would like to become successful at this and sell it for a living. She was wearing one of these items. I can only describe it as one of the most unique necklaces that I have ever seen. She had twisted some gold wire into intricate shapes, and as the necklace was turned, different animals appeared within the structure of the necklace. I admired the necklace and asked her how she had managed to create the unique and beautiful internal image and then transfer this to the outside in her careful manipulation of the gold wire.

The process within this session was to continue with the generative modelling work that I had done in the previous session and to use the metaphor of something she had created as a medium to validate and honour her uniqueness as a human being. At a psychodynamic level, my aim was to provide her with an experience of 'good mothering', unconditionally accepting her for herself and assisting her to find a space to develop her own sense of self.

> The following week, she came into the session and began to quietly cry. I sat with her for a while and finally she explained that her dream had returned, only this time a baby camel had appeared at the nomads' campsite. As it was being walked through the camp, the camel that had been around for years looked up and noticed it. As it did so, a tear appeared at the corner of its eye. As A relayed her dream to me, she became quite excited and said that she thought that the baby camel was in fact the long-lost baby of the adult camel, and it had recognised its own child. I agreed that this might be so, and A then spent the rest of the session excitedly making up stories of what might have happened to the baby camel in the period between losing its mother and finding her again.

The direct psychodynamic process within this session was that of the client acknowledging her own inner child through my validation of her, and once she had relayed this to me verbally she entered into a fantasy world to try to figure out the missing components of her own history that she had hitherto repressed.

At her fifth session in therapy, A talked a lot about her parents and their relationship. She described being aware of nudity in the family home from a very young age and not being bothered by it, but more recently this was beginning to bother her. Both her parents still walked in on her while she was taking a bath or using the toilet. We talked about how she might manage this situation now and she was at a loss as to what to do. At the same time, she also explained that she shared everything with her parents, including her therapy sessions with me. I was moved to operate from within my own countertransference and discussed with her my relationship with my own daughters and how I had learned to respect their growing up and needing to keep certain things private from myself and their father. She found this concept odd and asked me quite personal questions about how I felt about this and how I knew whether to trust them or not.

This was one of the more difficult sessions that I had with the client. I found her questioning quite intrusive and I was also wary of the level of personal disclosure that I was using as a therapeutic tool. As I continued further through the process with her, I recognised that the anxiety I was experiencing was part of her own projective process and I discovered in the following session that she had unconsciously needed to test out that I could appropriately contain her process.

She returned to therapy the following week and said that she wanted to talk about sex and its relationship to her OCD. She recognised that she had allowed herself to be violated in previous sexual relationships in a number of different ways, which had started with some very early sexual experiences; she was now finding this quite difficult to live with. She also shared with me that she was using chat rooms to act out some of her sexual fantasies and wanted to know whether or not I thought that this was appropriate. I again felt myself reacting from within my own countertransference and talked to her about keeping safe.

In this session, I moved to work predominantly through the psychodynamic process and contained her sufficiently that she could pursue whichever thought processes seemed relevant to her. At a neurological level, I was enabling her to reconnect the neural synapses that had been affected during her very early childhood, particularly in relation to her mother. It was important for her that she could begin a process of individuation and that I continued to respond to her transferential needs. During the following month she acted out this individuation through verbal and non-verbal processes.

Up until this point in therapy, I had found it difficult to develop an emotional connection to A and found her very controlling in the sessions, with her determining the course of dialogue that we would take. When she returned a week later, I immediately felt that something had changed and the session was emotionally charged throughout. I found her quite difficult to contain, as she would move very quickly from intense associated angry states to being highly dissociated and creating confusion. She ended the session abruptly and said 'I'm not important to you', and walked out. I found this difficult to manage as I was concerned that she might act out her anger in some way that would be harmful to her. The following week, she regaled me with tales of challenging her mother all week with major rows at home, developing an obsessive relationship with a man on the internet and having cybersex with him for hours on end. She felt that she was controlling him and loved the feeling of power it gave her. A few days later she called me to say she had gone away for a while and she would book an appointment on her return, and I was not to worry, but to trust that she would be OK. I was concerned that her OCD had moved to something that could potentially be dangerous for her if she were to act out her fantasies, and with good supervisory support I was able to contain this. On her return to therapy she said that she had been going to extreme lengths to shock me, and recognised that over the preceding weeks a bit of her had taken over and that she had felt it necessary for this bit of her to be given free reign for a while. She was sorry for trying to shock me, but was pleased that I had let her go. She then disclosed an abusive episode in her childhood and we spent some time working with healing her inner child using alignment processes over a number of sessions. She was able to move to a place where she identified that she wanted a relationship with a man that enabled her to have spiritual, sexual and emotional connection. At the end of five months in therapy, she no longer had obsessive thoughts or patterns of behaviour, had ceased her medication, had found herself a job away from home and was living in a flat with a new circle of friends, and had asked her husband for a divorce.

Although she was challenging as a client, I enjoyed working with A. The therapeutic process was contained through the psychodynamic interaction with the client and the neurolinguistic psychotherapy process enabled an outcome orientation to the therapy including neurological re-patterning. In summary, I operated predominantly within an Ericksonian mode during the relationship and found that the only way I could dialogue with A was by entering her model of the world. I worked only with the outcomes that she wanted and recognised very early that she needed to control our relationship. By utilising the scaling process, she had tangible evidence of things that she could control in her internal world, and it is interesting that once we agreed the scale and behaviours that she wanted to measure, we never revisited this during the rest of the therapy. When I asked her to spend some time thinking about what it was that moved her to positive emotions, my purpose was to enable her to find her own internal positive resources. This process in itself revealed the dream that she used as the metaphor for her life, which she had hitherto been unable to share with me, or herself. By continuing in my exploration of her positive resources, she was able to share with me her passion for jewellery-making, which I utilised within the therapy through a series of embedded commands to encourage her to bring to consciousness her own internal world. As we have seen, this had an immediate effect, enabling her to move her unconscious processing forward, bringing herself as a baby into the dream, which enabled the parenting process to begin. She was able to share with me her fantasies around her loss of the maternal object, and I moved into the parenting role, creating the space and trust within the therapy such that she could act out her attachment needs with me. As she worked this through, she was then able to access the core material and underlying emotional structures that had been created as a result of her childhood trauma of abuse, which we were then able to address in therapy. By resolving both her attachment issues and the underlying sexual trauma she was able to resolve her patterns of obsessive-compulsive behaviour, heal herself and move forward in her life.

Somatised conflict

The second case that I refer to provides insight into a psychotherapeutic process that stays within the bounds of purist neurolinguistic psychotherapy and a programmatic model of change.

J was referred to me by her workplace as she had been off for some considerable time with ME. Work wanted to support her and she had asked for therapy as she felt that there might be some underlying emotional cause behind her illness. She had tried a range of alternative approaches, had altered her diet and ensured that she rested regularly to manage her illness. She was currently experiencing mood swings, and found that television programmes or her friend's baby would trigger her to experience depressive episodes; she also noticed that she was getting quite angry and would often throw things. She denied any suicidal ideation, rather citing feelings of 'why me?'.

At this initial session, she was able to identify clearly an outcome and evidence procedure. She was aware of patterns within her life and was also prepared to take responsibility for herself, i.e., she was *At Cause*. She was self-containing and requested a model of change that was short term and outcome-focused, with her primary aim being to return to work in a measured and sustainable manner.

Her personal history was that she was the eldest of three children in a working-class family and she saw herself as being a 'pseudo-mother' to her siblings. Her mother had lost her first child in infancy, and J was premature, spending the first few weeks of her life in the special care baby unit. Her mother remained in hospital for a while after J was discharged to the care of her grandmother, with whom she developed a very close relationship. She recounted tales of refusing to be fed by her mother and screaming if her mother tried to pick her up. Her mother remained ambivalent towards her throughout her childhood.

It would have been relatively easy to make an assessment at this stage with regard to attachment disorders, and the subjective world of the client determined that she was clear about her goal and her desire to work towards achieving this. She was associated into her experiences as a very young child and had what she considered an appropriate level of emotion concerning these experiences. In terms of O'Hanlon and Gilligan's model, she was operating with an integrated sense of self.

At school she was bright and popular, but she used to avoid bringing friends home because she lived in a council house and was embarrassed that her family was not like other families: their house was regularly full of 'other people's kids, that mum looked after'. She had occasionally binged on food as a teenager and recalled three incidents of self-harm. She had been quite ill in her teens, and was hospitalised on a number of occasions. Interestingly it was usually her teachers that took her to hospital. J had been the first member of the family to go to university. During her investigations for ME, her GP said that she might have cancer, and her immediate reaction was, 'Oh good, that will teach her [mum] a lesson, now she might believe me'. She had done well at university and had met her husband there.

Within this aspect of her history she remained associated, and could contain this emotion relatively well. Occasionally she would interrupt the session to walk to another room 'to contain herself', or would walk to the window and look out until her emotion subsided. She was very clear that she did not want me to rescue her from this and that she wanted to deal with it in her own way.

Her husband's background was very different from hers and she had found this quite difficult in the early stages of their relationship, although she described a much warmer relationship with her husband's family compared to her own, which she voiced as 'I am drawn to people older than me, they can give me motherly advice'.

We discussed her reaction to TV programmes and her friend's baby and she said that she wanted to have a baby now, but knew it was not the right time as her friends with children said they mess up your life. Immediately prior to her marriage she had been diagnosed with polycystic ovaries, and she was concerned that this might affect her ability to conceive. Her sister-in-law had recently become pregnant and J was finding it quite difficult to observe the attention being paid to her. She voiced a view that if she got pregnant it would give her one thing in common with her mother, and it would give her mother an opportunity to make up for how she was in the past.

Comparing this with her previous statement when she thought she might have cancer, she has expressed a range of emotions towards her mother and a desire to heal this for the future. Had she had a less flexible perspective on her relationship with her mother, the therapeutic process would most likely have been more psychodynamic.

J was a very intelligent woman and wanted to consciously participate in and own the therapeutic process. We discussed the notion of values and she suggested that she might be experiencing conflict within her own family value set. She identified the following values:

- *everyone getting on*, which was away from feeling unwanted, inadequate or awkward

- *not wanting any ill feeling*, which was away from the way she had felt her entire life
- *not wanting her family to be her best friends*, which was away from being judged by her mother
- *supported* by her friends rather than her family as she felt that she carried the weight of her family's problems on her own
- *taking an active interest in her job and friends*, which would make her feel wanted and needed by other people
- *interested and involved with life not being a rollercoaster*, which was away from people not showing that they are interested in her
- *recognition and being treated equally*, which was away from her being valued only through money
- *no betrayal*, moving away from not trusting others and her mum telling everyone everything about her.

After we had elicited her values she became quite emotional and said that she found it very difficult to let people in. She confessed that 'I need the illness to get attention, it makes me feel needed'.

Following this session, J described it as being quite cathartic and agreed that she wanted to look at the core belief structure that was sitting under the 'away from' values. I used the prime concern elicitation process (James, 1996), and she accessed a core belief of 'I should be dead'. This resulted in a further cathartic release and we worked together to align and heal her inner child. During this time, she regressed into child-like voice qualities, became very emotional and said 'I need looking after'. She found this process insightful and following integration moved to being 'a whole person'.

Earlier in the therapy process it was quite clear that she had developed a series of strategies to ensure that I did not look after her, which was contrary to what she had been creating through her illnesses.

We then re-elicited her values which had changed to:

- *we all support each other and get on*, which was towards sharing achievements
- *showing an interest and caring about each other*, which was towards sharing feelings
- *giving recognition to each other*, which moved her towards feeling good about herself
- *we love each other*, which was about being part of a family, and provided her with grounding.

> Subsequent to this change work, J returned to work within two weeks, initially on a part-time basis and then full time. She recognised that she could not change her mother; rather she could change how she related to her mother, and she started to develop stronger, clearer boundaries with her husband's family based on equality of relationship rather than them constantly buying J and her husband things.

This case was a relatively straightforward process of working with the conscious mind of the client to recognise and realign unconscious patterns of behaviour. My role throughout the process was to hold the torch for J so that she could explore and reframe her inner world. The structure of the methodology of NLP enabled J to resolve a deeply held core belief that was creating conflict in her value structure. By working at pattern level, J was able to quickly enter into the process and through ecological change work, she could make the necessary changes without entering into a long-term therapeutic relationship, such that she could return to work.

Patterns of therapeutic process

Although each therapeutic encounter is very much working with the client's model of the world, I find it helpful to have an overview of the therapeutic process which I also provide to students. This is provided as a map rather than a territory, and like any map, all it can ever do is provide direction; it is entirely up to the therapist as to the mode of transport, speed of travel, or deviations and sights to see along the way. I very rarely use the map in its entirety; rather I allow the client's world and experience in the session to direct me to the page of the map that we might be on.

1   Contract with the client.

- Problem identification – big chunk.
- Outcome – evidence.
- Why therapy now?
- How long has the client had this problem?
- What has the client done about this problem?
- Ecology for self and client.
- Client at cause or effect.
- Does the client really want to let go of the problem? At this point I will often do a success analysis using Prochaska and DiClemente's (1992) model of change.

2   Sometimes I will ask a client to complete a pre-session questionnaire, particularly if they are work-referred clients. This will include the following questions.

- If you could have anything as a result of therapy, what would you want?
- What do you currently have in your life that you no longer want?
- What do you not have in your life that you want now?
- Write a short life history including any events that were significant to you (both positive and negative).
- What patterns have you noticed occurring in your life so far?

3 Initial session.

- Outline structure of therapy.
- Introduce the conscious and unconscious mind – verifying through reference experiences where they have had communication with their unconscious mind.
- Introduce prime directives of the unconscious mind and some of the presuppositions of NLP, particularly that the unconscious mind needs orders to follow, thinks in symbols, takes everything personally, represses memories with unresolved negative emotion for protection, and presents memories for resolution. Of the presuppositions I remind them that every behaviour has a positive intention, that everyone lives in their own model of the world, and that people are doing their best that they can.
- Introduce the concept of cause and effect.
- If they are consulting for a physiological symptom, I will cite Chopra and discuss how the unconscious mind controls the body. With physiological issues it is important to find out what happened one to five years before the first symptom.
- Confidentiality with exceptions such as harmful to self or others, and child protection.

4 Detailed personal history.

- There is no irrelevant information in a detailed personal history. Write everything down.
- Why is the client here? Why else? Why else? Elicit all reasons for the client being in therapy to enable full pattern recognition. Often the first reason isn't the real reason; it can be a smokescreen and it is often the real reason that underpins everything.
- If this problem were to disappear, completely, for good, right now, how would the client know that it had gone? What would they see, hear, feel, or notice?
- How does the client know they have this problem? (Elicit a reality strategy and any diagnosis made.)
- When do they do it?
- When don't they do it?
- How long have they had this problem?

- What have they done about it so far?
- Was there ever a time when they didn't have this problem?
- In each of these events, what is the relationship between the event and the current situation in life? (Elicit every single event and scan for patterns.)
- What happened the first time they had this? (for each event)
- What has happened since then? (for each event)
- What emotions do they have associated with this problem?
- What do they believe about the problem?
- Pattern of childhood in relation to the problem.
- Elicit history to trace the derivation of the problem or problems back to the source.

  - Family history – parenting, grandparenting
  - Siblings
  - Parents' relationships and grandparents' relationships with family and client
  - Pay particular attention to 0–7 imprint period, 7–14 modelling period and 14–21 socialisation period
  - Education – primary
  - Secondary
  - Tertiary
  - Social history – socialisation
  - Friendships
  - Separations
  - Illnesses
  - Relationships – personal
  - Sexual history
  - Marriage
  - Work history – job/career development
  - Health – beliefs about illness and wellness
  - Role models of illness.

- Ask client's unconscious mind when they decided to create this problem and for what purpose.
- What is a higher-level presenting problem of this, such that if the higher-level problem were to disappear all the lower-level examples would disappear too?
- Ask client's unconscious mind if it is totally willing to assist and support them in having an undeniable experience of this problem disappearing.

5 History of development of the problem.

- Circumstances related to the development of the problems.
- Dynamics at work/home when problem was created.

- What pattern echoes in childhood?
- Are there SEEs (significant emotional events) around the time of creation of problems?

6   Cause and effect.

- How has person created problem?
- What purpose is being served?
- Do they really want to change it?
- Listen for language of responsibility; are others to blame?

7   Secondary gain.

- What is this problem preventing the client from doing (that they don't want to do) which, if the problem disappeared, they would have to do?
- What is it that they're not doing because of the problem?
- What is it that they are doing, which they enjoy doing, that they won't be able to do if the problem disappears?
- Ask their unconscious mind if there is anything it wants them to pay attention to such that if they were to pay attention to it, it would cause the problem to disappear.
- What are they pretending not to know by having things be this way?
- Every presenting problem is an example of something. I share this diagram with the client (Figure 8.1).

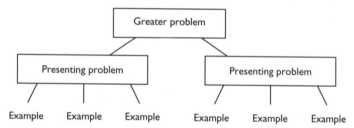

Figure 8.1 Patterns

8   Sourcing the problem: values elicitation.

- Elicit values hierarchy.
- Elicit motivation strategy.
- Elicit go/stay loop (threshold values).
- Elicit 'away from' values.

  - Listen for modal operators of necessity (got to, must, need, etc.)
  - Negative statements (e.g., 'not x')
  - Dissociated language (you, they, self by first name).

- Elicit complex equivalents of values.

9 Prime concern or core belief elicitation.

- Three primary energies – be – do – have.
- Prime concern elicitation process.
- Naturalistic elicitation.
  - Notice analogically marked-out words
  - Child-like voices
  - Semantically packed – physiological response (emotional response, tonal qualities)
  - Universals, modal operators of necessity, dissociated language
  - Deliberately vague language
  - SEEs
  - Vertical gestalts of meaning.

10 Collate information.

- Establish prime concern.
- Notice analogically marked-out words.
- Every presenting problem is an example of something.
- Check out semantically packed words.
- Check out double binds.
- Complex equivalence.

11 Interventions.

- Neurological re-patterning.
- Use least amount of change for maximum amount of benefit.
- Release all prime concerns.
- Release any negative emotions or limiting decisions.
- Integrate any parts elicited.
- Re-elicit values hierarchy, checking that all 'away from' values have disappeared or at least the balance is at 80% towards and 20% away from.
- Test and future pace by asking the client to review their previous problem state, and also by considering a time in the future when the previous problem might have occurred, running the client's reality and convincer strategies.
- Install any required strategies and new behaviours.
- Programme the future – checking for congruence.

I have presented the map of the methodology of neurolinguistic psycho-therapy in its entirety. This can only represent the science of therapy, whereas the development of sustainable relationships through healthy and happy lives is not a science. I have demonstrated, in the case studies throughout this book, the application of the science within an artistic flexible framework, much in the way that Erickson, Satir and Perls each put aside what they knew at a scientific level before they related to their clients at an emotional level.

Chapter 9

A postmodern approach

Energy and attention have gone into forcing yourself, because of a mistaken feeling of 'oughtness', along lines that run counter to your healthy interests. To the extent that you regain and redirect this energy, the areas of restored vitality will progressively increase. It is nature that cures – *natura sant*. A wound heals or a bone knits by itself. There is nothing the physician can do but clean the wound or set the bone. It is the same with your personality.

(Perls *et al.*, 1951, p. 112)

Postmodernism

A style or concept in the arts characterized by distrust of theories and ideologies and by the drawing of attention to conventions.

(*Oxford English Dictionary*)

Literature that reacts against earlier modernist principles by reintroducing traditional or classical elements of style.

(*American Heritage Dictionary*)

Recognising that my own bias would naturally elicit a preference for a constructivist model of working with unconscious processes, I have presented in this book the entirety of neurolinguistic psychotherapy from its roots through to current practice. Within this I have endeavoured to bring in a range of perspectives, making links with similarities that exist in other psychotherapeutic approaches and adding to current research into neuroscience.

There is a growing move among neurolinguistic psychotherapists to return to the principles of the original therapists that were modelled by Bandler and Grinder. In this final chapter, I present my own thoughts on how the modality of neurolinguistic psychotherapy can move forward. I return to the quote by DeLozier (1995) in the Introduction: 'the patterns of

NLP were not imparted to us, but unfolded in our learning'. NLP is not a pattern that can be taught; NLP is about self-learning and discovery.

As NLP developed through the 1980s and was adopted by therapists, for a time it appeared to lose the essence of what made the work of Erickson, Satir and Perls so effective. This has now re-emerged through the work of O'Hanlon, Gilligan, Dilts and, within the UK, Gawler-Wright. My aim in this book is to awaken in the hearts and minds of therapists the joy and compassion that was present in the therapy work of Erickson, Satir and Perls.

I consider that NLP as a methodology is effective as an applied psychology, and on its own it is not psychotherapy: a position that is in alignment with that of the original developers of NLP. To use it as such, for clients who need psychotherapy, it will enable short-term change and movement towards a solution state that may require conscious and regular reprogramming. If it is used on its own where clients have experienced developmental deficit, or have traumatic repressed experiences, it is likely to set up potential problems later on. These problems as they have been presented by some of my clients have ranged from unfulfilled expectations, a feeling of being let down, a belief that the therapy did not work, that the person themselves must be bad or wrong because they keep visiting the same problem, through to severe dysfunction and exacerbation of underlying pathology. Nowhere in the minds or work of Erickson, Satir or Perls was there a thought or belief that the therapy had the potential to resolve all of life's problems; rather they worked to support clients to gain a more useful perspective on their experience and develop healthier and happier lives.

While she agrees with me in terms of the pursuit of psychotherapy as practised by Erickson, Perls and Satir, conversations with Gawler-Wright reveal a different position towards the client and the therapist's diagnosis. Her credo for practice knowingly subjects itself to a chosen belief in the client's system as self-balancing. This belief creates a filter for the therapist whereby she responds to symptoms or deficits as being manifestations of compensating resourcefulness by the client. She therefore focuses not on the depth or seriousness of the client's difficulties as the limit to effectiveness of any psychotherapeutic approach, but instead on whether the therapist has respectfully modelled how the client is currently applying their resources and whether the therapist successfully stimulates the individual, through co-created relational activity, to engage in different applications of their strengths and attention. The relational activity may well involve programmatic 'games' in which the client is beheld as 'an artist creating themselves' through engagement in new sensory experiences and linguistic expressions. This difference in perception about the client, however, also places emphasis on the relational skills of the psychotherapist. It highlights, Gawler-Wright (2005) argues, the need in training for therapists to develop one of the core NLP skills identified by Grinder and DeLozier: to be knowingly at peace in a place of 'not knowing'. Hence Erickson's ability to facilitate highly distressed and even disturbed clients through both brief and sometimes longer-term intervention (in conversation, Gawler-Wright and Wake, May 2005).

Behaviourism vs. constructivism

Neurolinguistic psychotherapy appears to be trying to find a place that sits between constructivism, Ericksonian psychotherapy and behaviourism. For therapists who prefer a behaviourist approach this can provide a setting for therapy that takes account of the subjective nature of experience, with the therapist operating from a meta-perspective outside the system to influence change within the system. Behavioural modelling can work very effectively in enabling a client to alter their internal representations and strategies for 'doing' a specific problem, as highlighted in the case of the young man with Tourette's in Chapters 1 and 4. Where the therapist stays outside the system, and there is no relationship with the client other than at a secondary or superficial level, the therapist reduces the chance of reacting to countertransferential processes. However, this approach of bringing to consciousness that which is held within the unconscious may upset the equilibrium of the client's ecosystem such that they cannot function effectively. This raises questions about some of the more provocative pattern interrupts that behaviourally oriented therapists might use. Schore (2003, p. 51) has identified that mismatching a client may result in 'misattunement', which can create a 'stressful *desynchronization* between and destabilization within their right brains' (emphasis in original), resulting in the client either becoming distressed or detaching from the relationship with the therapist, i.e., not returning to therapy, which may mean that the therapist views the client as having achieved their outcome. Erickson himself expressed concerns about the use of conscious therapy to address unconscious material in his epilogue to Bandler and Grinder's work (1975, p. 256).

> Experimental investigation has repeatedly demonstrated that good unconscious understandings allowed to become conscious before a conscious readiness exists will result in conscious resistance, rejection, repression and even the loss, through repressing, of unconscious gains. By working separately with the unconscious there is then the opportunity to temper and to control the patient's rate of progress and thus to effect a reintegration in the manner acceptable to the conscious mind.
>
> (p. 256)

How then does a therapist who prefers behavioural modelling work within the metaphor of a client's reality? Even within a behavioural modelling approach, a therapist cannot not make meaning of what they perceive, and the perceptions of the therapist are based on what is already known by them. A therapist may view the microcosmos of the client's world and perceive a history of abuse or inability to maintain successful relationships. How does the therapist know whether what is perceived is in fact reality or their own projection onto the client?

In Chapter 7 I discussed the concept of splitting or parts of the personality and how this may be transferred to the therapist through projective identification. Programmatic therapy presents a dilemma for therapists who wish to work non-relationally with clients who have experienced trauma prior to verbal or cognitive ability. The client may only be able to communicate somatic markers of distress via the transferential relationship. If the therapist chooses to stay dissociated from the therapeutic relationship with clients, the opportunity to assist neurological re-patterning is missed. Schore (2003, p. 106) states that 'when such "nonconscious affect" . . . is interactively regulated, amplified, and held in short-term memory long enough to be felt and recognized, the patient's affectively charged but now regulated right brain experiences can then be communicated to the left brain for further conscious processing'. Basch (1985, p. 11) supports this and suggests that the clinician's role within this process is to 'act the part of the corpus callosum, so to speak, until that structure can take over and the patient can do for himself what he needed us to do with and for him'.

I would go further and say that non-relational therapy with a client who has evidence within their history of trauma and/or repression is likely to have a negative impact on the neurology and psychology of the client. Programmatic behavioural therapy can be very effective where the client has full conscious and unconscious acknowledgement of the presenting problem state. Any therapist risks working from within a blind spot, and this may be more likely to happen if therapy is offered from a dissociated or meta position. The therapist can counter this by ensuring that their personal supervision and/or therapy is embarked on with a relationally minded supervisor and/or therapist.

In considering the more constructivist and hypnopsychotherapeutic approach, the influence of Erickson, Satir and Perls is evident in the unconscious processes that flow throughout the foundation principles of NLP. Much of the therapeutic alliance of all three therapists was about right brain to right brain communication. It is this regulation process that enables the development of social and emotional growth with the client in the therapy relationship. I have worked with a group of my students to model the components of an effective neurolinguistic psychotherapist within the therapeutic alliance.

- The therapist operates from the three perceptual positions during the therapy process.
- The therapist suspends judgement.

- A process is developed that enables the therapist to develop an internal mechanism that lets her 'know how she knows' that what the client is presenting is representative of the client's reality rather than her own intersubjectivity.
- The therapist remains open to feedback from the client, the environment, her own internal mechanisms, her supervisor, her peers.
- There is alignment and congruence with the client's model of the world when the therapist is in second position.
- The therapist continually checks 'whose outcome is it?'.
- The therapist is willing to go where the client wants to go – regardless (i.e., the client leads the therapy process, including determining when it is appropriate for the therapist to lead).
- The therapist is aware of when she is not letting herself progress the therapy, i.e., she is stopping herself from going to the place that is required for therapeutic success.
- The therapist is 'just' – this was modelled through the group's experience and on researching this, it resonates closely with the Japanese haiku – an awareness of just this moment.
- The therapist becomes aware of stimuli that are 'not me', i.e., she responds to stimuli from the client.
- The role of the therapist is to create a vacuum or container for the client and remain aware of who fills the vacuum.
- In the Dyson model (therapists described this as if they were operating in a similar way to the inner workings of a Dyson vacuum cleaner) the therapist is absorbing information from the client at a number of different sensory levels.
- The therapist is willing to ask herself if 'she is fit for this' i.e., whether she is the right person to work with the client.
- The therapist is clear about her exit strategy.

Over and above these factors, the therapists recognised that it is important to create a container of ecology for themselves that includes:

- supervision
- ongoing learning
- experiential learning
- an attitude of courage, self-reflection, self-awareness, openness to learn, and a willingness and 'OKness' to say they had got it wrong
- recognition that they are part of an evolutionary process (Master Practitioner Class, Spring 2007, Awaken Consulting).

Working with unconscious processes may lay the therapist open to a degree of risk, of working blindly at times. Constructivism encourages therapists to stay in the 'now' with the client, yet if the therapist does not reflect and make meaning of their interactions with clients in supervision and personal therapy, how do they know whether they are projecting their reality on to the client in either useful or unuseful ways? Watzlawick (1978, p. 43) usefully summarises this in his acknowledgement that our world image changes on a day-to-day basis and:

> It is not *the world*, but a mosaic of single images which may be interpreted in one way today and differently tomorrow; a pattern of patterns; an interpretation of interpretations; the result of incessant decisions about what may and what may not be included in these meta-interpretations, which themselves are the consequences of past decisions.

For the therapist who is working through cognitive modelling, programmatic change may not be effective for a client who has never learnt to have trusting and intimate relationships with others. If the client holds an existing construct that they are alone in the world, cannot trust others, and have no internal construct of 'love', then it is the development of this that becomes the basis of therapy. Where clients have experienced developmental delay or deficit, combining neuroscience with psychodynamic and relational therapy, and some of the programmatic aspects of NLP, it is possible to offer a reflexive and effective model of therapy.

If a therapist stays within a purist constructivist approach, they may acknowledge the client's presenting construct as influencing their life negatively, and may, through their own life experiences, work within the metaphor with the client. Within their own neurology, they may hold an internal construct of a loving and intimate relationship that is dynamic and adult, and may project this onto their client in a way that causes the client to react negatively. Or they may facilitate the client to develop trust with themselves as the therapist and create the 'collaborative dance' as described by McDermott and Jago (2001, p. 86). Schore (2003, p. 268) suggests that the optimum place for a therapist to operate is perhaps in both: that where 'genuine dialogue' exists, the patient will bring to the therapy 'an inner word and then into a spoken word what he/she needs to say at a particular moment but does not yet possess as speech'. Schore emphasises the role of the therapist in this interaction: that if the client's world is validated and empathised with, the affects as they have been held can then be moved to a bodily sensation and then articulated through logical verbal processes, what in NLP terms is called 'proper naming'. Without this, the client's world remains repressed.

Subjectivity in the therapeutic space

Where it is customary to speak of the 'client–therapist relationship', we want to draw attention to our understanding that the interaction between

> the two constitutes an active system created by and between the two individuals. As with other systems, there is mutual influence, and, as the word 'system' implies, there are also implicit and explicit structures which affect both parties. There are assumptions (about the nature and role each has, about the purpose and process of therapy, about change, about the self) and there are rules. While some are overt (for example, what happens if either party has to cancel, how payment is made), others, although not spelt out, are present nonetheless – Does the therapist interpret? What amount of silence is acceptable? In what ways is it acceptable for the client to influence the therapist? Perhaps the most significant implication of a systemic approach is the interaction between the two parties is recognised as mutually regulating; therapy is not a treatment which the client 'receives', the therapist 'gives' or even 'offers', but rather an ongoing collaborative dance.
>
> (McDermott & Jago, 2001, p. 86)

McDermott and Jago highlight here the dilemma that is presented to the neurolinguistic psychotherapist and how he relates within the client–therapist system. Both client and therapist will have their own experiences of reality, both of their life and what has brought them to this point where they have connected with each other in a shared reality, and also how they experience what they perceive as the shared reality of therapy. Both parties in the system will have a set of rules, some of which are consciously known by the individual and some of which are outside conscious awareness. Unconscious rules can affect therapy much more than either party is aware. The client may have unwritten rules about what is and is not acceptable to be discussed with another. The same principle applies for the therapist. Is a therapist willing to explore, recognise and challenge what some of his unwritten rules might be? Do therapists readily explore their own internal subjective processes through supervision and therapy, or do they make the assumption that their own map is good, right, robust and ecological?

To highlight the influence that rules can have in the therapy setting, I illustrate two cases, the first being a client that had an internal value structure and set of rules about being a father that prevented him from moving on within his grieving process. As a therapist and former nurse, I too had a set of rules about length of time for grieving processes and how soon somebody could or should move on.

> The client was referred to me through his workplace to enable him to address some behavioural difficulties that had been of increasing concern to his manager. Historically he had always been political at work and was renowned for voicing his opinion; recently this had turned into what were perceived as uncontrollable levels of anger.

There had been two recent incidents at work where his behaviour was deemed to be unacceptable. The client attended for his first session and was fully aware of the problems that his behaviour had created at work. He was quite clear about the change that was required in him and felt that things had spiralled out of control; he described feeling a permanent state of apprehension that he could not understand. We talked about his anger and he explained that he did not understand where it was coming from. As we discussed this further it soon became apparent that he was stuck in a grieving process. His daughter had been killed in a car accident two years previously, while on holiday and although he felt that he had grieved for her, it seemed that he was still very angry.

As soon as I became aware of what I perceived to be the cause of his anger, I focused on it. This was contrary to what the client wanted to focus on. He was in the latter years of his working life and wanted to retain his job such that he could move into a secure retirement.

In my own mind I considered this would be a relatively straight-forward therapeutic process, yet the client seemed to want to focus on his anger towards some of his colleagues at work. I initially found it quite difficult to stay focused on his work relationships when I knew that he was experiencing unresolved grief [in my model of the world]. When I was able to put aside my own rules and expectations with regard to grieving and stayed with the client in his space of anger and irritation at his workplace, we very quickly developed a strong thera-peutic bond. In one of the subsequent sessions, while we were talking about his workplace and colleagues, who in his mind were belligerent and lazy, he suddenly became very distressed. When he finally com-posed himself he shared with me that he could not move on with regard to his daughter, because he could not condemn the driver of the car that his daughter was travelling in. He was scared that I might judge him for what he was thinking and felt demonised by his thoughts.

He articulated back to me my own projection from the first session. I had judged him in that session; I had made an assumption about the cause of his anger and what he needed to do to resolve it. It was only when I moved away from my own prejudices that he could then work within his own world in the therapeutic space. Even though his anger was stemming from the death of his daughter, it was up to him to realise this and not have me point it out for him.

> He explained to me that his son had been driving the car and he was distraught that if he became angry with his son, he might lose him as well as his daughter.

This complex double bind meant that he was stuck within his grief and could not see a way out; additionally my own rule structure concerning grief and my desire to enable him to address it quickly prevented him from sharing some of his thoughts with me.

> Becoming more flexible and giving him the space to lead the therapy gave him permission to own his anger about his daughter's death. I was able to contain it in the therapeutic space and he was able to work through his anger. As we moved to conclude the therapy, he learnt to develop a new set of rules regarding being a father to his son, based on an adult–adult relationship.

This case example demonstrates how a rule that I consciously knew about affected my work, and in the following example I share with you client work where my own unwritten and unconscious rule as a therapist prevented me from working effectively with a client.

> A client presented with relationship difficulties. He found it difficult to manage his partner's temper. She would become very challenging at times, and his own stress levels generated at work meant that he wanted his time at home with her to be peaceful and enjoyable. The effect that this was having on their relationship was apparent in a number of areas including their sexual relationship. She was becoming very concerned that he was looking at other women in a way that was sexual, and in her words was 'mentally undressing every woman you meet'. He denied seeing any of these women in a sexual way and said, 'They are just beautiful, I never think sexual thoughts about any of them'. She was becoming increasingly distant to him and what little time they had together was becoming tense and unproductive. Within his own construct, the client recognised that he was becoming less committed to the relationship and was becoming quite 'hung-up' on the sexual difficulties that were being presented.

The client was very clear about his outcome for therapy, and also his presenting problem. At this initial session, I perceived that this would be a relatively straightforward process and that he would quickly resolve his issues and move forward in his life.

> He willingly explored his issues in therapy and after some time, we reached an impasse. It was as if we were getting to the point of resolution and then something would happen to prevent this. This occurred over a couple of sessions and I recognised that he was becoming increasingly frustrated with me. I took the case to super-vision and within this context recognised that I was avoiding a close therapeutic relationship with him as I was concerned that I might find him sexually attractive.

I had acted out for him exactly the process that he had been doing with females around him. Within my own construct, I had an unwritten rule that 'forbade' me from finding clients sexually attractive, in the same way that he could not accept that he could find people outside of his immediate relationship attractive. This resulted in his process being avoided by me as the therapist, and once I internalised my own sexual feelings, he successfully addressed the issues in therapy.

Schore (2003, p. 56) describes this process of the therapist getting in the way of the therapy for clients as follows: 'Cycles of organization, disorgan-ization, and reorganization of the intersubjective field occur repeatedly in the treatment process'. He suggests that our ability to manage this and work with the feelings of others is dependent on 'our capacity to tolerate varying intensities and durations of countertransferential states marked by discrete positive affects, such as joy and excitement, and negative affects, such as shame, disgust, and terror'. The therapist's ability to deal with this process will be in accordance with their own imprinted experiences, of which they may or may not have knowledge. Schore (2003, p. 56) confirms my own view: 'for this reason, I believe personal psychotherapy is a pre-requisite for anyone entering the field'. Yet neurolinguistic psychotherapy is promoted as a modality of therapy that requires minimal personal therapy of the therapist by NLPtCA, which at the time of writing is a total of 12 hours for the four-year duration of training. Kristeva (2001, p. 111) highlights a dilemma that is faced by therapists, and particularly those who do not have personal therapy as part of their training, i.e., that very few therapists can work with the 'limits of primal repression, the point at which the symbolic character of human nature collapses into chaos as the client's affective state changes . . . without drowning'. Yet if neurolinguistic psychotherapists enable clients to access and resolve primal states of being as outlined in Chapter 6, they risk losing themselves in the chaos of the client's inner world.

If neurolinguistic psychotherapists were more willing to explore their own internal constructs and develop even stronger flexibility in moving between first, second and third perceptual position (O'Connor, 2001, p. 33), they would be enabled to work relationally with others. This process would facilitate very effective neurological re-patterning through the identification and resolution of somatic markers of distress. BeeLeaf Institute for Contemporary Psychotherapy, a UKCP Training Member Organisation in neurolinguistic psychotherapy, centralises this development of the self and use of the self through somatic marker and cognitive naming. Assessment criteria and learning outcomes of their second year of a four-year training process utilise Dilts and DeLozier's (2000) qualities of mastery as a solid basis on which to build the required personal characteristics of a skilled and safe psychotherapist of any modality (Gawler-Wright, 2004).

Research into neurolinguistic psychotherapy

Compared to other modalities of psychotherapy, neurolinguistic psychotherapy is incredibly young, having developed a separate therapy arm to the voluntary body that regulates NLP in the early 1990s. Because of its brief history as a modality of psychotherapy it has difficulty in demonstrating its effectiveness in sufficiently large numbers to be considered as a therapy of choice, particularly within the NHS. A limited number of studies are available on the internet that, in the main, have researched specific aspects of NLP as a methodology. This has resulted in the development of The Institute for the Advanced Study of Health's (IASH) Research and Recognition Project, whose aim is to 'define and support feasible health projects involving NLP presuppositions, distinctions and processes in order to make discoveries in the systems of influence effecting health and healing'. IASH has commenced a project that aims to develop scientifically based research on the efficacy of NLP as a series of potential treatment protocols. The site is linked to the University of Surrey, which has an educational research project, and also to an Australian research and training organisation, Inspirative, that lists over 100 research papers on the use of specific NLP technologies with certain conditions.

- www.nlp.de/cgi-bin/research/nlp-rdb.cgi
- www.nlpco.com/pages/research/index.php
- www.nlpiash.org
- www.inspirative.com.au

Much of the available research concerns the use of specific techniques within the methodology and very little is psychotherapy-specific, reinforcing my view that it is an applied psychology; however, the IASH project may well demonstrate its effectiveness as a psychotherapy over time. There is evidence of only one controlled trial of neurolinguistic psychotherapy, conducted by Genser-Medlitsch and Schütz (1997), and no studies exist of its efficacy compared to other therapeutic approaches.

One of the first reviews of NLP research literature was conducted by Sharpley in 1984, who proposed that there was little supportive evidence for, particularly, the assumption of a preferred representational system, and in fact proposed that a substantial amount of data opposed it as a model of processing information. By 1987, Sharpley had continued his critique of NLP; he proposed that it 'had little to support [it] and much to answer to in the research literature' and suggested that a meta-analysis be conducted of the large amount of data already available. One of the major critiques of the research completed in these early days was that it reviewed one aspect of the methodology when in fact there are so many other contributing factors that affect outcome. In 1985 (pp. 589–596) Einspruch and Forman supported Sharpley's concerns about the methodology used in their review of 39 studies on NLP. They identified that although NLP is 'in theory, testable and verifiable . . . past research was fraught with methodological confounds' and as such they concluded that it was 'not possible at this time to determine the validity of either NLP concepts or whether NLP-based therapeutic procedures are effective for achieving therapeutic outcomes' and that 'only when well-designed empirical investigations are carried out may we be assured of NLP's validity as a model of therapy'. Einspruch and Forman (1988, pp. 91–100) continued their research and were able to demonstrate marked improvement in a group of 31 phobic patients within a multifaceted treatment programme using NLP and Ericksonian approaches. Measurement instruments used were 'Mark's phobia questionnaire' and 'fear inventory', and the 'Beck depression inventory' pre- and post-treatment. The researchers concluded that 'NLP holds promise for becoming an important set of therapeutic techniques for treating phobias'. This then places the more programmatic elements of neurolinguistic psychotherapy alongside CBT as an easily learned and applied model that can be used in a structured way to treat low-level generalised anxiety disorders.

Genser-Medlitsch and Schütz's (1997) study demonstrated through a comprehensive evaluation of 55 patients that neurolinguistic psychotherapy is an effective modality of therapy in accordance with its therapeutic objective. The clients all had severe DSM-IV conditions, such as schizo-affective disorder, psychosis, psychosomatic tendencies, depression or dependency problems (American Psychiatric Association, 1994); most of them were also on medication. Patients in the control group all had milder symptoms. At three points in time, measurements were conducted of changes in individual complaints, clinical psychological symptoms, individual coping strategies, and locus of control tendencies, using the linear rating scale model (LRSM) and the linear partial credit model (LPCM). After therapy, the clients who had received NLP scored significantly higher (76%) in each of the measured areas and experienced a reduction in clinical symptoms. The researchers concluded that 'It could be established that, in principle, NLP is effective in accordance with the therapeutic objective'. What is missing from this study is a definitive description of the therapeutic process and whether it was predominantly programmatic, the history of the patients included in the study or the degree of disturbance. A longitudinal follow-up study of this group of patients would be beneficial in demonstrating effects of therapy over time and whether there is any recurrence of symptoms.

Bolstad and Hamblett (2000) have demonstrated the effectiveness of one-off treatment sessions using the phobia cure for those experiencing PTSD, which was later developed by Muss who completed a pilot study using the process with members of a police force experiencing PTSD. This study demonstrated 100% effectiveness in resolution of symptoms, which was sustained over a period of time. The study does not determine that there was any developmentally associated event prior to the one that was thought to trigger the PTSD, suggesting that as a stand-alone treatment for single factor events of PTSD, NLP as an applied psychology is effective. Bolstad (2002) has continued to support research into a number of the tools and techniques used in NLP, and reports on research dated between 1984–2001. He quotes from a variety of sources as wide ranging as the use of anchoring to access a self-caring state in adult children of alcoholics; the treatment of phobias including PTSD; and the treatment of asthmatics using time line therapy that resulted in a near zero use of asthma inhalers in the NLP group compared to fewer changes in the control group. This analysis of Bolstad's suggests that there is potential for using NLP as an applied psychology in specific disorders; however, it does not demonstrate neuro-linguistic psychotherapy.

Bolstad also describes variations on NLP, such as EMDR (eye movement desensitisation and reprocessing) and thought field therapy, for which there is substantial research demonstrating effectiveness when combined with other psychotherapeutic approaches that address the relational aspects.

For neurolinguistic psychotherapy to be taken seriously and to have its place as an effective and respected modality, the profession might consider two approaches to developing research into it. Further research could be conducted into specific tools and techniques used for specific problem states or behaviours, within the spectrum of behaviourist approaches as discussed earlier. This would develop NLP as an applied psychology and would present the field with a dilemma concerning its use. At the time of writing, applied psychology as a professional activity is being brought into a statutory regulation system. NLP has so far evaded attention, yet as more and more psychologists and psychotherapists are starting to use aspects of the technology, the field will be required to be more accountable for how the methodology is taught and principles of practice. Alternatively, research can be developed into its effectiveness as a psychotherapeutic process, including the role of the therapist within the relationship.

One of the challenges that the therapy field, and within it neurolinguistic psychotherapy, is faced with is the desire to use scientific measures of observation for a therapeutic process that is not scientific. As I have demonstrated in this book, the therapist plays an active role in the development of the brain where affective states are present. A number of studies could be conducted, including the perceptions of therapists themselves of the role of the therapist within neurolinguistic psychotherapy. Levels of recurrence of symptoms or presenting problems would provide insight into the differences arising from length of time in therapy, and therapist awareness of transferential and countertransferential processes.

Final thoughts

> What you don't realize, Sid, is that most of your life is unconsciously determined.
>
> (Erickson, in Rosen, 1982, p. 25)

> The capacity for experience-dependent plastic changes in the nervous system remains throughout the life span.
>
> (Schore, 2003, p. 202)

O'Hanlon and Martin's (1992) early work on modelling Erickson's solution-oriented hypnosis summarises the different perspectives of the unconscious as they are held by Erickson and Freud. 'In the Ericksonian approach, when we use the word "unconscious", we mean something different from the Freudian view of repressed urges and primal urges that the ego or superego have to deal with' (p. 108). They define the unconscious as:

- a repository for those things that you don't keep in your conscious mind, but could recall if you wanted
- it is your deeper, wiser self
- holding the sensory memories from life.

I end this book by returning to the concept of the unconscious mind. O'Connor and Seymour (1990, p. 6) refer to it as 'All the life-giving processes of our body, all that we have learned, our past experiences, and all that we might notice, but do not, in the present moment'. Erickson was a master at working with the unconscious and some of the presuppositions are derived from his respect for his clients' unconscious minds. He believed that there was a positive intention to all of the behaviours that they presented to him, and that individuals were making the best choices that they could at the time. His work focused on enabling the client to access more of their unconscious resources such that they could have a greater repertoire of choice. What I have demonstrated in this book is that if neurolinguistic psychotherapists stay within a programmatic model of working, they are not honouring Erickson's work and most importantly are staying out of rapport with a client's unconscious. It is only when the therapist develops a truly responsive relationship of trust and understanding with clients that the unconscious can become conscious; what is held non-verbally and somatically can be sponsored and validated.

By utilising the principle of systems theory it is important that clients are encouraged to access their unconscious and view their subjective experience from within the principles of cybernetics. It is more enabling for a client to have choice about how they react to their reactions than to change their reactions *per se*. Gilligan has expanded this and through self-relations, clients are encouraged to validate, sponsor and heal disintegrated and fragmented aspects of themselves. This supports the principles of cybernetics, where clients develop a healthy relationship to their emotions and aspects of themselves that they have been previously told are bad or wrong.

I would urge neurolinguistic psychotherapists to accept and place in context the programmatic modelled aspects of NLP, which is an applied psychology. By including relational therapy within their repertoire of skills it is possible to aid development of neural synapses and neurological re-patterning, emerging with a psychotherapeutic process that honours the work of Erickson, Satir and Perls, and the fundamental presuppositions that:

- enable the client to acknowledge all their internal states and external behaviours as positive resources
- respect the client's model of the world through inclusion.

References

Ader, R. and Cohen, N. (1982) 'Behaviourally conditioned immunosuppression and murine systemic', *Lupus Erythematosus*', *Science*, 215: 1534–1536.

Adler, A. (1992) *Understanding Human Nature* (C. Brett, Trans.), Oxford: Oneworld Publications. (Original work published in 1927.)

American Psychiatric Association (1994) *Diagnostic and Statistical Manual IV*, Washington, DC: APA.

Amsterdam, B. (1972) 'Mirror self-image reactions before age two', *Developmental Psycholbiology*, 5: 297–305.

Amsterdam, B. and Levitt, M. (1980) 'Consciousness of self and painful self-consciousness', *Psychoanalytic Study of the Child*, 35: 67–83.

Aristotle (389–322 BCE) *Causation in the History of Western Philosophy*. Retrieved August 9, 2006, from http://en.wikipedia.org/wiki/causality

Bandler, R. (1985) *Using Your Brain for a Change: Neurolinguistic Programming*, Moab, UT: Real People Press.

Bandler, R. and Grinder, J. (1975a) *Patterns of the Hypnotic Techniques of Milton H. Erickson, M. D., Volume 1*, Capitola, CA: Meta Publications.

Bandler, R. and Grinder, J. (1975b) *The Structure of Magic, 1*, Palo Alto, CA: Science and Behavior Books.

Bandler, R. and Grinder, J. (1977) *Patterns of the Hypnotic Techniques of Milton H. Erickson, M. D., Volume 2*, Capitola, CA: Meta Publications.

Bandler, R. and Grinder, J. (1979) *Frogs into Princes*, Moab, UT: Real People Press.

Basch, M. (1995) 'Kohut's contribution', *Psychoanalytic Dialogues*, 5: 367–373.

Basch, M. F. (1985) 'New directions in psychoanalysis', *Psychoanalytic Psychology*, 2: 1–19.

Bateson, G. (1972) *Steps to an Ecology of Mind*, New York: Ballantine Books.

Bateson, G. (2000) *Steps to an Ecology of Mind: Collected Essays in Anthropology, Psychiatry, Evolution and Epistemology*, Chicago: University of Chicago Press.

Bateson, G. (2006) *Global Vision*. Retrieved April 30, 2006, from www. global-vision.org/bateson.html

Beck, A. T. (1976) *Cognitive Therapy and the Emotional Disorders*, New York: International Universities Press.

Beck, D. E. and Cowan, C. C. (1996) *Spiral Dynamics: Mastering Values, Leadership and Change*, Oxford: Blackwell.

Berne, E. (1957) *A Layman's Guide to Psychiatry and Psychoanalysis*, New York: Grove Press.

Bion, W. R. (1984) *Learning from Experience*, London: Karnac.

Bodenhamer, B. G. and Hall, L. M. (1999) *The User's Manual for the Brain, Volume 1*, Bancyfelin, UK: Crown House Publishing.

Bollas, C. (1987) *The Shadow of the Object*, New York: Columbia University Press.

Bolstad, R. D. and Hamblett, M. (2000) 'Developing NLP based treatment programs for fast resolution of psychological trauma', *NLP World*, 7(1): 5–22.

Bolstad, R. D. (2002) *Resolve: A New Model of Therapy*, Bancyfelin, UK: Crown House Publishing.

Bowlby, J. (1969) *Attachment, Vol. 1 of Attachment and Loss*, London: Hogarth Press.

Bucci, W. (1997) *Psychoanalysis and Cognitive Science*, New York: Guilford Press.

Buck, R. W. (1994) 'The neuropsychology of communication: Spontaneous and symbolic aspects', *Journal of Pragmatics*, 22: 265–278.

Byrom, T. (1976) *The Dhammapada: The Sayings of the Buddha*, New York: Vintage.

Cameron-Bandler, L., Gordon, D. and LeBeau, M. (1985) *The Emprint Method*, San Rafael, CA: FuturePace.

Cameron-Bandler, L. and LeBeau, M. (1987) *Emotional Hostage: Rescuing Your Emotional Life*, Moad, UT: Real People Press.

Carroll, R. (2002) 'Neuroscience and psychotherapy', *The Psychotherapist*, 18: 17–19.

Charvet, S. R. (1995) *Words That Change Minds*, Dubuque, IA: Kendall Hunt.

Chen, J. (2002) *A Quantum Theoretical Account of Linguistics*. Retrieved December 17, 2006, from http://nats-www.informatik.uni-hamburg.de/~joseph/di/dis/node26.html

Chomsky, N. (1957) *Syntactic Structures*, The Hague, The Netherlands: Mouton & Co.

Chopra, D. (1989) *Quantum Healing: Exploring the Frontiers of Mind/Body Medicine*, New York: Bantam Books.

Chopra, D. (1995) *The Way of the Wizard: Twenty Spiritual Lessons for Creating the Life You Want*, New York: Harmony Books.

Chugani, H., Behen, M., Muzik, O., Juhasz, C., Nagy, F. and Chugani, D. (2001) 'Local brain functional activity following early deprivation: A study of post-institutionalised Romanian orphans', *Development and Psychopathology*, 6: 533–549.

Clyman, R. (1991) 'The procedural organisation of emotions', in T. Shapiro and R. Emde (Eds), *Affect: Psychoanalytic Perspectives*, New York: International Universities Press.

Damasio, A. (1994) *Descartes' Error: Emotion, Reason and the Human Brain*, New York: Penguin.

Darwin, C. (1998) *The Expression of the Emotions in Man and Animals* (with introduction, afterword and commentaries by P. Ekmen), Oxford: Oxford University Press. (Original work published 1955.)

DeLozier, J. (1995) 'Mastery, new coding and systemic NLP', *NLP World*, 2: 1.

Descartes, R. (1991) (J. Cottingham, R. Stoothoff, D. Murdoch and A. Kenny,

Trans.) *The Philosophical Writings of Descartes*, Cambridge: Cambridge University Press.

de Shayzer, S. (1988) *Clues: Investigating Solutions in Brief Therapy*, London: W. W. Norton.

Devinsky, O. (2000) 'Right cerebral hemisphere dominance for a sense of corporeal and emotional self', *Epilepsy and Behaviour*, 1: 60–73.

Dilts, R. (1990) *Changing Belief Systems with NLP*, Capitola, CA: Meta Publications.

Dilts, R. (1999) *Sleight of Mouth: The Magic of Conversational Belief Change*, Capitola, CA: Meta Publications.

Dilts, R., Hallbom, T. and Smith, S. (1990) *Beliefs: Pathways to Health and Wellbeing*, Portland, OR: Metamorphous.

Dilts, R. B. and DeLozier, J. (2000) *Encyclopedia of Systemic NLP and NLP New Coding*, Scotts Valley, CA: NLP University Press. Available online at http://NLPuniversitypress.com (retrieved December 1, 2006).

Edelman, G. (1987) *Neural Darwinism: The Theory of Neuronal Group Selection*, New York: Basic Books.

Edelman, G. (2004) *Wider Than the Sky: A Revolutionary View of Consciousness*, London: Penguin Books.

Einspruch, E. L. and Forman, B. D. (1985) 'Observations concerning research literature on neuro-linguistic programming', *Journal of Counselling Psychology*, 32(4): 589–596.

Einspruch, E. L. and Forman, B. D. (1988) 'Neurolinguistic programming in the treatment of phobias', *Psychotherapy in Private Practice*, 6(1): 91–100.

Ellis, A. (1962) *Reason and Emotion in Psychotherapy*, Secaucus, NJ: Lyle Stuart.

Erickson, M. H. (1985) (Eds E. L. Rossi and M. Ryan) *The Lectures, Seminars and Workshops of Milton H. Erickson. Vol II. Life Reframing in Hypnosis*, New York: Irvington.

Erickson, M. H. and Rossi, E. L. (1989) *The February Man: Evolving Consciousness and Identity in Hypnotherapy*, New York: Brunner/Mazel.

Fields, R., Taylor, P., Weyler, R. and Ingrasci, R. (0000) *Chop Wood, Carry Water*, Los Angeles: Jeremy P. Tarcher.

Foundation for Inner Peace (1972) *A Course in Miracles*, Mill Valley, CA: Foundation for Inner Peace.

Freud, S. (1904) 'Freud's psycho-analytic procedure', in J. Strachley (Ed. and Trans.), *Standard Edition of the Complete Psychological Works of Sigmund Freud* (Vol. 7), London: Hogarth Press.

Freud, S. (1926) 'Inhibitions, symptoms and anxiety', in J. Strachley (Ed. and Trans.), *Standard Edition of the Complete Psychological Works of Sigmund Freud* (Vol. 20), London: Hogarth Press.

Freud, S. (1933) *New Introductory Lectures on Psychoanalysis* (W. J. H. Sprott, Trans.), New York: W. W. Norton.

Freud, S. (1957) 'The unconscious', in J. Strachley (Ed. and Trans.), *Standard Edition of the Complete Psychological Works of Sigmund Freud* (Vol. 14, pp. 166–204), London: Hogarth Press.

Freud, S. (1958) 'Recommendations to physicians practicing psycho-analysis', in J. Strachey (Ed. and Trans.), *Standard Edition of the Complete Psychological Works of Sigmund Freud* (Vol. 12, pp. 111–120), London: Hogarth Press.

Freud, S. (1959) 'Inhibition, symptoms and anxiety', in J. Strachey (Ed. and Trans.), *Standard Edition of the Complete Psychological Works of Sigmund Freud* (Vol. 20), London: Hogarth Press.

Gawler-Wright, P. (1999) *The Skills of Love*, London: BeeLeaf Publishing.

Gawler-Wright, P. (2004) *Intermediate Contemporary Psychotherapy, Volume 2*, London: BeeLeaf Publishing.

Gawler-Wright, P. (2005) *A Time Machine between Your Ears*. Presentation to the Independent NLP Conference, London.

Gawler-Wright, P. (2006) *Wider Mind: Ericksonian Psychotherapy in Practice*, London: BeeLeaf Publishing.

Gawler-Wright, P. (2007) *Intermediate Contemporary Psychotherapy, Volume 2, 2007 Edition*, London: BeeLeaf Publishing.

Genser-Medlitsch, M. and Schütz, P. (1997) *Does Neuro-Linguistic Psychotherapy Have Effect? New Results Shown in the Extramural Section* [online article], Austria: EANLP.

Gerhardt, S. (2004) *Why Love Matters: How Affection Shapes a Baby's Brain*, London: Routledge.

Gilligan, S. (1997) *The Courage to Love: Principles & Practices of Self-Relations Psychotherapy*, New York: W. W. Norton.

Goleman, D. (1996) *Emotional Intelligence*, London: Bloomsbury.

Graves, C. W., Huntley, W. C. and LaBier, D. W. (1965) *Personality Structure and Perceptual Readiness: An Investigation of Their Relationship to Hypothesized Levels of Human Existence*. Union College. Retrieved September 20, 2007, from www.clarewgraves.com/articles-content/1965_GHL/1965_GHL1.html

Haley, J. (1993) *Uncommon Therapy: The Psychiatric Techniques of Milton H. Erickson, M.D*, New York: W. W. Norton.

Hargaden, H. and Sills, C. (2002) *Transactional Analysis: A Relational Perspective*, London: Routledge.

Heisenberg, W. (1932) (Trans. C. Eckart and F. C. Hoyt) *Physical Principles of the Quantum Theory*, Toronto: General Publishing Company.

Hesse, H. (1965) *Steppenwolfe*, London: Penguin Books.

Hoffman, H. S. (1987) 'Imprinting and the critical period for social attachments: Some laboratory investigations', in M. H. Bornstein (Ed.), *Sensitive Periods in Development: Interdisciplinary Studies* (pp. 99–121), Hillsdale, NJ: Lawrence Erlbaum Associates Inc.

Hudson, P. and O'Hanlon, B. (1991) *Rewriting Love Stories: Brief Marital Therapy*, New York: W. W. Norton.

Hudson, P. and O'Hanlon, B. (1996) *Stop Blaming: Start Loving*, New York: W. W. Norton.

Huxley, A. (1954) *The Doors of Perception and Heaven and Hell*, New York: Harper Collins.

James, T. (1996) *Prime Concerns: Using Quantum Linguistics to Increase the Effectiveness of the Language We Use*, Honolulu, HI: Advanced Neurodynamics.

James, T. (2003) *Time Line Therapy*® *Practitioner Training*, Series Notes. Version 6.26, August 2003, London: NLP World.

James, T. and Woodsmall, W. (1988) *Time Line Therapy and the Basis of Personality*, Capitola, CA: Meta Publications.

James, W. (1884) 'What is an Emotion?', *Mind*, 9: 188–205.

Jelem, H. and Schutz, P. (2007) *Neuro-linguistic Psychotherapy (NLPt)*. Retrieved September 20, 2007, from www.eanlpt.org

Jung, C. G. (1961) *Memories, Dreams, Reflections*, New York: Random House.

Jung, C. G. (1971) *Psychological Types*, London: Routledge & Kegan Paul. (Original work published 1921.)

Keirsey, D. and Bates, M. (1984) *Please Understand Me: Character and Temperament Types*, Del Mar, CA: Promethus Nemesis.

Kelly, G. A. (1991) *The Psychology of Personal Constructs*, Vol. 1, London: Routledge.

Kernberg, O. (1976) *Object Relations Theory and Clinical Psychoanalysis*, New York: Aronson.

Klein, M. (1932) *The Psychoanalysis of Children*, London: Hogarth.

Klein, M. (1946) 'Notes on some schizoid mechanisms', *International Journal of Psycho-Analysis*, 27: 99–110.

Klein, M. (1952) 'Notes on some schizoid mechanisms', in J. Riviere (Ed.), *Developments in Psychoanalysis*, London: Hogarth.

Klein, M. (1960) *Our Adult World and Its Roots in Infancy*, London: Tavistock.

Kohut, H. (1984) *How Does Analysis Cure?*, Chicago: University of Chicago Press.

Korzybski, A. O. (1948) *Science and Sanity*, Fort Worth, TX: Institute of General Semantics. (Original work published 1933.)

Kosslyn, M., Ganis, G. and Thompson, W. L. (2001) 'Neural foundations of imagery', *Nature Reviews Neuroscience*, 2: 635–642.

Kostere, K. and Malatesta, L. (1990) *Maps, Models and the Structure of Reality: NLP Technology in Psychotherapy*, Portland, OR: Metamorphous Press.

Kovelman, J. A. (1998) *Once upon a Soul: The Story Continues . . . Science, Psychology and the Realms of Spirit*, Carson, CA: Jalmar Press.

Kristeva, J. (2001) *Melanie Klein*, New York: Columbia University Press.

Lawley, J. and Tompkins, P. (2005) *Metaphors in Mind: Transformation through Symbolic Modelling*, London: The Developing Company Press.

Lawley, J. and Tompkins, P. (2006) 'What is therapeutic modelling? A dialogue with James Lawley & Penny Tompkins', *Resource*, 8: 35–39, London: Porto Publishing.

Layden, M. A., Newman, C. F., Freeman, A. and Byers Morse, S. (1993) *Cognitive Therapy of Borderline Personality Disorder*, Boston: Allyn & Bacon.

Lazarus, A. A. (1971) *Behaviour Therapy and Beyond*, New York: McGraw-Hill.

Lazarus, A. A. and Abramovitz, A. (1962) 'The use of "emotive imagery" in the treatment of children's phobias', *Journal of Mental Science*, 108: 191–195.

Lazarus, J. (2006) *Ahead of the Game: How to Use Your Mind to Win in Sport*, Penryn, UK: Ecademy Press.

Leary, T. (1988) *Change Your Brain*, Berkeley, CA: Ronin Publishing.

Lewis, M. (1982) 'Origins of self-knowledge and individual differences in early self recognition', in J. Suls (Ed.), *Psychological Perspectives on the Self* (Vol. 1, pp. 55–78), Hillsdale, NJ: Lawrence Erlbaum Associates, Inc.

Lilly, J. (1968) *Programming and Metaprogramming in the Human Biocomputer: Theory and Experiments*, New York: The Julian Press. Retrieved October 21, 2006, from http://www.futurehi.net/docs/Metaprogramming.html

Lorenz, K. (1935) 'Der Kumpan in der Umwelt des Vogels: Der Artgenosse als auslösendes moment sozialer verhaltensweisen', *Journal für ornithologie*, 83: 137–215, 289–413.

Lorenz, K. (1970) *Studies in Animal and Human Behaviour* (Vol. 1), Cambridge, MA: Harvard University Press.

Lowen, A. (1972) *Cognitive Therapy of Borderline Personality Disorder*, Boston: Allyn & Bacon.

Mahler, M. A. (1980) 'Rapprochement subphase of the separation–individuation process', in R. Lax, S. Bach and J. A. Burland (Eds), *Rapprochement: The Critical Subphase of Separation–Individuation* (pp. 3–19), New York: Jason Aronson.

Martin, M. and O'Hanlon, B. (1992) *Solution Oriented Hypnosis: An Ericksonian Approach*, New York: W. W. Norton.

Maslow, A. (1943) 'A theory of human motivation', *Psychological Review*, 50: 370–396.

Massey, M. (1979) *People Puzzle: Understanding Yourself and Others*, Reston, VA: Reston Publishing Co.

McDermott, I. and Jago, W. (2001) *Brief NLP Therapy*, London: Sage.

Mearns, D. and Cooper, M. (2005) *Working at Relational Depth*, London: Sage.

Meltzer, D. (1979) *The Kleinian Development*, London: The Clinic Press.

Miller, G., Galanter, E. and Pribram, K. (1960) *Plans and the Structure of Behaviour*, New York: Holt, Rinehart and Winston.

Mollon, P. (2001) *Releasing the Self: The Healthy Legacy of Heinz Kohut*, London: Whurr Publishers.

Mollon, P. (2004) *EMDR and the Energy Therapies: Psychoanalytic Perspectives*, London: Karnac Books.

Moore, S. M. (1998) 'How can we remember but be unable to recall? The complex functions of multi-modular memory', in V. Sinason (Ed.), *Memory in Dispute*, London: Karnac Books.

Moreno, J. L. (1977) *Psychodrama: First Volume*, New York: Beacon House.

Myers, I. (1962) *The Myers-Briggs Type Indicator*, Palo Alto, CA: Consulting Psychologists Press.

NLPtCA (2007) *What is Neuro Linguistic Psychotherapy & Counselling?* Retrieved September 20, 2007, from http://nlptca.com/whatisnlpt.php

O'Connor, J. (2001) *NLP Workbook*, London: Harper Collins.

O'Connor, J. and Seymour, J. (1990) *Introducing NLP: Psychological Skills for Understanding and Influencing People*, London: Thorsons.

O'Connor, P. (1985) *Understanding Jung, Understanding Yourself*, New York: Paulist Press.

O'Hanlon, B. (1997) *Guide to Possibility Land: Fifty-One Methods for Doing Brief, Respectful Therapy*, New York: W. W. Norton.

O'Hanlon, B. (2000) *Do One Thing Different*, New York: Harper Collins.

O'Hanlon, B. (2002) *Even From a Broken Web: Brief, Respectful Solution Oriented Therapy for Sexual Abuse and Trauma* (2nd edn), New York: W. W. Norton.

O'Hanlon, B. (2003) *A Guide to Inclusive Therapy*, New York: W. W. Norton.

O'Hanlon, B. and Bertolino, B. (1988) *Even From a Broken Web: Brief, Respectful Solution-Oriented Therapy for Sexual Abuse and Trauma*, New York: W. W. Norton.

O'Hanlon, B. and Rowan, T. (2003) *Solution Oriented Therapy for Chronic and Severe Mental Illness*, New York: W. W. Norton.

O'Hanlon, B. and Weiner-Davis, M. (1999/2003) *In Search of Solutions: A New Direction in Psychotherapy*, New York: W. W. Norton.

O'Hanlon, W. H. (1987) *Taproots: Underlying Principles of Milton Erickson's Therapy and Hypnosis*, New York: W. W. Norton.

O'Hanlon, W. H. and Martin, M. (1992) *Solution Oriented Hypnosis – An Ericksonian Approach*, New York: W. W. Norton.

Panksepp, J. (1998) *Affective Neuroscience: The Foundations of Human and Animal Emotions*, Oxford: Oxford University Press.

Pansepp, J., Siviy, S. M. and Normansell, L. A. (1985) 'Brain opioids and social emotions', in M. Reite and T. Field (Eds), *The Psychobiology of Attachment and Separation* (pp. 3–49), Orlando. FL: Academic Press.

Pareto, V. F. D. (1935) *Mind and Society* (Vol. 3), Kila, MT: Kessinger Publishing.

Parlett, M. and Hemming, J. (1996) In W. Dryden (Ed.), *Gestalt Therapy*, London: Sage Publications.

Pavlov, I. P. (1927) *Conditioned Reflexes*, London: Routledge. (Original work published 1904.)

Perls, F., Hefferline, F. and Goodman, P. (1973) *Gestalt Therapy: Excitement & Growth in the Human Personality*, New York: Julian Press Dell Publishing. (Original work published 1951.)

Perls, F. S. (1969) *Ego, Hunger and Aggression: The Beginning of Gestalt Therapy*, New York: Vintage Books.

Pert, C. (1997) *Molecules of Emotion: Why You Feel the Way You Feel*, London: Pocket Books.

Piaget, J. (1968) *Genetic Epistemology: A Series of Lectures Delivered by Piaget*, New York: Columbia University Press.

Pinker, S. (1994) *The Language Instinct*, New York: Morrow.

Plutchik, R. (1983) 'Emotion in early development: A psychoevolutionary approach', in R. Plutchik and H. Kellerman (Eds), *Emotion: Theory Research and Experience* (pp. 221–257). New York: Academic Press.

Prochaska, J. L. and DiClemente, C. C. (1992) 'Stages of change in the modification of problem behaviour', in M. Hersen, R. Eisler and P. M. Miller (Eds), *Progress in Behaviour Modification* (Vol. 28), Sycamore, IL: Sycamore Publishing Company.

Robbins, A. (1991) *Awaken the Giant Within*, New York: Fireside.

Rogers, C. (1974) 'In retrospect: Forty six years', *American Psychologist*, 29(2): 115–123.

Rogers, C. R. (1951) *Client Centred Therapy*, London: Constable.

Rosen, S. (1982) *My Voice Will Go with You: The Teaching Tales of Milton H. Erickson*, New York: W. W. Norton.

Rothschild, B. (2000) *The Body Remembers: The Psychophysiology of Trauma and Trauma Treatment*, New York: W. W. Norton.

Rycroft, C. (1995) *A Critical Dictionary of Psychoanalysis* (2nd edn), London: Penguin.

Sands, S. (1995) 'Self psychology and projective identification – whither shall they meet? A reply to the editors', *Psychoanalytic Dialogue*, 7: 651–668.

Satir, V. (1972) *Peoplemaking*, Palo Alto, CA: Science and Behaviour Books.

Satir, V. and Baldwin, M. (1983) *Satir, Step by Step*, Palo Alto, CA: Science and Behaviour Books.

Schore, A. (1996) 'The experience-dependent maturation of a regulatory system in the orbital prefrontal cortex and the origin of developmental psychopathology', *Development and Psychopathology*, 8: 59–87.

Schore, A. N. (2003) *Affect Regulation and the Repair of the Self*, London: W. W. Norton.

Schrödinger, E. (1958) *Mind and Matter*, Cambridge: Cambridge University Press.

Sharpley, C. F. (1984) 'Predicate matching in NLP: A review on the preferred representational system', *Journal of Counselling Psychology*, 31(2): 238–248.

Sharpley, C. F. (1987) 'Research findings on neurolinguistic programming: Nonsupportive data or an untestable theory?', *Journal of Counselling Psychology*, 34: 103–107.

Skinner, B. F. (1961) 'Teaching machines', *Scientific American*, 205(5): 90–107.

Sluzki, C. E. and Ransom, D. C. (1976) *Double Bind: The Foundation of the Communicational Approach to the Family*, New York: Crune & Scratton.

Stern, D. (1985) *The Interpersonal World of the Infant*, New York: Basic Books.

Stern, D. (1998) *The Motherhood Constellation: A Unified View of Parent–Infant Psychotherapy*, London: Karnac Books.

Stewart, I. and Joines, V. (1987) *TA Today*, Nottingham: Lifespace.

Strauss, C. L. (1963) *The Structural Study of Myth*, New York: Basic Books.

Trevarthen, C. (1993) 'The self born in intersubjectivity: The psychology of an infant communicating', in U. Neisser (Ed.), *The Perceived Self: Ecological and Interpersonal Sources of Self-knowledge* (pp. 121–173), New York: Cambridge University Press.

Trevarthen, C. and Aitken, K. J. (2001) 'Infant intersubjectivity: Research, theory and clinical applications', *Journal of Child Psychology and Psychiatry and Allied Disciplines*, 42(1): 3–48.

Tudor, K. and Worrall, M. (2006) *Person Centred Therapy: A Clinical Philosophy*, London: Routledge.

Twitmeyer, E. B. (1902) *A Study of the Knee-Jerk*. Unpublished doctoral dissertation, University of Pennsylvania, USA.

Von Foerster, H. (2003) *Understanding Understanding: Essays on Cybernetics and Cognition*, New York: Springer-Verlag.

Watzlawick, P. (1978) *The Language of Change: Elements of Therapeutic Communication*, New York: W. W. Norton.

Winnicott, D. W. (1958) 'The capacity to be alone', *International Journal of Psychoanalysis*, 39: 416–420.

Winnicott, D. W. (1986) *Home is Where we Start From: Essays by a Psychoanalyst*, New York: W. W. Norton.

Wright, C. I., Fisher, H., Whalen, P. J., McInerny, S. C., Shin, L. M. and Rauchs, S. L. (2001) 'Differential pre-frontal cortex and amygdala habituation to repeatedly presented emotional stimuli', *NeuroReport*, 12: 379–383.

Zinker, J. (1977) *Creative Process in Gestalt Therapy*, New York: Brunner/Mazel.

Index

Note: Page numbers in **bold** refer to figures and information contained within tables.